WITH CORDS
of
LOVE

WITH CORDS

of

LOVE

A WESLEYAN RESPONSE TO RELIGIOUS PLURALISM

AL TRUESDALE *with* KERI MITCHELL

BEACON HILL PRESS
OF KANSAS CITY

ISBN-13: 978-0-8341-2306-9
ISBN-10: 0-8341-2306-1

Printed in the
United States of America

Cover Design: Darlene Filley
Interior Design: Sharon Page

Library of Congress Cataloging-in-Publication Data

Truesdale, Albert, 1941-
  With cords of love : a Wesleyan response to religious pluralism / Al Truesdale, with Keri Mitchell.
    p. cm.
  Includes bibliographical references.
  ISBN-13: 978-0-8341-2306-9 (pbk.)
  ISBN-10: 0-8341-2306-1 (pbk.)
  1. Religious pluralism—Methodist Church. 2. Methodist Church—Doctrines. 3. Religious pluralism—Holiness churches. 4. Holiness churches—Doctrines. 5. Wesley, John, 1703-1791. I. Mitchell, Keri, 1979- II. Title.

  BX8331.3.T78 2006
  261.2—dc22

                                                                    2006100364

10 9 8 7 6 5 4 3 2 1

CONTENTS

Acknowledgments 7

Introduction 9

PART I: UNDERSTANDING RELIGIOUS PLURALISM 15

1. The Profile of Religious Pluralism 19
2. The Christian Faith in a Field of Diversity: The Historical
   Development of Religious Pluralism (Snapshots) 31
3. Finding Truth Along Many Paths: Plurality, Postmodernity,
   and a New Opening for the Gospel.................................... 47
4. Responses to Religious Pluralism Within Christianity.............. 65

PART II: THE NEW TESTAMENT AND RELIGIOUS PLURALISM 77

5. What Is the Gospel of God? 79
6. A Missional People: The New Testament Church
   in a Pluralistic Context 89

PART III: PLURALISM AND REDEMPTION
FROM A WESLEYAN PERSPECTIVE..101

7. Why Our History Matters 103
8. Amazing Grace: The Wesleyan Way of Salvation...................119
9. A Wesleyan Response to Religious Pluralism.....................143
10. Telling the Gospel Story in a Wesleyan Way 157

PART IV: STORYTELLERS: CHRISTIAN LIFE AND WITNESS
IN A RELIGIOUSLY PLURALISTIC WORLD 169

11. Christian Formation: Shaped by the "Real World".............171
12. Living the Story in a Religiously Pluralistic World...........183
13. Anticipating the Story's End 193

Conclusion..205

Notes 207

Bibliography...247

ACKNOWLEDGMENTS

I am indebted to numerous persons for their assistance in writing *With Cords of Love* and want to register my deep appreciation for their friendship and service.

Pat Wright, Smithville, Illinois; Louise Biederman, Beaufort, South Carolina; Elsie Ours, Dunbar, West Virginia; Omajean Smith, Cross Lanes, West Virginia; and Bob Gunno, Charleston, West Virginia; read an early draft of the book and made valuable suggestions for improving the document.

Later in the writing process, Marlene Custer of Wooster, Ohio, and Betsy Ballard, Dwain Butler, and Royece Cox of Vicksburg, Mississippi, carefully critiqued the manuscript and offered many helpful suggestions for making it readable by and useful to clergy and laypersons.

What a delight it has been to work with Keri Mitchell, a diligent and bright young editor with a can-do attitude. As long as the Lord continues to grace the Church with young professionals like Keri, we should be joyfully confident. She is a compliment to the journalism program of Southern Nazarene University.

The creativity, patience, and encouragement a writer encounters when working with Bonnie Perry of Beacon Hill Press of Kansas City sparks motivation when the internal fires burn low. Thanks, Bonnie.

As with all that I write, my wife, Esther, has again proved to be my best critic and supporter. Her ability to read what I have written and then send me "back to the drawing board" is always appreciated, even if not always enjoyed.

Special thanks from Keri Mitchell to her grandfather, Rev. Bobby G. Robison: You have spent your life changing the world, one person at a time, by showing each one the love and hope of Christ, and I pray I will spend my life following in your footsteps.

Introduction

During a stopover in Japan, thinking we could do Tokyo in a day, my wife and I hustled to keep up with the Japanese tour guide steering us through the cultural and historic sites. We wandered through the grounds of the ancient Imperial Palace, watched a fireworks show from atop the Tokyo Tower, and made ourselves look silly while trying to order from a Japanese menu. Between tour bus stops our guide pointed out sites from more recent history—Christian churches—indicating the one where he was a member.

So his actions surprised me when we approached an ancient gate leading into a Shinto shrine. The gate consisted of two ornately carved wooden columns standing roughly 20 feet apart. Our guide's gaze carefully traced the columns all the way to the top, then soared beyond. Turning to us, he enthusiastically explained that the gate opens to the heavens. "That's why no crossbar is at the top," he said. It was obvious that he bought into his explanation. He turned to those of us standing nearby and confided, "Left to itself, Christianity is incomplete, too narrow. It needs the help of other religions." He went on to describe the Shinto elements that supplement his Christian lifestyle as though he had gone through a religious cafeteria and carefully selected from the menu to create a comprehensive spiritual diet. "God tells us to pray," he said, "and then leaves it up to us to use our reason for deciding which parts of which religion to embrace." For our guide, a smorgasbord of religious expression—I'll take the broccoli, hold the potatoes—was his chosen fare for daily life.

Our Tokyo guide typifies people all over the world who believe the diverse array of religions should be embraced and appreciated for their respective "truths." Religions should listen to and learn from each other, they believe, and abandon the outdated practice of trying to evangelize people of different faiths. Such a practice is primitive, they say, and reveals both an arrogant disregard for other people's deeply held values and a lack of understanding regarding how religions arise. This, in a nutshell, depicts the ideology of religious pluralism.[1]

Alan Race, a well-known British writer on interfaith dialogue, defines religious pluralism as a crowded "marketplace of religious possibilities" where religions "jostle with each other" and compete for shoppers' attention.[2] The market scene signals to Christians that "the days of religious and cultural isolationism are at an end."[3] Christianity no longer exists in a bubble protected from the impact of other religions. The bubble has burst, the landscape has changed, and the earth has shifted under our feet.[4]

OUR PLURALISTIC WORLD

Metropolitan areas all over the United States and Europe exemplify the phenomenon of increasing religious diversity. Take the hilly terrain of Kansas City in America's heartland. The city's Islamic center and a corresponding school for Muslim children are situated near the top of one slope, while the Community of the Good Shepherd Lutheran Church lies at the foot. Just down the road sits a Jehovah's Witnesses Kingdom Hall, and a nearby hilltop offers views of the impressive Unity Village tower, world headquarters for the independent Unity religion.

The scene looks a little different in the antebellum town of Beaufort situated on the coast of South Carolina. The majestic steeples of St. Helena's Episcopal Church and First Baptist Church tower over the town's historic district, bearing elegant witness to a traditionally dominant Christian voice. Nestled in the Bible Belt, Beaufort is liberally supplied with churches of all kinds. Among them are praise houses where the Gullah-speaking slaves once worshiped[5] and where some African-Americans still do on special occasions.

But looks can be deceiving. The following announcement recently appeared within the folds of Beaufort County's *LowCountry Weekly:* "The Salt Marsh Alternative Religions Group invites you to enjoy a cup of tea and networking with like minds about Shamanism, Wicca, earth-based religions and other forms of paganism. Tea and chat discussion groups meet Wednesdays at 6:30 p.m. All paths and levels welcome."[6]

Religious pluralism may sound like a vague abstraction until we put it in the context of places like Kansas City, Beaufort, and others all over the world. Mere decades ago in the two-fire-truck town where I was reared, religious pluralism would have referred to the Jewish, Catholic, and Protestant communities. We distinguished between the Methodists who each year were *revived* and the Baptists who *rededicated.* This was the situation for much of America. But times have changed. Islamic mosques and schools, Hindu and Buddhist temples, Sikh communities and meditation centers have become fixtures in American communities. The impact has not been limited to populous cities. Great Falls, South Carolina—an old mill town with roughly 2,100 residents—recently found its Christian customs challenged in court by a Wiccan priestess. In 2001 Darla Wynne filed a lawsuit declaring it unconstitutional for the town council to continue its longstanding tradition of opening meetings with prayer in Jesus' name. Federal judges and appeals courts ruled that the practice advanced one religion over the others. The town fought the suit all the way to the U.S. Supreme Court, which indirectly declared Wynne the victor in June 2005 by refusing to hear the case.

The religious landscape is diversifying right before our eyes. In addition to the traditional world religions, which are themselves undergoing change, new religions are forming. David B. Barrett, editor of the *World Christian Encyclopedia*[7] and a former missionary to Africa, says that "enormous religious change [is] going on across the world, all the time. It's massive, it's complex, and it's continual." Barrett backs his claim with a team that has identified 9,900 distinct religions in the world—a colossal number that continues to increase by two or three new religions every day.[8]

In most European countries where either Protestantism or Catholicism once reigned, the ebbing Christian tide is giving way to energetic Islam, eastern religions, and reinvention of ancient pagan religions. An immigration upsurge within the European Union is largely responsible for Muslims now comprising 3 to 5 percent of the population—somewhere between 15 and 20 million people. People in the know expect these numbers to increase dramatically. Between now and 2015, declining birth rates will cause Europe's population to drop roughly 3.5 percent, but the Muslim population will double. If current birth rate trends continue, Europe will have a Muslim majority by the end of the 21st century.[9] Time will tell if the term *Eurabia,* coined by Egyptian-born scholar Bat Ye'or, proves to be prophetic.[10] Far more severe is the assessment by renowned Italian journalist Oriana Fallaci. She contends that Europe is on the verge of becoming a dominion of Islam and that Europeans lack the moral and religious strength needed to ward off an approaching Islamic "conquest."[11]

Consider the United Kingdom, which has witnessed a tenfold increase in the number of British Muslims and Muslim immigrants over the past 40 years. Though the Anglican Church is the established church in Great Britain, more of the country's Muslims attend weekly religious services than do its Anglicans. And, needless to say, Muslims far outnumber Methodists in the land of the Wesleys.

In North America, religions that were small just a few years ago now challenge some traditional Jewish and Christian groups in size. More than 300 Buddhist temples are located in Los Angeles, home to the greatest variety of Buddhists than any other city in the world. Muslims residing in the United

States now outnumber the nation's Episcopalians, Jews,[12] or Presbyterians. Rochester, Minnesota, has seen its Muslim population grow from less than 50 in the early 1990s to roughly 5,000 today and will soon have a mosque blended into its skyline. The $4 million facility—three stories tall, topped by a large dome and flanked by 180-foot-tall minarets—will accommodate 1,800 worshipers.[13]

"The world has never seen a nation as religiously diverse as the United States," *TIME* magazine reported in recent years.[14] Diana Eck, director of the Pluralism Project of Harvard University, agrees.[15] Forty years ago the Civil Rights Movement inspired Congress to pass and President Lyndon Johnson to sign the Immigration Act of 1965, which dramatically changed the method by which immigrants are admitted into America. The bill decreed that future immigrants were to be welcomed based on their skills and professions instead of their countries of origin. Consequently, people from countries with dominant religions other than Christianity began to arrive in larger numbers. Annual immigration figures rose as well; according to the U.S. Census Bureau, the number of immigrants entering America tripled between 1970 and 2000. So in 40 years' time, millions of Muslims, Buddhists, Hindus, Sikhs, Jains, Zoroastrians, and others have come to the United States from all over the world, significantly altering the religious landscape.[16]

If the New Testament presented the gospel of Jesus Christ as one of many acceptable religious options, then we could treat religious pluralism as no more than a historical reality Christianity needs to absorb. But this is not the case. The New Testament instead makes comprehensive and exclusive claims regarding Jesus. So the expanding reality of religious pluralism raises questions and presents challenges to which we simply must respond—fairly and candidly. Stewardship of the gospel requires this. Failure to respond faithfully and intelligently would leave the Church ineffective in its witness and sidelined on the current religious playing field.

THE JOURNEY AHEAD

The subsequent chapters will help us learn to distinguish between substantial Christian faith and the mix-and-match approach of the religious atmosphere in which we live. One of this book's goals is to inform. But its more important purpose is to equip Christians for effective witness in the world. In a pluralistic and postmodern context (postmodernity will be discussed in chapter 3), we are interested in knowing how to tell the Story of God in a manner faithful to Jesus Christ.[17] We will do this from a Wesleyan perspective, relying upon the Scriptures, our doctrinal commitments, and the rich resources of our heritage.

At a minimum, religious pluralism calls upon Christians to carefully consider how to deal with the reality as well as the prominence of traditional world religions such as Hinduism and Islam. But it requires more. Contemporary religious pluralism calls upon us to raise the same question with reference to scores of newer religions, such as the Baha'i faith,[18] the Church of All Worlds, the neo-pagan Druids, and the Covenant of the Goddess.[19] Wilfred Cantwell Smith correctly observed in 1972, "From now on any serious intellectual statement of the Christian faith must include, if it is to serve its purposes among men, some doctrine [appraisal] of other religions."[20] These other religions are not going away. As a matter of fact, they are thriving in our hometowns.

The distinctive convictions that characterize the Wesleyan tradition rule out all misrepresentation of other religions as well as any hint of oppression, coercion, and meanness of spirit. Because of the way we believe God works in the world, our doctrinal tradition makes possible both listening and proclamation, both respect and conviction. To borrow words from theologian Karl Barth, we Wesleyans believe that God leads with cords of love (see Hos. 11:4).[21]

PART I

UNDERSTANDING RELIGIOUS PLURALISM

"Welcome! Greetings in the bounty of the Earth Mother, the blessings of the Gods, and the Way of the Wise" (A welcome to inquirers, from the neo-pagan Druids).[22]

If we want to take religious faith seriously, we must pay close attention to the questions posed by religious pluralism, says Paul Knitter, emeritus professor of theology at Xavier University in Cincinnati. But why should we heed Knitter's warning? Don't Christians possess the truth? Isn't the gospel meant for all people, and doesn't it rule out all religions other than Christianity?

The apostle Paul, when preaching in Athens—then a center of religious and philosophical pluralism—made claims about Jesus he believed to universally apply to all people within earshot. Some of them labeled him a "babbler." Nevertheless, he told them, "While God has overlooked the times of human ignorance, now he commands all people everywhere to repent, because he has fixed a day on which he will have the world judged in righteousness by a man whom he has appointed, and of this he has given assurance to all by raising him from the dead" (Acts 17:30-31).[23]

If Paul was correct—if God wants all people everywhere to repent and believe in the risen Christ as the Savior of the world—why not just faithfully proclaim the gospel, dismiss all other religions, and be done with it? Many Christians have chosen to do just that. But we misunderstand Paul if we read this text and assume he simply wrote off other religions and philosophies.

Paul believed—and this is key—that God had been at work in his hearers long before Paul arrived on the scene. The numerous gods worshiped by the Gentiles did not make them total strangers to Christ in Paul's view, but it evidenced their hunger for the one true God, a hunger produced by God himself (v. 28). Take the neo-pagan Druid welcome quoted above. Paul would have considered it indicative of the Holy Spirit's efforts to lead all people to salvation. He used such religious ideas to create bridges between the gospel and the beliefs of those to whom he spoke, trusting that his proclamation would build upon the Spirit's preparation.

We must also recognize that the success of Paul's mission to the Gentiles resulted not only from his knowledge of the gospel but also from his knowledge of the cultural, religious, and philosophical contexts in which he spoke. If not for him, spreading the gospel into the Gentile world would have been very difficult because the other apostles (perhaps excepting Barnabas) did not understand Hellenistic culture the way Paul did. He took seriously the defining themes of Greco-Roman culture and knew how to connect the dots between that culture's religious longings and the message of new life in Christ Jesus.

No less is required of us in a similar and, yet, significantly different 21st-century pluralistic context. Anyone who prides himself or herself on ignorance of other world religions has stepped out of Paul's company.[24]

In today's climate, Paul's claims about Jesus Christ are often considered oppressive, intolerant, uninformed, and hopelessly narrow. Many people, including a large number of Christians, consider religious pluralism to be more than a temporary phenomenon. Religious pluralism "seems to be of the very stuff of reality, the way things are, the way they function."[25] Rev. Dr. George F. Regas concurred with this statement from the influential pulpit of the Washington National Cathedral. Regas, rector emeritus of All Saints Church in Pasadena, California, said acceptance of religious pluralism sets him free from the narrow restrictions of traditional Christianity. It liberates him to recognize that God is greater than his limited Christian understanding.[26]

Observers note that despite decades of blood, sweat, and tears contributed by Christian missionaries, they have barely made a dent in Buddhism, Hinduism, and Islam. "When confronted by living religions, especially if they are undergirded by some kind of intellectual system," Knitter says, "Christian missionaries have had practically no success at conversions."[27] Adding insult to injury, Muslims, Hindus, and Buddhists now freely communicate their faith to people in traditionally Christian lands.

Perhaps equally sobering is the fact that in many European countries that were once missionary sending centers, Christianity is being largely shoved aside by secularism, neo-paganism, Islam, Buddhism, and the rest.[28] Religion writer Jeff M. Sellers says discouragement is the primary reason missionaries to Spain stick around just two years on average. High proportions of Spaniards who appear to come to faith subsequently deny it under family pressures and other stresses. Scattered miracles of faith are often followed by scattered denials of faith.[29] This from a country that in the 16th and 17th centuries zealously sought to incorporate Christianity into every aspect of its culture.

1
THE PROFILE OF RELIGIOUS PLURALISM

In the early part of the 17th century, Puritans in the Massachusetts Bay Colony called Rhode Island "the sewer of New England." How did the young colony earn such scorn? It was willing to harbor fleeing religious dissidents like Roger Williams, who advocated a strict separation from the Church of England, and Anne Hutchinson, who claimed to receive special revelations from the Holy Spirit. Williams fortified the Puritans' sour estimate of him when he eventually embraced complete religious toleration for people in the colony, including Jews and Muslims.[30]

Almost four centuries later in Nashville, Joyce Jackson appeared on the front page of the *Tennessean*'s religion section. Jackson is a member of the Baha'i faith, and the article depicted her as a symbol of religious diversity in Nashville as well as the entire United States. Baha'i teaches that there is only one God and one human family, and that all religions are spiritually united— a creed that would cause the Puritans to roll over in their graves.[31] Reflecting the current pluralistic mood, the article assumed that both Jackson and Baha'i are as much a part of America's religious mosaic as are Nashville's Methodists and Baptists.[32]

DEFINITIONS

The basic meaning of *pluralism* is something that exists in more than one form—the condition of being plural. We are focusing on a specific form of pluralism—religious. Sociologist Peter Berger defines *religious pluralism* as the "wide variety of religious and other reality-defining agencies that compete" for people's allegiance today.[33] This definition gets us started but doesn't go far enough. So far we have described religious pluralism mainly as religious diversity, but it is crucial to understand that for many it includes much more. For many people, religious pluralism is also an ideology, a philosophy regarding how religious diversity *ought* to be understood. The basic concept has been around for centuries, but in recent decades it has expanded into a popular field of study and attracted an entire throng of devoted researchers, writers, sociologists, and theologians—many referring to themselves as "religious pluralists." One such researcher, D. A. Carson, describes religious pluralism as a set of ideas that insist that tolerance *must* be granted to all religions because none of them can justifiably claim to be "the true one."[34] Religious pluralists claim that this position *ought* to be promoted by all open-minded and culturally sensitive people.[35] They argue that because of intrinsic limitations, no set of religious beliefs can legitimately claim to be the standard for assessing other sets of religious beliefs.

It's not that people who buy into the ideology of religious pluralism discount the importance of religion. Just the opposite. Most religious pluralists believe strongly in the importance of religion, but this belief is coupled with the conviction that each religion is valid and should be respected. Maybe some sort of absolute truth unifies the many religions; maybe it doesn't. But for religious pluralists, that's beside the point. Their critical point is that no single religion possesses truth in such measure that it can challenge the legitimacy of other religions. According to their ideology, the missionary who sets off for Thailand to convert Buddhists to the Christian faith is a Neanderthal in the evolution of religious sensitivity. Proponents of religious pluralism believe that no single religion holds the secret to salvation. A person who thinks otherwise is considered by them to be something of an oppressive hayseed.

According to the ideology of religious pluralism, religions are both formed and limited by their cultural and historical locations. In other words, the truth of your religion is limited to the confines of your community. It is "true" to the extent that it helps your community find answers to fundamental questions and pathways to salvation. A particular religious story may energize, guide, and define you and your community, but beyond your religion's city limits, it is not binding on anyone else. Each religion is limited by the religion next door, and you must adhere to the No Soliciting sign posted on your neighbors' front doors.

This ideological stance is comparable to my penchant for chocolate. Chocolate ice cream has a tremendous hold on me, but I recognize that it does not have the same hold on other people. My wife, for example, craves strawberry ice cream, and I would be foolish to try to convince her that chocolate ice cream is superior. It's a matter of taste. No matter how significant chocolate is to me—especially when you add almonds into the mix—its powers are lost on nonchocoholics.

Keep in mind that no matter how popular the claims regarding religious pluralism may be, they are just that—claims. The ideology of religious pluralism has behind it the weight of strong public opinion, particularly in the West and in other secularized nations such as Japan. But no matter how strong the public opinion, it doesn't verify the ideology of religious pluralism. Had the strength of opinion carried the day, the Christian faith would have died in its cradle. No matter how offensive some people may consider the New Testament claims regarding Jesus Christ,[36] their aversion is no reason to overrule what the living God has chosen to do in His Son. The Early Church confronted widespread ridicule of the gospel and went on proclaiming Christ as Lord anyway.

OUR MODEL: THE EARLY CHURCH

Responding to religious pluralism is nothing new for Christians. "How should we proclaim the gospel of Christ in our world?" is a question the Church has raised since the first century. The Early Church was keenly aware of the competing religious claims vying for acceptance. Those initial Christians could have presented the gospel as one more religious alternative in an already crowded marketplace. They could have carved out a niche for their story and left it at that.

But this was not an option for the apostles and other Christian leaders we meet in the New Testament. They believed that, in Jesus Christ, God had accomplished something involving all people, nations, cultures, and times. The birth, life, death, and resurrection of Jesus were universally important. Paul told Timothy that God our Savior "desires everyone to be saved and to come to the knowledge of the truth. For there is one God; there is also one mediator between God and humankind, Christ Jesus, himself human, who gave himself a ransom for all" (1 Tim. 2:4-6). On the Day of Pentecost, when the promised Holy Spirit was given to the Church, the nations were represented. They heard the good news in their own languages. Peter told them the universal reign of God was present in the risen Christ. The Holy Spirit was now confirming that Jesus is the Redeemer of the world (Acts 2:1-13).

The Church itself, the New Testament says, is a sign that God is now drawing all things into unity through Christ Jesus. Paul made a statement— radical at the time—that "there is neither Jew nor Greek, slave nor free, male nor female" because all people are "one in Christ" (Gal. 3:28, NIV). Through Him and by the Spirit, the Father is now reconciling "to himself all things, whether on earth or in heaven, by making peace through the blood of his cross" (Col. 1:20).

Consider the dichotomy within the ragtag bunch we know as Jesus' first disciples. At one end of the spectrum was Matthew, a Jew who, before Jesus called him, collected taxes for the Roman Empire. His job would have publicly marked him as a sinner and invited the Pharisees' scorn. At the other end was Simon the Zealot (not to be confused with Simon Peter). The surname "Zealot" identifies Simon as someone who rigorously observed all aspects of Jewish law and, consequently, would have viewed Matthew with religious contempt. Yet Jesus called both men to be His disciples. In Him they found common ground—breaking bread together and later proclaiming the gospel in the power of the Spirit (Acts 5:31-33). Out of this kind of diversity, Paul said, God in Christ has created one new humanity (Eph. 2:15).

If the first Christians' beliefs regarding God's universal deed in Christ were true, then other religious stories that claimed to be adequate independent of Christ were false. Peter wrote to young Christians who had recently left Greco-Roman religions and cults and said Christ had "ransomed [them] from the futile ways inherited from [their] ancestors" (1 Pet. 1:18). Paul left no doubt regarding the implications of the Christian gospel for other religions. "Indeed, even though there may be so-called gods in heaven or on earth—as in fact there are many gods and many lords—yet for us there is one God, the Father, from whom are all things and for whom we exist, and one Lord, Jesus Christ, through whom are all things and through whom we exist" (1 Cor. 8:5-6).

The New Testament simply and consistently permits no plurality of creators and redeemers. There is only one—the sovereign God revealed through Jesus Christ. People can reject the New Testament's message as hopelessly parochial, outdated, and erroneous, but they cannot successfully integrate it into a compilation of religions.

THE FIRST-CENTURY "MARKETPLACE" OF RELIGIONS

Earlier, we heard Alan Race describe the 21st-century scene as a "marketplace of religious possibilities." In it religions "jostle with each other," competing for attention from "shoppers."[37] Race could just as easily have been describing the 1st-century Greco-Roman world into which the gospel was born. It, too, resembled a crowded marketplace spilling over with religious wares. The options were almost unlimited. In the first century, separation of religion and state as we know it today was unimaginable, and "nothing in public life was undertaken without first seeking to determine whether the enterprise enjoyed divine favor."[38] In addition to free food, jugglers, magicians, speeches, and so forth, local celebrations included sacrifice to the local deities. Except for the Jews, worship of one God who trivialized all other so-called gods was nonexistent.

The closest thing approaching a world religion was the religion of imperial Rome—the imperial cult, established under the reigns of both Julius Caesar (100-44 B.C.) and Caesar Augustus (63 B.C.-A.D. 14).[39] Augustus declared himself lord and savior of the whole world. He established his own cult and the cult of the goddess Pax (the Roman goddess of peace) in Rome and throughout the empire. The universal reign of the Peace of Rome (the Pax Romana) was thought to be willed by the gods and was expected to last forever. People believed that the empire's grandeur verified these beliefs. Accepting the imperial religion by worshiping the gods of the state[40] was expected of everyone, and refusing to do so was considered treasonous. At the same time, the Romans assumed that every nation they conquered had its own god(s) and did not interfere with the national religious practices of these groups.[41]

With the primacy of the Roman state religion in place, the religion of imperial Rome could make room for many other gods and lords. This held so long as they accepted Roman rule and superiority[42] and "so long as they remained merely local, personal or private, and made no counter claims about universal truth and world dominion. Ultimately all gods and lords would have to serve and sustain the cause of the Roman Empire." This made the religion of imperial Rome the "world religion" of the day.[43] No wonder John the Revelator proclaimed that the Incarnate God who is Lord of all could never be successfully folded into that arrangement.

At the heart of every imperial city were temples and shrines dedicated to Augustus Caesar or some other emperor, and one or more of the Greek and Roman deities who had willed Rome's worldwide reign. Cities such as Ephesus, where emperor worship began in 29 B.C., competed for permission to build temples to the emperors. Residents of Ephesus devoted themselves to Artemis, a cosmic queen who mediated between individuals and their fate.[44] In Corinth, citizens visited the sanctuary of Asclepius, the god of healing, to seek relief from their aches and pains.[45] They also frequented the temple of Aphrodite, the goddess of love and beauty, where hundreds of sacred prostitutes served the male worshipers. And the Athenians were so addicted to worshiping gods that they had erected an altar to an unnamed god—just in case someone didn't know which god to thank or appease (Acts 17:22-23).

Besides the more traditional and official deities, numerous newer religions known as mystery religions had emerged. To feed the masses' religious hunger, mystery religions promised salvation, community, and communion with deity. People were initiated through secret rites, and as they came to understand the mysteries, they were redeemed. Mystery religions offered ecstasy and supreme visions to ordinary folk and, not surprisingly, enjoyed enormous appeal.[46] As if this were not enough, the empire was also well-stocked with "religious associations, seers and oracles, magicians and astrologers, miracle workers and philosophers." The whole cosmos was thought to be saturated by gods and evil spirits.[47]

People freely mixed religions and formed strains that were unique to a particular city, region, or populace. Augustine described how pagans would take popular religious stories and combine them "with their sacred rites and ceremonies."[48] We call such mixing syncretism. Gnosticism, which borrowed freely from Christianity, was an example of this. Jesus Christ played a very important role in Gnosticism, but He was completely reengineered and converted into a lesser being by the time the Gnostics were through with Him.

So the first-century Greco-Roman world was a religious alphabet soup— you could move a spoon around and spell almost anything. And people were free to embrace numerous religions without contradicting their allegiance to any of them. The Roman Empire expected the religions to respect one another. So long as Christians were considered a sect of the Jews, they were protected by Roman recognition of the Jews as a religion. But once that identity was stripped away, they became the ultimate "outsiders"; they simply did not fit into the multicolored picture we have described and so were persecuted for numerous reasons.[49] They would not submit to the requirements of the imperial cult. They would not endorse and participate in the assumed religious diversity and tolerance, because they would not permit their Christ to become just another player on the religious stage. They absolutely would not have Him bow before the gods of Rome. And they would not attend the temples and shrines dedicated to the emperors.[50] Christianity didn't even look like a religion because it didn't constitute a single ethnic group, such as the Jews. Consequently, Christians could not celebrate ancestral rites in a temple presided over by priests. They could not even show their critics an image of the Christ they claimed to worship. If ever there were a bunch of atheists who posed a grave threat to social order, Christians fit the bill.[51] Additionally, Christians were so diverse they couldn't even constitute a *collegium,* a legal organization of people who shared common characteristics such as place of origin, occupation, or an interest in the theater or athletics. When groups met that had no such common ties, the Romans suspected they were meeting for troublesome political reasons. To top it off, public activities included the worship of local deities, but the standoffish Christians would not participate. So they earned from their pagan neighbors the contemptuous label, "haters of the human race."[52]

In this eclectic and fluid atmosphere, the young Christian Church proclaimed Jesus Christ as Lord and Savior. The odds stacked against Christians make their faithfulness all the more remarkable. The Church had to guard against those who wanted to blend foreign elements with the gospel. Paul's letter to the Christians in Colossae chastised the false teachers who told young Christians to worship other beings in addition to worshiping Christ, claiming that only then would they be complete (Col. 2:8-23). Opportunities to corrupt the gospel waited at every turn, but the apostles worked tirelessly and tenaciously to protect its integrity.

DÉJÀ VU

"Like our sisters and brothers in the other Neopagan movements, we're polytheistic Nature worshipers, attempting to revive the best aspects of the Paleopagan[53] faiths of our ancestors within a modern scientific, artistic, ecological, and holistic context. Like our predecessors and namesakes the Druids, we're people who believe in excellence—physically, intellectually, artistically, and spiritually."

With some modification, this statement could pass for one of the first-century religious options. Instead, it appears on the Web site of the neo-pagan Druids, just one of many forms of neo-paganism—religious movements attempting to revive ancient pagan religions—that are currently thriving in Europe and North America.[54] The similarity between the century into which the gospel was born and ours is striking. Then as now, many religions share the same political and social spaces. Names and forms have changed, but the phenomenon remains much the same.

One major distinction between the Church in the first century and our situation today is that the Early Church had no part in shaping Mediterranean culture the way Christianity has shaped the West.[55] Ironically, this distinction makes our mission both easier and more difficult. On the bright side, many people are already somewhat familiar with the Christian story and its values. The Christian faith can point to many justifiable reasons for saying it has richly benefited humanity, such as widespread affirmation of the dignity and worth of each person. This value, so deeply enshrined in Western democratic institutions, is incomprehensible apart from what philosopher Alfred N. Whitehead called "the Galilean vision" that extended the good news of God's love to all people—no exceptions.[56]

On the other hand, we also have to contend with a darker side of Christianity's involvement in society. Muslims rightly remember the oppression the Crusades spawned. Jews remember a long history of anti-Semitism. Many people in lands once colonized by European "Christians" recall a legacy of exploitation and dismissal of their cultures. Musa Dube quotes an African proverb that pointedly makes this clear. "When the missionaries came, we had the land and they had the Bible. When the missionaries left, they had the land and we had the Bible."[57] Women recall how the Bible and Christianity have often been used to deny them both a full-fledged place at the table of human dignity and the Pentecostal promise of their ministry in Christ's Church.

Those who sally forth into a pluralistic world in Christ's name while ignoring the mixed Christian record will go ill prepared. They should not be surprised if they repeat longstanding errors and obstruct rather than communicate the gospel of liberation.

Today, in the presence of other religions, Christians must confront the history of a relationship between church and culture that has often compromised their witness. As Dietrich Bonhoeffer signaled so clearly, our task of disengaging from a pagan culture is quite different from the task of the Early Church. In the West we have so often allowed the world's political and economic powers to shape the gospel that we must now relearn the difference between the two.[58] Think of how easily some of us equate the gospel's success with our church budgets and membership numbers, ignoring the clear New Testament teaching that the way of discipleship is the way of the Cross. Many Christians who live under persecution are puzzled by our simplistic equation. Some Christians act as though the gospel of Jesus Christ is in danger if the secular state doesn't back it. At a time when the Nazis were persecuting faithful German Christians, Bonhoeffer asked, "How much space must the church have?" He answered, "Only as much space as it takes to faithfully proclaim the gospel of Jesus Christ."

We must also candidly confront a history where, in the name of Christ, Christians have often cooperated with political powers to subdue and convert people of other religions. Our use of "unholy alliances" must be confessed, regardless of whether other religions have done the same.[59]

Another distinction 21st-century Christians face in their mission is the prevalence of mixing Christian beliefs with ideas contrary to the Scriptures and the creeds, known as syncretism. Tendencies toward syncretism have existed since the first century, as we previously noted. But today, in the absence of any kind of church council control, syncretism is rampant. Given this, we should not be surprised if the term *Christian* seems ambiguous to many.

On a daily basis, 15 to 20 million viewers in at least 133 countries hang on every word of a modern-day syncretist—Oprah Winfrey, host of the highest-rated show in television history. She was raised in a Baptist church in Mississippi, and though she is quick to express appreciation for her Christian background, along the way Winfrey concluded that Christianity as she knew it was too hung up on the notion of a jealous God. "Come on—let's get over it!" she was quoted as saying in an article titled "The Gospel According to Oprah." And get over it she has. The God to which the Baptists introduced Winfrey has taken on revised characteristics. "Oprah's clothes may bear labels," Marcia Nelson says admiringly, "but her faith does not."[60] Her gospel doesn't require specific "doctrinal commitments or a community."[61] On her show, Oprah identifies God as "the FORCE." God doesn't have an ego problem, Winfrey said, so He doesn't care what you call Him. If you believe in a rhythm of nature and in love, then you believe in God.[62]

Winfrey is not alone in her stance. After participating in Christian services on Sunday—complete with scripture reading and confession of the Nicene Creed—a considerable number of Christians will engage in Buddhist or Hindu practices later in the week. They will read books that identify and explain the role of cosmic powers, and they harmonize all of this with the confessions they make on Sunday. Tying up loose ends is not essential when it comes to syncretism as long as it makes sense to you or your community.

Even recognized religions have sprouted from syncretism. The Church of Jesus Christ of Latter-Day Saints is one example; the Baha'i faith to which Joyce Jackson belongs is another. Baha'i draws from Buddhism, Christianity, Islam, and an astonishing mix of other religions. Though Jackson was raised Southern Baptist, at age 19 she became a member of the Baha'i faith. Why? Because she "longed for a closer connection to Christ and his teachings." Jackson said that she "wasn't getting what she needed from Christianity in general." But, she said, in Baha'i she found answers for her questions.[63] Author Bill Easum labels this kind of syncretism "designer faith."[64]

Syncretism also rears its dangerous head in more inconspicuous ways. Christian missionary and church historian Floyd Cunningham is baffled by one of his brightest Protestant seminary graduates who avoids a particular tree when he returns to his hometown because he believes a spirit inhabits it. Cunningham also knows of one Protestant church that refused to disturb a termite mound because the congregants were certain that dwendes, or spirit-dwarfs, lived there. "On an intellectual level," Cunningham observes, "most of these Christians would be reluctant to recognize anything good in another religion."[65]

The error of syncretism isn't limited to the spirit realm. If we aren't careful, we Christians can attach so much significance to a political party or country that it begins to assume religious qualities. This happened openly during World War II when many German Christians tried to mix Christianity with National Socialism (Nazism). Their mantra was: "Germany the end, Christ the means!"

Christians also need to pause before jumping on the latest self-improvement bandwagons. Some books, for example, to which Christians give almost addictive attention, even some that claim to be Christian, actually compete with orthodox Christian faith. Recognizing syncretism is often a case of specks *versus* logs; it's easier to spot in someone else than in ourselves.

Just as the Early Church found ways to tell and faithfully live the story of God in its pluralistic setting, so must we. And just as the Holy Spirit empowered and gave wisdom to the early Christians, so will He empower us today. The resurrected Christ, who was Lord over the Church and the world then, is still Lord of lords now. One day, every knee shall bow and every tongue confess that Jesus alone is the Christ, to the glory of God the Father. For there is but "one God and Father of all, who is above all and through all and in all" (Eph. 4:6).

For Reflection and Discussion

1. Explore and discuss the amazing diversity of religious options by using the links at <http://www.pluralism.org/resources/links/index.php>.
2. What is the difference between the fact of religious pluralism and the ideology of religious pluralism? Why is the distinction important?
3. Practically, what would be required for Christians to live as counterculturally as did the first-century Christians? Are there historical factors that limit our ability to bear witness as they did?

4. What are some of the ways in which Christians have in the past and in the present exhibited conduct that obstructs the gospel?

5. Syncretism can take many forms, both open and subtle. What are some of its current expressions in your culture and within the Christian church?

2

THE CHRISTIAN FAITH IN A FIELD OF DIVERSITY:
THE HISTORICAL DEVELOPMENT OF RELIGIOUS PLURALISM (SNAPSHOTS)

They had anticipated a weeklong wedding celebration with a friend in Bangalore, but Doug and Angie Flemming, Christian missionaries in Southeast Asia, instead found themselves stuck in Bangkok.[66] Soon after they boarded their Air India flight, a voice came over the intercom system announcing mechanical difficulties. After a two-hour standstill on the runway, the passengers were taken to a hotel to wait out the delay.

Hours turned into three days, giving Doug and Angie plenty of time to get acquainted with their fellow passengers who came from all over the world. Most were en route to Whitefield, a famous Indian ashram, which is a secluded place to which persons can retreat for instruction in Hinduism. At Whitefield they would listen to and learn from the Hindu teacher Sri Sathya Sai Baba. They represented numerous religious backgrounds and cultures, but a desire to study at the feet of the teacher united them.

Never had Doug and Angie encountered such a diverse group. There was a Muslim cleric from Malaysia, a Portuguese-Thai businessman from Brazil, and a young Catholic exchange student from the United States. The pilgrims also included an Indian-Australian computer technician from Sydney, a Buddhist monk from Thailand, an Indian-Fijian doctor from New Zealand, and a well-known Hindu research physician associated with the World Health Organization.

"They were open to any and all ideas," Doug said of their fellow travelers. "They found merit in all religious teachings. Truth, they believed, can be found along many paths. So they insisted on tolerance for other beliefs and practices."

Although Doug and Angie's story was set in Bangkok, the religious diversity, openness, and mutuality it reveals just as easily marks London, Amsterdam, Atlanta, or hundreds of additional American cities and towns. Their experience symbolizes the seismic shift in the way much of our society approaches religion—a shift that has taken place over centuries and deserves, if not demands, our attention.

As we have noted, religious variety is nothing new. What is relatively new, particularly in what was once called the Christian West, is the conviction held by many that no single religion contains truth that people of other religions *ought* to embrace. Instead, the truth of each religion is relative to the community that finds fulfillment in it. For more than a millennium, Christianity was the dominant religion in Europe and in some of its colonies. In Europe other religions were often excluded, greatly restricted, or, as in the Jews' case, persecuted. But in more recent centuries our society began moving toward toleration and eventually arrived at the present where many people consider all religions equal.[67]

How did we shift from a time when the Church uniformly believed in Christ as the Redeemer of all people to a time when many Christians embrace the ideology of religious pluralism?[68]

Paul Knitter answers the question with one word: "knowledge."[69] Our knowledge of other religions and cultures, he says, has turned the age-old fact of religious diversity into "a newly experienced reality." Expansion of our knowledge is traceable. Christians have been more or less acquainted with other religions from the beginning, with Jews as neighbors since the first century and Muslims since the seventh century, for example.[70] Early in the second millennium extensive overland East-West trade expanded Christian Europe's knowledge of Islam, Zoroastrianism, Buddhism, and Manichaeism.[71] Exploration and colonization in the 16th and 17th centuries produced a torrent of geographical and cultural literature that led many people to question the absolute validity of Christianity.[72] Emergence of the science of religions[73] in the late 19th century accelerated opportunities for becoming acquainted with the religions next door as well as those further away. Today, scholarly and popularly written books that deal with the world's religions elbow for space on bookstore shelves, particularly in Europe and North America. Translations of the Bhagavad Gita, the Tao-Te-Chin, and the Koran are readily available. Terms from Eastern religions—*karma, reincarnation, nirvana*—have found their way into the English language. Your neighbor across the street may have been raised a Christian but has since added Buddhism[74] to his or her religious world and also participates in a branch of the Sufi Order International.

Author Charles Davis notes that, because of increasing religious knowledge, many Christian students are not content to have their religious questions answered solely within the framework of Christian ideas. They require comparisons with other religions. "Religious pluralism," he says, "has undoubtedly entered into the consciousness of the younger generation."[75]

Just half a millennium ago, when European countries began "discovering" new continents, the Western world became conscious of existing civilizations in places like the Americas and Asia. This awakening was followed by colonialism and missionary activity. Christians were already familiar with other religions, but familiarity expanded greatly as a result of missionary activity.[76] Over time the dominion of Western colonizers gave way to independence movements in the colonies. Cultures demanded that their distinctive character be respected. Eventually the stories of Buddhists, Sikhs, Hindus, African religions, and others were heard, and these competing voices often drowned out the efforts of Christian missionaries. Dominance gave way to a demand for tolerance, and in many instances tolerance developed into established pluralism.

HISTORICISM

One of the principal engines driving the formation of religious pluralism as an ideology is *historicism*. Historicism is the belief that social structures—including religions—are best understood in the context of their historical origins. The Italian philosopher and historian Giambattista Vico (1668—1744) is credited as the father of historicism. In his book *The New Science*,[77] Vico taught that to understand the things we accept as true and certain today, we must peel back centuries of layers from institutions, beliefs, texts, and so forth. The passage of years produces changes in language and customs, Vico said, overlaying humankind's beliefs and institutions with error. Humans created history, and that creation must now be rigorously and scientifically examined—a process that will lead to wisdom. For Vico, the scientific study of causes didn't rule out divine influence upon history. In fact, he believed history reflects the presence of a divine order or providence guiding the development of human institutions.

For Christians, historicism has often acted as a stepping-stone rather than a stumbling block. It taught us how to learn about and listen to other religions without simply reading them through Judeo-Christian eyes. It promotes awareness, sensitivity, and careful examination. If our faith is as strong as we say it is, then understanding religious origins is something we should welcome.

Because of historicism we have gained a much better understanding of the early Christian community and can better understand the gospel as the New Testament presents it. Examining the first-century Greco-Roman world shows us, for example, that it was built on a patron-client structure. Fathers were considered patrons, or benefactors, of the family, and children were clients, or recipients of benefits. Fathers provided for their children, but they owed him as a result. The emperor would have been society's chief patron as well as the client of the gods. A person might be a client in one setting (a citizen before the governor) and a patron in another (a father in a family). Your ambition in the first century was to increase your gifts to people but not necessarily for altruistic reasons. By giving gifts you gained power and influence because you increased a person's indebtedness to you. Christ comes along and turns that social structure on its head. He cares for children, elevates women, and heals lepers and paralytics who have nothing of material or social significance to give in return. He says to His disciples, "Forgive everyone indebted to [you]" (Luke 11:4), and "You call me Teacher and Lord—and you are right, for that is what I am. So if I . . . have washed your feet, you also ought to wash one another's feet" (John 13:13-14). Jesus' gospel and the way of life He established for His disciples were something a patron-client structure would never permit. The system locked people into a hierarchical order and made it difficult for them to advance. Yet Jesus, the Lord and Master, grabbed a bowl and towel, washed His disciples' feet, and undercut the establishment.

Setting aside the dietary and table rules was another radical subversion on Jesus' part. The laws governed how, what, and with whom righteous Jews could eat, and their adherence to these laws decided their religious purity. Eating with sinners meant you had crossed religious boundaries and defiled yourself before God. Jesus came along and threw all that unnecessary baggage overboard because it weighed down the gospel He proclaimed. He freely extended God's love and fellowship to people such as a disreputable woman (Luke 7:36-39) and Zacchaeus (19:2-10) who could not have even begun to measure up to the established rules of membership. Twice (Mark 6:33-44; 8:1-10) Jesus crossed the purity lines by feeding the multitudes out in fields, abandoning concern for both ritual hand washing and receiving people according to whether they qualified as righteous. Even more radical, the second feeding occurred in a predominantly Gentile community. Unless we are familiar with the importance attached to dietary and table rules, and why Jesus dismissed them, the significance of these stories skips right past us. Jesus' actions made clear that the kingdom of God has no room for exclusiveness. The Kingdom doesn't depend upon what or with whom one eats. It is not what goes into a person that defiles a person—it's what comes out (Matt. 15:10-11). Scholars' use of historicism has helped them, and us, understand all of this.

Historicism has also had a profoundly positive influence upon the way we read the Bible. Using the tools of modern historical research, biblical scholars have helped us understand how the various writings that comprise the Bible were developed. The Gospels of Matthew, Mark, and John, for example, conform to the first-century biography genre, which differs greatly from 20th-century forms of biography. Today's biographies focus on a person's psychological motivations, childhood influences, and individual accomplishments or failures. But biographers in the Greco-Roman world were primarily interested in the *significance* of a famous person's career and how that person died, which was regarded as a measure of his character. Biographers measured an individual's importance according to the group with which he identified and often used the biography to express what was valued or urged in that community. In the Book of Mark, the significance of Christ is that He intentionally makes His way to the Cross, signifying to the original readers that to be a disciple of Christ is to take up the cross. There is no way we could simply read the Gospels and know all of this, but when the scholars explain genre characteristics, it helps unlock the gospel for us.

Scholars have also used methods of historical research to decipher how Jewish and Christian communities influenced the formation of the biblical texts. Jesus lived during an era known as second Temple Judaism, referring to the Temple the Jews rebuilt after returning from exile. The grand expectation during this period was that the exile would end and the kingdom of God would be inaugurated when God returned to the Temple and forgave the sins of the people. So when Jesus forgives sins and declares that He is the embodiment of the new Temple, we understand that He is ushering in the kingdom of God. God has returned to the Temple, not as the Jews expected, but in the person of Jesus.

REDUCTIONISM

In the 19th century, under the influence of intensifying atheistic secularism, historicism often became *reductionistic*.[78] Reductionism is the belief that

the world and human existence can be either adequately or completely understood within (reduced to) the limits of the world itself. People don't need to
and shouldn't go beyond the limits of this world to understand the world. So
social institutions, social values, religions, texts such as the Bible, and so
forth, have no causes other than those found in history—in this world alone.

In its reductionist form, historicism applied the cause-effect theory used
in the natural sciences. For every effect, reductionists believed, a natural
cause can be found that completely accounts for the effect. Explanations that
don't rely upon natural causes—such as appeal to divine activity—are only il-
lusory, mythical, or superstitious. So Vico's confidence that history shows the
presence of providential order was discarded. Historicism in its reductionistic
form is often called "nothing but-ism," meaning that there is nothing more to
institutions—including religion—than their historical causes.

Using this thought process, all religions can be fully explained by examining and understanding their historical origins.[79] Many people believe that
the Jews adopted monotheism from the Egyptians who enslaved them. Their
belief in one God did not come from heaven or some sort of revelation but
derived from the Egyptian belief that the universe originated from one deity
who created everything. The same kind of mythmaking process can be applied to Buddha's conception and birth. Many Mahayana Buddhists believe
that one day while Buddha's mother-to-be was sleeping, her attendants saw a
white elephant descend from heaven and enter her womb through her side,
resulting in Buddha's miraculous conception. The white elephant was none
other than the divine being who, out of compassion for humankind, came
down from heaven.

Christianity has similar mythmaking origins according to reductionist
historicism. Many people believe that the idea of Christ's resurrection derived
from a group of disenchanted and confused disciples who could not come to
grips with their own bitter disappointments. They coped by creating a story—
their crucified Messiah was no longer dead but miraculously alive again—that
bolstered them and saved them from despair. Reductionists point to the differ-
ing accounts of Christ's resurrection in the Gospels that don't agree on such
details as who went to the tomb first. Through the mythmaking process the Jesus of history, the great Jewish teacher who died—and whose flesh rotted like
any other mortal—became the Christ of faith.

Reductionists maintain that this mythmaking process occurs in all religions. Miraculous explanations are completely unnecessary. Explainable caus-

es can account for each religion's origins, so adding divine or transcendent causes would be foolish. As many 19th- and 20th-century people embraced a reductionist view of religions, it became more difficult to accept traditional beliefs in the superiority of one religion over another. The Holy Spirit caused Mary to conceive, and a divine being in the form of a white elephant entered the womb of the Buddha's mother—now which one do you want to believe?

We can see how this more extreme form of historicism would contribute to the emergence of religious pluralism. All divine explanations for religion have been brushed aside. According to this idea, the truth is that all religions are purely accidental. The events that brought them into existence could just as easily have been different. Just as history is manmade, so are religions. And because no religion can rise above its historical contexts, none of them—including Christianity—possess divine and binding truth that people of other religions *ought* to accept.

Take the following story from church history, which illustrates how reductionist historicism reaches its conclusions. Early in the fourth century, a bitter controversy erupted among Christians over whether Christ is fully God or whether He is the first and highest of all God's creatures. The Arian party, named after the Egyptian Arius (c. A.D. 250-336), taught that while Christ is the Savior of the world, He is still a creature—God's first and highest creation. Another group, under the strong influence of Athanasius (A.D. 296-373), taught that Christ is fully God, just as the Father is God. The debate was the centerpiece of the Council of Nicaea in A.D. 325, which rejected the Arian position and affirmed that Christ is fully God. We Christians affirm this stance in the Nicene Creed.

The council's decision was supposed to have ended the controversy. It didn't. The Arians (mostly in the eastern part of the empire) who denied Christ's deity didn't just fade away. Instead, for over 50 years they and their sympathizers offered stiff opposition. If an emperor (such as Constantius in the East) threw his support to the Arians and their sympathizers, that position became orthodox and the Nicene party fell out of favor. But if an emperor (such as Constans in the West)[80] backed the Nicene position, it was declared orthodox. This battle, which often included political and ecclesiastical intrigue on both sides, continued until Emperor Theodosius came to power in 380. He forcefully supported the Nicene position, a position reconfirmed at the Council of Constantinople in 381. But for half a century, orthodoxy had depended upon what the emperor in question happened to support.

Observing all this, a strict historicist would say, "Don't you Christians get it? Surely you are not so blind. What you affirm today as having been 're-vealed' by God depends completely upon ancient political happenstance. One more roll of the political dice, such as military success by the Arian Valens (364-378), and maybe you would now be affirming the 'revealed' truth that Christ is a creature, and not God."[81]

Some efforts were made during the 19th century to make room for all other religions under a Christian umbrella. But by the late 19th century, main-stream modern thought had judged these efforts as failures. The prevailing be-lief was that it is not a common "god" that all religions share but historical happenstance and heated human creativity. Author Joseph O'Leary, adopting the extreme historicist explanation of religion, says that if Christians will only recognize the many forms their own religion has taken, and that Christianity occupies only one spot on the large religious landscape, they will see how they are just as confined to history as any other religion.[82] History has pro-duced many forms of Buddhism and Hinduism (often described as a family of religions) over time, amid diverse mind-sets and social strata, and Christianity is no different. It consists of Roman Catholics, Eastern Orthodox, and many forms of Protestants whose beliefs often conflict with each other. One segment believes God loves and wants to save a limited number of people, and another believes God loves and wants to redeem all people. Following the 16th-centu-ry Reformation, Christians killed hundreds of thousands of other Christians—all in the name of divine revelation. But somehow they are able to overlook all of this. Christianity no more needs a god to explain itself than does Hinduism or neo-paganism. Christians, O'Leary says, need to grow up "historically."[83]

THREE IMPORTANT CONTRIBUTORS: SCHLEIERMACHER, DILTHEY, AND MAURICE[84]

Friedrich Schleiermacher (1768—1834), a German theologian, is known as the father of modern theology. He represents the first major step toward recognizing religious pluralism within Christianity. The 18th-century Enlight-enment raised the question, "How could a loving God fail to offer salvation to all within their own historical and cultural settings? Wouldn't God speak to people from within the historical context in which they exist?"

Schleiermacher answered that all persons have a "feeling of God con-sciousness." There are different stages of development in this feeling of God consciousness, with the monotheistic religions being the highest. Religions representing the lower stages will eventually advance to monotheism, he believed. The Christian religion is the ultimate stage of religion's development; Schleiermacher asserted that Jesus' God consciousness was perfect. Nevertheless, God is redemptively present in some measure in all religions, he said, so His presence in all religions should be respected.[85]

Even though Schleiermacher made a place for other religions, he still thought of Christianity as superior. So while historicism affected his estimate of other religions, it did not come to full flower. He still implicitly depreciated other religions in favor of Christianity.

Toward the close of the 19th century, German philosopher Wilhelm Dilthey (1833—1911) stressed the fundamental importance of our social relationships—the family, community, tribe, and clan relationships from which our values emerge. The reality of life is that we live in a particular region, within a particular geography, and are born into a particular social and cultural structure. If you want to understand a person's values and religion, you have to take these contexts into consideration. So the fundamental meaning of "history" is not some grand story, so to speak, but the crib or womb in which we come to know ourselves. We recognize how rich that is but also how limited.

I came to understand myself in a Christian setting. I was taken to a church rather than a mosque, and my family celebrated Christmas rather than Ramadan. Given my social situation, it's not hard to understand why I'm a Christian. Dilthey said this consciousness of our historical limitations should keep us from making absolute claims about what other people should believe and how they should act. We were nurtured and shaped in a particular social womb, and that's how we became who we are. And we should realize that is happening to other people in other contexts all over the world. That context, however, may mistakenly teach its people that its beliefs are absolute. Chinese people were taught for centuries to believe that China is the center of earth. Soldiers in Japan were once taught that people from other cultures and countries were subhuman, so from their perspective they weren't doing anything wrong when thrusting a bayonet through the womb of a pregnant Filipino mother. Some children in *madrassas,* or religious schools, in certain Islamic countries are being taught from the Koran that the West is Satan's citadel and should be destroyed, while many children in Christian Sunday Schools are taught that only Christians truly know God.

We live in a particular historical era, and we are bound by its limitations. The next historical era will surpass what we now know. When I was growing up in the Jim Crow South, Blacks could not eat in my grandmother's dining room. They had to eat in the kitchen. Black field hands could not eat inside houses; they had to eat on the back steps or in the yard. These "laws" were as much a part of my religious convictions as the laws "Honor your father and your mother" (Exod. 20:12) and "Remember the sabbath day, and keep it holy" (v. 8). No sharp distinction was made between the two; both were grounded in my understanding of how the world *ought* to be. But, thank God, through the years these "laws" crumbled, largely because of the power and benefits of the Civil Rights Movement. This experience illustrates Dilthey's claim that history is an "immense field of ruins."

Recognizing historical limitations, Dilthey taught, is the key to understanding cultures and religions. No matter how rich they may be, all cultures and religions are necessarily limited. The discrepancies between various beliefs and systems we observe should make us skeptical regarding what we claim to know. Universally valid truth still exists, but because we are planted in and limited to our own historical and cultural contexts, the best we can ever hope to accomplish is an approximation of truth.[86] Wide-ranging humility is required.

In the middle of the 19th century, Anglican theologian J. F. D. Maurice (1805-72) spoke of the "actual presence" of the kingdom of Christ in the world.[87] He believed God's supreme self-disclosure happened in Christ. What was only anticipated in other religions was made complete in Christianity. Nevertheless, Maurice said, we should recognize that in the world religions there are "precious fragments of truth" (e.g., the Buddhist belief that love is the essence of ultimate reality) reflecting the kingdom of Christ. We should recognize that Islam, Hinduism, and Buddhism can and do serve God's purposes. Missionaries should build upon this foundation.

SCIENCE OF RELIGION

In the last third of the 19th century, a new academic discipline known as the science of religion was born, and its heyday lasted until the beginning of the 20th century. Known also as the History of Religion School, it contributed much to the evolution of religious pluralism. The school rigorously applied the principles of historicism to Christianity and other religions.[88] Ernst Troeltsch (1865—1923)[89] was one of its most distinguished representatives. He was interested in the role religion played in human intellectual development and the historical process by which religion came to be. Troeltsch, a confessing Christian, said we humans are purely historical and cultural creatures. Therefore, all our religious claims regarding the divine are no more than culturally conditioned stories, or myths. A person's religious experience may lead him or her to think he or she has attained knowledge of the absolute and true God. But the naïveté embedded in such certainty would be clear if only he or she could recognize that people of other religions have similar experiences and reach similar conclusions. Informed people will take the additional steps of embracing religious pluralism, recognizing the immensity of God, and confronting the historical quality of human experience. They will then see how historical and critical study discredits religious dogma.[90]

Normally, Troeltsch thought, Christians are ignorant of their historical limitations. They think they exist as an exceptional island in the stream of world religions. Blind to the truth about their own religion, they evaluate other religions historically but can't apply this assessment to their own.[91]

Late in life Troeltsch came to believe that in the next world, in the heavenly kingdom, the religions would be united. In anticipation of this, the world religions should show tolerance toward each other, a tolerance built upon love.[92] Even with this belief, O'Leary says, Troeltsch was still not sufficiently pluralistic. Troeltsch, he says, still tended to impose a hierarchical order on the family of religions.[93]

THE FIRST WORLD PARLIAMENT OF RELIGIONS IN CHICAGO (IN CONNECTION WITH THE COLUMBIAN EXPOSITION OF 1893)

The first World Parliament of Religions is credited with being a major catalyst in spurring the growth of religious pluralism in North America. Propelled by 19th-century American religious fervor, the parliament contributed importantly to a shift away from the dominance of Anglo-Saxon Protestantism and to the beginning of a multireligious society. All the major religions of the world were represented. The words of Mal. 2:10 appeared on the cover of the parliament's proceedings: "Have we not all one father? hath not one God created us?" (KJV). Author Richard Seager said, "After the Parliament, there were many ways to be religious."[94] In his address to the delegates, Swami Vivekanandam, a Hindu who subsequently toured the United States and Europe as a popular speaker, quoted from a hymn he learned in India as a child: "As the different streams having their sources in different places, all mingle their water in the sea. Sources in different tendencies, various though they appear, crooked and straight, all lead to Thee."[95]

TWENTIETH CENTURY: FROM EAST TO WEST

During the 20th century religious pluralism became more and more readily embraced. Courses in world religions became commonplace, even in high schools, and the classes' ground rules required that all religions be taught comparatively and without any preferential treatment. China began to open as its postwar isolation and fear of foreigners subsided. Westerners traveling in the Orient became more common, and opportunities to observe other religions up close expanded. The numbers of students coming from the East to study in the West, and vice versa, escalated. As people from the East and Middle East came to the West, they brought their religions and built impressive temples and mosques. A steady stream of movies and books favorably and informatively presenting other religions also contributed to global awareness. The monumentally popular book *Siddhartha* (1922) by Hermann Hesse exposed Westerners to a young man's journey along the path of Eastern spirituality toward enlightenment. *Gandhi* (1982), the widely acclaimed movie telling a riveting story of Mahatma Gandhi, was influential in illuminating the teachings of Hinduism. Another popular movie, *Kundun* (1997), gave an intriguing account of the 14th Dalai Lama.

IMMIGRATION TO EUROPE

Edwin de Jong, Christian pastor in Gottmadingen, Germany, observes that after World War II, economic factors in Europe played a role in the growth of religious pluralism. Rebuilding Europe after the war took an enormous amount of money and labor. Through the Marshall Plan, the United States contributed large sums of money for rebuilding. But because many men had died in the war and many others were unwilling to work in low-paying jobs, a labor shortage occurred.

The solution was to import cheap labor, especially from Turkey and Morocco. Starting in the 1950s and booming in the 1960s, many foreign laborers came to work in Europe. The plan was that workers would be in Europe only temporarily. But many of them stayed and brought their families. With the growing population of Muslims, Europeans began to grow accustomed to the presence of a religion other than Christianity. The process intensified when several African countries gained independence (e.g., Algeria), and many of their citizens moved to Europe, bringing their faith with them.[96]

Second Vatican Council (1962-65)

One of the most important 20th-century contributors to a growing sensitivity to non-Christian religions was the second Vatican Council, which generated major reforms in Catholic doctrine. Although Vatican II did not support the ideology of religious pluralism, it did establish a positive role for non-Christian religions in "advanced cultures." The Declaration on the Relation to Non-Christian Religions *(Nostra Aetate)* states:

> The Catholic Church rejects nothing that is true and holy in these religions. She regards with sincere reverence those ways of conduct and of life, those precepts and teachings which, though differing in many aspects from the ones she holds and sets forth, nonetheless often reflect a ray of that Truth which enlightens all men. Indeed, she proclaims, and ever must proclaim Christ "the way, the truth, and the life" (John 14:6), in whom men may find the fullness of religious life, in whom God has reconciled all things to Himself.[97]

Vatican II left no doubt about the missionary character of the Church. "The pilgrim Church is missionary by her very nature, since it is from the mission of the Son and the mission of the Holy Spirit that she draws her origin." Conversion to Christ and forsaking other religions remained an undeniable missionary goal. However, Vatican II asserted that missionaries would discover "grace among the nations."

Catholic scholars agree that the Vatican II documents teach that devotees of other religions can be saved. But they disagree over whether Vatican II teaches that other religions are redemptive in themselves. The official position is that the other religions are not redemptive. A vocal minority of scholars argues to the contrary.[98]

Postcolonial Criticism

A fairly recent form of social analysis known as postcolonial criticism is another contributing factor in the emergence of religious pluralism. Postcolonial criticism exposes the many ways colonial powers imposed their own cultures upon the cultures of the people they colonized. Postcolonial studies draw attention to "the importance and presence of minority and subjugated voices which have been lost, overlooked, or suppressed"[99] in the texts, histories, and narratives of the colonizers. The colonizers' disposition, partially fed by a sense of religious superiority, led them to believe that they possessed the truth and that the colonized countries were inferior. The colonial powers disregarded these countries' established education systems, religion, and values, replacing them with "superior" Western values, such as technology, democracy, and Christianity.

This disregard comes under severe criticism in the 2002 movie *Rabbit-Proof Fence*. Set in 1930s Australia, the movie takes a critical look at colonial British authorities who believed that children born out of illicit relationships between whites and Aboriginals threatened to corrupt the pure European race. They rounded up the children like cattle and placed them in schools that trained them to accept a lesser role in society and to refrain from intermarrying or producing other mixed-race children. The rabbit-proof fence, built to keep rabbits from invading cropland, symbolized the children's plight.

Postcolonial criticism encourages people to retell and reembrace their stories, to confront the ways their own cultures were suffocated and denied in the interest of Western "superiority." Examining the ways in which colonizers imposed their beliefs upon the religions of those colonized is part of this process. Postcolonial criticism seeks to expose the domination that occurred and to give uncensored voice to the religions and cultures of the colonized.

INTERNET ENCOUNTERS

Finally, the dissemination of information and globalization of cultures ignited by the Internet have probably contributed to religious pluralism more extensively than anyone can measure. A Google search of "Christianity" turns up 33.2 million Web sites, "Islam" turns up 46.2 million sites, "Hindu" 17.2 million, and "Buddhism" 15.5 million. And those numbers don't include the millions of other Web sites devoted to thousands of other religions.

Wadi Haddad, president of Knowledge Enterprise, Inc., says this free global flow of information has resulted in an international culture that offers people an opportunity to explore other cultures without leaving the comforts of home. You can sign up at www.dailyom.com to receive a continual e-mail flow of inspirational thoughts that will nurture your mind, body, and spirit. You can visit www.beliefnet.com—with chat rooms and articles devoted to 17 religions—and find a guide to evangelical Christianity alongside a guide to kabbalah. Or you can log onto www.pluralism.org and gain a solid introduction to world religions thanks to the Pluralism Project of Harvard University.

All this exposure has multiplied our opportunities for learning about and experiencing the various religions, and it has contributed to the prevalent belief that selecting a religion (or religions) is simply a matter of personal taste, psychological disposition, and values. This plethora of information has in some instances shaken individuals' allegiance to their traditional religions.[100]

While all of these 20th-century shifts were taking place, the West was experiencing a crisis of public confidence. Two world wars jolted Westerners' confidence in the superiority of their own civilization and in the capability of the Judeo-Christian tradition to resolve social conflict. "Many who survived the Second World War found themselves unable to believe in a loving *and* powerful God who [would permit] the horrors of war and the unspeakable reality of genocide—to say nothing of the absurd specter of nuclear holocaust," says Calvin College professor Richard J. Plantinga.[101] A book titled *The Disappearing Heaven* by Dutch author H. W. von der Dunk traces Europe's loss of hope and confidence in modern ideals. Antonie Holleman reported on the book and summarized the author's conclusion: "The feeling of most people at the end of this dramatic century is that humanity has lost heaven; no God, no objective truth, no meaning, no metanarrative [overarching story by which to live]."[102]

Roman Catholic theologian Karl Rahner looked at this long process and concluded, "The West is no longer shut up in itself." We can no longer think of ourselves as occupying the center of world history and the center of culture.[103]

For Reflection and Discussion

1. What are the implications of the relativity of all religions for the Christian faith?

2. Are you aware of additional contributors to the development of religious pluralism that have not been discussed in this chapter? For example, can you think of additional movies and lyrics of popular music that contribute to an increased awareness of other religions?

3. Christians in the first century encountered a religiously diverse world and so do we. What are some of the major differences and similarities between the two experiences?

4. Among the factors that have contributed to the emergence of religious pluralism in the West, are there some you believe to be more influential than others? If so, why?

5. Are there forms of reductionism that you encounter in public evaluations of religion (e.g., on television, in film) and in your reading and/or academic studies?

3

FINDING TRUTH ALONG MANY PATHS:
PLURALITY, POSTMODERNITY, AND A NEW OPENING FOR THE GOSPEL

"I know you're out there. I can feel you now. I know that you're afraid. You're afraid of us, you're afraid of change," says Neo in the closing moments of *The Matrix*,[104] the 1999 film directed by Larry and Andy Wachowski.

Anyone who has watched the movie knows that Neo addresses his threats to the Matrix. But what is the Matrix? And why should it fear Neo?

According to Mark Tabb, writing in the *Kansas City Star,* the Matrix is modernity run amok, symbolized by an omnipotent machine that distorts reality and enslaves humankind.[105] But postmodernity, symbolized by Neo and the other rebels, has entered the picture and seeks to expose modernity's threat to the human spirit. Neo, the film's main character, continues the indictment: "I don't know the future. I didn't come here to tell you how this is going to end; I came here to tell you how this is going to begin. Now, I'm going to hang up this phone, and I'm going to show these people what you don't want them to see. I'm going to show them a world without you."

During the modern era, many people boasted that humankind's rational mind would set humanity free from the constraints of religion and superstition. But postmodern observers say that an arrogant misuse of reason has not produced freedom but instead restricted the human spirit by reducing what people can believe and know to the confines of this world. Instead of setting people free, they say, modernity made them little more than part of a great cosmic machine. The consequent irony, numerous postmodern thinkers point out, is that freedom, a major hallmark of modernity, is now being squelched by the very system that was supposed to protect it.

"The Matrix is everywhere," says Morpheus, Neo's teacher. It's "all around us. You can see it when you look out your window or when you turn on your television. The Matrix is the world that has been pulled over your eyes . . . There's something wrong with the world."

Early in the film Morpheus asks Neo, "Do you know what I'm talking about?"

Do *we* know what Morpheus is talking about? Whether the judgments postmodernity levels against modernity are fair, or the conflict between them as severe as Neo claims, is subject to intense debate. But the differences are important enough to warrant our attention because they will help us understand the context of religious pluralism and how to tell the gospel story within that context.

Postmodern is a term many of us are still getting to know. We hear it more and more often because many people believe we are experiencing a historic shift from one era (modernity) to another (postmodernity). In varying degrees the change affects us all, though not everyone is in agreement regarding its nature, its importance, or even what it should be called. Some Christians argue that, far from passing away, modernity still has lively contributions to make.[106] We are simply witnessing modifications in modernity, which has morphed into "hypermodernity," they say. And clearly the confident atheism that marked earlier moderns like Sigmund Freud and Karl Marx hasn't evaporated in a postmodern dawn.[107] But others argue that we are undergoing a transition similar in magnitude to the shift from the Middle Ages into the Modern era. We should recognize modernity's sunset and not lament the emergence of postmodernity, they say.[108] I have no interest in trying to decide the extent to which the world is still modern and to what extent it has become postmodern. I believe the postmodern markers are sufficiently evident and important to justify serious attention, especially as they bear on the role of religion in human life. Rather than fear postmodernity, I believe that it presents the Christian faith with opportunities for proclaiming the gospel that modernity in some of its essential features opposed. Our goal is to identify and understand these opportunities. But to do this we must first give attention to the rise and decline (or crisis) of modernity.

EMERGENCE OF THE MODERN ERA

Some changes in history are so seismic in their impact that they rearrange the way people understand themselves, their societies, and the world. Theologian Alister McGrath says that as a result of such major changes, what seemed believable in the past now becomes unacceptable, eccentric, and even irrational.[109] The emergence of the modern era was such an occasion.

Modernity flowered in the 18th and 19th centuries as a fruit of the Age of Reason (c. 1685—1789), also known as the Enlightenment.[110] Modernity is sometimes spoken of as "the Enlightenment project."[111] Preceding the Age of Reason were the Wars of Religion that ravaged Europe in the name of God and revelation and, consequently, discredited Christianity in many people's eyes.[112] The Wars of Religion culminated in the savage Thirty Years War (1618-48).[113] Religious conflict had left thousands dead and most of Europe hopelessly divided over what it meant to be Christian. Understandably, many thoughtful people viewed the Church as having obstructed human progress. It had fought internal wars over dogma, often cast its lot with oppressive monarchs, and protected clergy privileges. It had too often supported the political and intellectual status quo.[114]

Around this time, philosophers and scientists such as Francis Bacon (1561—1626), Galileo (1564—1642), Johann Kepler (1571—1630), and Isaac Newton (1642—1727) began studying the observable world and turning to nature for answers about nature. This was not characteristic of the Middle Ages, a time when people turned mostly to church teaching and philosophers such as Plato and Aristotle for answers to their questions about the world. But as these men studied, they found that they could use reason to comprehend the laws of nature because nature itself is rational, just as humans are. Though these early scientists believed their studies glorified God, they learned that the mind, when used properly, is not dependent upon church tradition for all answers concerning the observable world. English philosopher John Locke (1632—1704) went so far as to say that placing revelation above reason is like asking a person to blind himself. God has given reason, hence reason *is* revelation. Let those who would seriously search for truth take heed: removing reason "to make way for revelation puts out the light of both."[115] Assertions such as these signified a move away from dependence upon ecclesiastical authority as a principal source of knowledge and opened up the possibility of applying reason in other arenas. Thoughtful people began to ask: "What if humankind were to apply the laws of nature and the rules of empirical science to the social realm—economics, education, politics, family life, and so forth? Could the order found in nature transfer to society?"

Numerous events—including these men's studies—are suggested as the beginning of the modern era, but no one can find its birth certificate. It might have been born in 1436 when Johann Gutenberg invented movable type and the printing press or when Martin Luther broke from the Roman Catholic Church in 1520 or perhaps at the end of the Thirty Years War in 1648. We do know that modernity's roots can be traced back at least to the close of the Middle Ages (15th century), to the Renaissance (15th and 16th centuries), and to the Protestant Reformation (16th century). We also know that modern science dates back to the late 16th century and that exploration and colonization of the New World in the 16th and 17th centuries played an important role in modernity's formation. But we don't know exactly when it began. All we know is it showed up and stuck around.

The Launching

"Animal trainers." That's essentially what the Enlightenment philosopher Immanuel Kant (1724—1804) called the church authorities, civil authorities, and philosophers who, he said, had erroneously tutored the Christian West for hundreds of years. The Church especially, he said, had treated people more like domesticated animals than free people whose minds are capable of thinking. This treatment had intimidated people so much that they were afraid to take a single step without the Church's permission. It had warned people of the horrible consequences—including hell—that would follow if they tried to think and walk on their own. But because of the Enlightenment, Kant said, the long, dark night of infancy, intimidation, and fear is over. If people exercise their reason and declare independence from their "animal trainers," they will learn to live on their own. After falling on their faces a few times, they will learn to act bravely and creatively.[116]

Kant, and many others before and after him, set out to teach people how to walk unaided by anything but adherence to reason.[117] Weak people, he recognized, would still need miracles and irrational religious dogma, but in Kant's view, religion, tradition, and political privilege had had their day and had failed. The frequently violent conflicts in the Church, its thirst for privilege, and its abuse of power had left it largely discredited. The track record of alliances between religious and political authorities was particularly galling. Conflicting claims among the philosophers had discredited their claims to know. The human mind, Voltaire declared,[118] deserves freedom, and the human community deserves peace and progress.[119] Let the age of mental enslavement end and the age of enlightenment begin! "Enlightenment," Kant announced, "is man's emergence from his self-incurred immaturity. Humankind's inability to use its understanding without the guidance of another is over. Dare to reason!"[120] How liberating the Enlightenment's theme!

As we can see, classical Christian faith did not fare well under the critical eye of many Enlightenment figures. They confidently believed that applying reason would emancipate humankind from the chains of irrational religion. But it would be a mistake to think of the Enlightenment simply as an enemy of the Christian faith. Even Kant wanted to retain religion, as long as it submitted to the strict discipline of reason.[121] Similarly, the Frenchman Pierre Bayle (1647—1706), a puzzling French Protestant, had a rigorous faith in God and revelation. But he delighted in puncturing what he saw as contradictions between much Christian dogma and the self-evident dictates of reason. There is, he said, much in Christianity that is downright irrational and unbelievable.[122]

Some Enlightenment figures believed reason alone could replace orthodox Christian faith altogether, but many others used reason not to abolish God "but to see him in a clearer light."[123] Predecessors of the Enlightenment such as Copernicus (1473—1543), Galileo (1564—1642), and Kepler (1571—1630) had already identified reason as a gift from God. They saw no conflict between exploring the natural order and being Christian, and in fact believed their endeavors would glorify God.

The Goal and the Path

If the framers of modernity were to succeed, then the oppression and retardation that had crippled Christian-dominated lands would end, and a glorious future would emerge. The hallmark of modernity was confidence that developing and applying objective reason to all spheres of life would yield a secular form of the kingdom of God on earth. The exercise of unfettered reason would release people from the prejudices of religion, tradition, and political intrigue. If confidence was modernity's hallmark, steady progress would be its path. Progress would take place along broad fronts, including education, morality, government, economics, community life, and individual happiness. Universal moral ideals based on reason would replace parochial and often contradictory moral teachings based on Christian dogma.[124]

Modern confidence received a shot in the arm in the form of high-octane fuel after Charles Darwin published *The Origin of the Species* (1859). Richard Hofstadter, late professor of American history at Columbia University, says that many people consulted this book "with the reverence usually reserved for scripture," believing that evolution "guaranteed the final fruition of human virtue and the perfectibility of man."[125] Darwin's study of biological history had uncovered what he believed to be a fundamental law of nature—adaptability—and people interpreted this law to guarantee human progress just as it guaranteed the progress of the Galapagos Islands finches, with one major difference. Humans, they believed, can make intentional progress by looking for ways to adapt within their environment and maximizing these possibilities. This notion was expanded in the latter part of the 19th century when social theorists adopted evolutionary theory and made it the basis for the young science of sociology.

We are probably most familiar with how the natural and social sciences apply reason to accomplish their goals. Remember elementary science fair experiments? Your teacher asked you to observe the world around you and to come up with a question that you could test, such as: Do plants grow faster under bright light? You developed a hypothesis, or educated guess, to answer this question, then tested your supposition by planting seeds under varying amounts of light. A few weeks later you examined your data, which might or might not support your hypothesis, and formed a conclusion. This system was anticipated by Francis Bacon (1561—1626) who in the *New Organ* (1620) laid down principles for studying the world. His new way of learning rejected the prejudices of the past and relied instead upon a careful study of nature itself. In the modern era, Bacon's approach matured into the scientific method. It became the defining way for learning what was truly worth knowing.

The fruit of the Enlightenment drove the expansion of the empirical and social sciences, gave birth to the Industrial Revolution, and prompted the growth of democratic societies.[126] It spawned great social welfare and prison reforms, opened education up to women as well as children of all races and classes, spurred the growth of unions, and increased consumer protection, all of which has benefited humankind.

The technology of modernity was so captivating and inspiring that it sometimes tended to take on godlike characteristics. Authors J. Richard Middleton and Brian J. Walsh illustrate this by describing the Crystal Palace Exhibition in Hyde Park, London, during the 19th century. The exhibition celebrated the technological marvels of the modern era. On May 1, 1851, Queen Victoria attended the opening event. After being greeted by a blast of trumpets, she was seated on a raised platform in front of a crystal fountain, reminiscent of the "sea of glass, like crystal" in Rev. 4:6. Later, the queen noted in her diary that the scene "was magical . . . so vast, so glorious, so touching. One felt—as many did whom I have since spoken to—filled with devotion, more so than any [religious] service I have ever heard." What sparked her wonder? The accomplishments of "this 'peace festival,' which united the industry of all nations of the earth." The next day, the London *Times* also described the scene, but in even grander terms. The exhibition "included all that is useful or beautiful in nature or in art." The *Times* reporter compared the exhibition to "that day when all ages and climes shall be gathered round that Throne of their Maker." Modernity, it seemed, was ushering in the kingdom of God![127]

Modernity's Rebels

As modern ideals spread, other claims to knowledge—including religion—that failed to conform to reason as modernity defined it were usually reduced to marginal importance. This thrust was certainly not without its rebels. The late 18th- and early-19th-century Romantic Movement, for instance, revolted against what it believed to be a one-sided stress on reason to the exclusion of other important aspects of humanity and knowledge. The German Romantic poet Novalis charged Enlightenment thinkers with a strict emphasis on reason that "stripped Nature, the earth and the human soul of its poetry." They had "erased every trace of the holy."[128]

Coming from another direction, Englishman Robert Malthus (1766—1834) placed an impressive speed bump across the highway of confidence in human progress. In 1798 he published his famous *Essay on the Principle of Population.* Throughout human history, Malthus said, more mouths are produced than the earth is able to feed. During good times when a surplus of food is available, humans tend to overproduce. So when misery enters the picture in the form of famine, poverty, disease, and war, the people on the bottom of the food chain die—and no amount of progress will be able to change that. Inevitably and repeatedly, Malthus said, nature works to check the population imbalance. Nature's use of misery to ease population pressure provides an unavoidable obstacle to uniform progress and lasting social improvement. Modernity tended to support the notion that humankind is perfectible within the bounds of history, and the powers for perfecting lie within humanity's grasp. Malthus came along and said, "Not so fast!" Many people will always be left behind; it's built into the structure of the world.[129]

No historical era advances evenly in a society. In the modern era there were people and populations that rejected all or parts of its program. My uncle John, for instance, was born early in the 20th century and rejoiced over the marvels of the radio but would neither believe that man had landed on the moon nor accept daylight saving time. "How," he once asked me in all seriousness, "would I ever be able to explain to my pigs why they weren't being fed on time?"

More "Secular" than "Religious"

Unlike the Middle Ages that viewed the world mostly in religious terms, the post-Enlightenment Western world increasingly came to be understood in secular terms. The *secularization of life* is virtually synonymous with *modernity*. The word *secular* should not be seen as something bad; it simply means "what pertains to" or "is of" the world, in contrast to the realm of the holy or sacred. The secularization of life describes the modern experience of coming to understand the world more and more in terms of the secular rather than in terms of direct religious or divine causes. We as Christians subscribe to many secular explanatory processes. We want a secular constitution instead of the divine right of kings. When a child has epilepsy or an infant is born with Down syndrome, we seek secular explanations, not religious ones. But doing so doesn't infringe upon our faith in God.

In one famous story, the French mathematician Laplace (1749—1827) appeared before Napoleon to present the results of his study of Newtonian mechanics. Laplace explained to Napoleon the motions of celestial bodies. When his presentation was complete, Napoleon reportedly asked, "But man, where is God?" Laplace answered, "Sir, I have no need of that hypothesis." In the narrow sense, he was correct. He wasn't making an atheistic statement. His knowledge of the heavens, and ours, simply did not require divine explanations for understanding why the planets revolve around the sun. His explanations were secular.

Secularization should not be confused with secularism. Secularism is an ideology that completely dismisses God from the universe and the stage of human affairs and then ironically assumes a religious certainty all its own. It looks at the world and draws the conclusion that the world is all there is, and everything must be understood on the basis of answers the world can provide. Many modern people embraced secularism but by no means all people. Recognizing the important role of the secular doesn't necessitate secularism, as many of today's scientists and statesmen who believe in God demonstrate.

Many of modernity's spokesmen, such as Karl Marx (1818-83), Friedrich Nietzsche (1844—1900),[130] and Sigmund Freud (1856—1939) did subscribe to secularism, believing that all religions are deceptive and oppressive. We should recognize, Nietzsche said, that "God is dead." Western man slowly "killed God" by squeezing His space until He no longer had a place to stand. He died in the same way a tooth fairy dies when a child reaches adolescence. Nietzsche believed that the very concept of God was hostile to human life.

Marx thought religion would continue only so long as humankind had not fully found itself at home in the world. One day that problem would be solved and atheism would replace religion. Freud also predicted a dire future for religion. Religion results from a universal neurosis that can and will be cured, he said. Once the sickness is cured, the symptom (religion) will go away.[131]

It is important to understand that the philosophy these men embraced—there is no one here but us—was gospel for them. It represented liberation from religious and superstitious constraints and supposedly made it possible to carefully think through what it means to be human without reference to God. In fact, they believed God must die so that man can live; the two were incompatible in their eyes. This kind of opposition to Christianity may be hard for us to understand today, but we must recall the often ugly religious history with which most of them were familiar. Think of the revulsion against Christianity provoked by present-day infighting among numerous Protestant Christians, the vicious clashes between Protestants and Catholics in Northern Ireland, or the angry reactions ignited by the recent failure to protect children against sexual abuse in some parts of the American Roman Catholic Church. We can begin to understand the disdain many early moderns had for Christianity if we realize the problems the Church faced then were in many ways even more extensive. In response, many shapers of modernity minimized, or tried to eliminate, Christianity's role in society and sought to replace it with the far more dependable guides of social and empirical sciences. In other words, many moderns placed secularism in the driver's seat. Religion, if allowed to ride at all, was buckled into the backseat—all for the sake of human safety.

Yet we need to be careful not to paint with a broad brush. Though the major shapers of modernity did not assign God a major role in the march of human progress, we should be careful not to overlook the many benefits the modern era has visited upon us. Christians in the West, for example, don't have to live with the fear that another denomination can successfully appeal to the state to crush one's own denomination. We should also recognize that many moderns continued to make an important place for religion by embracing modernity and religious faith. Often this resulted in a strict application of reason that either minimized or redefined religion's role. Samuel Taylor Coleridge (1772—1834) called for a "reasoning faith" but added that reason alone can't disclose all spiritual truth that should be apprehended. Sociologist Emile Durkheim (1858—1917) thought religion had an important, but decreasing, role to play. Even so, he said, we have learned religion's secret. Society, not God, is the source of religion.

Reformation historian Diarmaid MacCulloch identifies John Wesley (1703-91) as an illustration of how some Christian leaders creatively and critically harnessed the modern era's benefits for enriching the Christian faith. Wesley digested much of the Enlightenment's exploration of knowledge and used that knowledge in many of his writings to instruct Methodists in England and the American colonies.[132] "Enlightenment for the common man" is the way one historian of the Enlightenment describes it.[133] Henry D. Rack credits the Enlightenment, in part at least, for one of Wesley's central convictions. In sharp contrast to the bitterly extensive divisions Christendom had absorbed since the 16th century, Wesley concentrated on a few agreed upon truths of Christianity and exercised toleration of differences in other matters. Wesley was, says Rack, a "reasonable enthusiast."[134] Wesley would have applauded Francis S. Collins, a contemporary child of the Enlightenment. He is the director of the National Human Genome Research Institute (USA) and has no problem balancing his work as a scientist with his freely confessed Christian faith.[135]

Modernity in Full Flower and Its Wilting

The 19th century witnessed modernity's full flower as well as signs of its wilting bloom. Based on Enlightenment hopes, modernity crafted a grand, overarching story (a narrative) it thought the whole world should embrace. The gospel of modernity—progress through a confident application of objective reason—transformed people and institutions both in the West and in colonized lands.

As impressive as the modern project has been, for decades the West has been living through a crisis in modernity and, many believe, its passing. The crisis has to do with an erosion of confidence in some of the pillars upon which modernity's house was built. Modernity itself has been the principal source of its undoing. In the name of objective reason and progress, modernity promised entirely too much. Many critics say that in its secularist form modernity even acquired the characteristics of a religion—complete with dogma, heresies, and priests.[136] As has happened to other great programs in human history—such as efforts by the ancient Persian and Roman empires to create universal civilizations—events demonstrated that modernity had overreached.

I had an aunt notorious for her visits to other family members. A solitary guest room wasn't good enough for her; she had to dominate the whole house. She would move in and take charge and because of this has become a legend in our family.

Many observers think that's what modernity in its arrogant form tried to do[137]—create a "single system of truth based on universal reason, which tells us what reality is really like."[138] Modernity should have modestly claimed just one room for reason, leaving space for other forms of knowledge. But it couldn't resist moving in, taking over, and trying to toss out the other residents—religion, especially classical Christian faith, being one of the first to go.[139] Herbert A. Hauptman, who shared the chemistry prize in 1985 for his work on the structure of crystals, is an excellent contemporary example of this posture. During a 2005 scientific conference at City College of New York a student asked, "Can you be a good scientist and believe in God?" Hauptman's response was quick and sharp. "No!" he declared. Belief in the supernatural, especially belief in God, is not only incompatible with good science, "this kind of belief is damaging to the well-being of the human race."[140]

Sooner or later, a wide-ranging revolt against modernity's sweeping claims for reason and progress could have been anticipated. Even in the 19th century, modernity's failures to deliver on some of its promises caused many thoughtful people to question some of its claims. The exploitation of workers —including women and children—during the Industrial Revolution and the social misery rampant in many European and North American urban centers set off alarms announcing that something had gone horribly wrong with the modern promise. In the 20th century the wrongs associated with subjugating non-Western cultures and the horrors of two world wars that heinously employed the fruit of reason sounded the alarms even louder. So did the pollution of our atmosphere and a growing awareness that deep-seated problems exist in the human predicament that reason and social solutions alone could not resolve.

The most widespread and telling judgments against modernity's excessive claims occurred in the late 20th century. The 1960s hippie movement confronted what it believed to be a sterile and oppressive technocracy.[141] It was a time of massive disenchantment over the excessive use of force in settling world conflicts and the excessive use of technology without concern for human and ecological values. Joined by singers such as Bob Dylan, Joan Baez, Arlo Guthrie, and Peter, Paul, and Mary—musicians who helped shape the counterculture—the hippies turned their disenchantment into a revolution. They revolted against businesses polluting the rivers and the atmosphere with no ecological controls. They revolted against a government that was seemingly controlled by powerful industrial interests. They revolted against capitalism because they believed it opposed the simple values of community, caring, and love. They largely rejected Christianity for what they perceived as its failure to live and speak prophetically against injustice, rampant individualism, materialism, and militarism. And so for their religious resources they turned east, and to Native American religion, rather than to Christianity. Then as now many people shrug off hippies as drug addicts who advocated free love, but what drove them philosophically was their disgust with an abuse of nature and people that they attributed to modernity. For them and many others the public exposure of modernity's excesses and failures signaled its passing and the emergence of its successor—postmodernity.

The reality of postmodernity came home to me one evening about a decade ago during a graduate seminar I was conducting. I was talking about historical progress and must have been rattling on like a good modernist, when a female seminarian in her late 20s abruptly interrupted me. "We don't know what you're talking about," she said, speaking for herself and her peers. "The world in which we were raised has given us no reason to trust in progress. You must remember that we were raised in the context of the lies our government told during the Vietnam War, the polluted land that science gave us at Love Canal, the near catastrophe of Three Mile Island, and the radioactive atmosphere produced by the Chernobyl explosion. Ours is a postmodern world."

The Postmodern Turn

At the beginning of this chapter, we noted that people argue over whether or not we have moved beyond modernity, a debate that only time will settle. I, along with many others, believe that we have. However, even if we are moving into a postmodern world, modernity will not just disappear; much of what was modern will be retained and will carry over into the next era. And even if much of the world is taking a postmodern turn, not everyone will make the move. As we also have noted, no era advances evenly.[142] Muslim extremists, for example, reject not only postmodernity but also modernity. And the Flat Earth Society in Europe, North America, and Australia claims to reject a round Earth.

If a major change in eras is happening, we are still in its early stages. So we should not be overly confident about knowing its profile. Nevertheless, we can already detect some of its distinguishing characteristics and how they affect telling and living the Christian story.[143]

Moving Beyond Modernity's Failures

Postmodernity is marked by a broad exposé of modernity's alleged failures and a desire to transcend them. Postmoderns claim that some of modernity's most distinguishing features were actually arrogant, self-deceptive, and injurious. Modernity not only put too much stock into what reason can accomplish, they say, but also arbitrarily imposed limits on what is worth knowing.

Many moderns, the indictment runs, failed to recognize that there are many things worth knowing far beyond what reason alone can establish. Religious stories, communal wisdom preserved and transmitted through stories, the rhythms of nature, and intuition all provide knowledge essential for human wholeness. And while reason is one important pathway to knowledge, it is by no means the only or even most important one. Non-Western cultures that listen to patterns in nature and cultures that rely upon myths about the meaning of life have pathways to knowledge that are just as important as the pathways the Enlightenment stressed. Moderns also failed to realize there are many more ways to recognize what is valuable and lasting.

I have heard seminary students, whose natural frame of reference is postmodernity, describe modernity's excesses by alluding to *The Matrix,* the movie discussed at the beginning of this chapter. Like the *Kansas City Star* reporter, they interpret the "matrix" as the modern conspiracy to confine the range of human thought, freedom, spirit, and mind within narrow and sterile boundaries that can be controlled by political, academic, corporate, and religious elites.

Pointing Fingers in the Wrong Direction

Theological prophets such as Karl Barth and Reinhold Niebuhr who wrote before postmodernity emerged boldly reaffirmed that humankind's fundamental problem is *religious,* not social, rational, or educational. Against the tide that attributed evil to a lack of education, unfair wages, inadequate housing, and so forth, theologians recovered and reaffirmed the reality of original sin. They warned apostles of modernity such as American philosopher John Dewey to recognize the error of trying to reduce original sin to a lag in social evolution. Dewey identified "difficulties [standing] in the way of social alteration" that have everything to do with deficient education, unjust social conditions, a lack of imagination, and so on—not some "aboriginal curse." These hindrances have kept natural creative tendencies in humans from being carried forward to fruition. We should, Dewey said, intelligently and justly use the resources at our disposal—such as education and social reform—to remove the obstructions to human progress.[144]

We agree that Christians ought to encourage and contribute to improvements in the human community through education, political reform, and the sciences. But contrary to what Dewey thought, none of these can resolve humankind's root problem—sin. That requires a Redeemer.[145]

The "Return" of the Sacred

Life overcame the efforts of many moderns to exclude "god." During the last three decades of the 20th century it became increasingly clear that the obituaries written for religion by people such as Friedrich Nietzsche, Karl Marx, and Sigmund Freud were vastly premature. Anglican theologian Alister McGrath says the atheism these men promised would dominate humankind's future is now "aging gracefully in the cultural equivalent of an old folk's home."[146]

Contrary to the notion that religion would decline in importance as humans advanced, the postmodern situation points in another direction. Harvard theologian Harvey Cox observed in 1988 that far from disappearing, humankind's religious traditions seem to be "leaping into a period of resurgence."[147] Now it is quite common for people in many walks of life to recognize religion as essential for understanding what it means to live in community. In 2005 the Duke University Clinical Research Institute released a scientific study conducted at leading academic medical institutions across the United States to assess the impact of intercessory prayer and healing touch on patients undergoing certain heart procedures. This project illustrates that in a postmodern climate, modernity's restrictive appraisal of reality is rejected in favor of a more holistic one. "Prayers for the sick and healing-touch are among the most widely practiced healing traditions around the world," said Dr. Mitchell Krucoff, an interventional cardiologist at Duke and lead author of the study.[148]

Who among those who came of age during the Cold War could have anticipated that today's Russian president, Vladimir V. Putin, would have a personal spiritual adviser in the Russian Orthodox Church? Atheism as championed by the Communists in the Soviet Union was supposed to have been the wave of the future. But today not only does the Russian president identify himself as a Christian, but members of his government and a great many others are also encouraged to receive Christian baptism. Paul Starobin, writing in the *Atlantic Monthly,* says that many Communists who grew up as atheists have embraced Christianity, necessitating the adult-size baptismal fonts that have become common in Russian Orthodox churches.[149]

Openness to the religious dimension, to "the transcendent," is a prominent feature of postmodernity. To be sure, how the religious dimension is defined, expressed, and celebrated is amazingly diverse. This is one place where religious pluralism enters the postmodern picture. The prevailing postmodern sentiment is that humankind tells and lives by many complementary religious stories, all of which must be respected and none of which should be either elevated or excluded. These stories may be embraced by well-educated people with careers as scientists or university professors—people who are in many respects modern but who now as postmoderns make a place for religion that would not have been characteristic of modernity. Postmoderns have recognized that when moderns squeezed out religion, they squeezed out essential dimensions of meaning.

Exposing the Myth of Objectivity

One of modernity's fundamental doctrines was that reason, unlike religion and political tradition, could demonstrate complete objectivity. Objectivity in the sciences and in their application elsewhere would release humankind from oppressive and crippling prejudices. Reason could rise above personal biases, nationalism, ethnic divisions and above all, religion.

Toward the end of the 20th century, social critics began to show how modernity's claim to be able to achieve complete objectivity was a myth. They pointed out how the work of physical, biological, and social scientists could be, and often had been, strongly influenced by their social and historical starting places. All of us, modernity's critics argue, begin our reasoning from contexts restricted by gender, social class, places of residence, temporal eras, and so forth. Everyone starts somewhere. And our starting places affect both what we look for and what we find. We reason from within a particular story that is layered with assumptions, biases, and values. More often than not, we aren't even aware of these layers. But they nevertheless influence our perspectives on the world.[150]

The credibility and importance of the sciences was certainly not dismissed. But critics of modernity began to recognize that even research interests often reveal prior values and interests. Consider the pharmaceutical companies that often seem more concerned about increasing their profits than developing drugs that will treat and eradicate rare but deadly diseases.[151] Or consider the powerful pharmaceutical lobby in Washington that often protects profits in the guise of public interest.[152] How many erectile dysfunction commercials do we have to watch before the priority of profit sinks in? In a recent article, orthopedic surgeon Dr. David B. Carmack hailed antibiotics as one of the "most significant advances in medical treatment in the past 70 years" that has "saved millions of lives."[153] But a few paragraphs later he noted that pharmaceutical development of antibiotics is drying up. It's not because people no longer need antibiotics. In fact, bacteria are growing increasingly resistant to antibiotics currently on the market, necessitating further research. Sadly, Carmack said, "Pharmaceutical companies have lost interest in the antibiotics market because these drugs simply are not as profitable as drugs that treat chronic conditions and lifestyle issues."

Postmoderns argue that modern confidence in reason and progress naively misjudged humankind's ability to place reason in the hire of self-serving and evil interests.[154] Reason can be subverted just as easily as any other dimension of the human spirit, a fact forcefully pointed out by theologian Paul Tillich even before postmodernity arrived on the scene. Reason, just like religion, can become idolatrous and demonic.

During the Industrial Revolution in the late 18th and 19th centuries, people saw how reason in the form of economic interests could be used to oppress men, women, and children. The world watched as scientists and dictators placed reason in the service of devastating world wars. The world was shocked to learn how reason had been used to try to engineer a superior race and to devise methods for eliminating European Jewry. Time and again we learned how reason had been purchased and prostituted by multinational corporations, how people could be oppressed in the name of science.[155] Use of "research" by the tobacco industry to hide its crimes against humanity has been particularly appalling. These realities led people in many camps to recognize that evil can take possession of reason, just as it can any other part of creation. The myth of achieving complete objectivity was unveiled, and modernity's claims of neutrality were punctured.

No More "Big Story"

Modernity's intention was to produce one grand narrative for the whole world: a one-size-fits-all account of life. It was supposed to apply to all nations and all cultures, and everyone was supposed to welcome it. Philosophers call this supposed comprehensive story a metanarrative, meaning an "overarching story." By adhering to the modern explanation of life—the concept that the West had the market cornered on technology, government, psychology, education, and everything else of real importance—people and cultures everywhere could progressively improve themselves and their communities. The big story was supposed to have flawlessly steered us forward in politics, morality, and social organization. But as modernity's grand claims became threadbare, critics exposed just how partial and ethnocentric the comprehensive story really was.

Theologian Robert W. Jenson says that in its time of crisis, modernity lacked the resources necessary for renewing its "moral and intellectual capital."[156] Modernity had tried to create a universal story for the world without reference to God. It failed. If the world's story doesn't come from God, Jenson says, "then it has none." Neither science, nor reason, nor talented statesmen "can so shape the world that it . . . makes narrative sense."[157]

Some postmodern critics have gone even further. They challenged the very notion of a comprehensive story of any kind—religion included—that claims to hold the truth for all people. They recognize that interpretive stories are extremely important. Without them we could not live meaningfully, but their truthfulness depends upon those who receive them and want to be shaped by them. This applies to religious truth as well because it, too, is socially constructed. In a postmodern atmosphere it is common to hear that although the Judeo-Christian story once served as the West's metanarrative, it no longer does or should. Instead, societies should protect a person's right to embrace a religious story of his or her choosing, while making sure he or she doesn't try to impose it on other people who don't embrace it, either because they live by other religious stories or none at all. It is easy to see how postmodernity lends itself to the ideology of religious pluralism.

Through the process of secularization the West's dependence upon the Christian story eroded to where we now commonly speak in one way or another of "the loss of metanarrative." Christians often comment on this as they interact with a culture that is increasingly post-Christian in character. The biblical story that was once an essential part of our social fabric is growing less and less familiar. As our media so clearly demonstrates, we are experiencing a deep "loss of Christian memory." Adam Nicolson, writing in the *Wall Street Journal,* put it this way: "I would guess that on the whole, and outside committed Christian groups, biblical literacy is a thing of the past. That long moment of Christian civilization is over."[158]

Clearly, anyone who hopes to tell the Christian story in a postmodern and pluralistic world must understand from the onset why the notion of a metanarrative seems so offensive. The postmodern philosopher Jean-François Lyotard even defined *postmodernity* as "skepticism toward all metanarratives."[159] History, postmoderns observe, is littered with the wreckage of metanarratives. Consider these carcasses that lie alongside history's highway:

- Only men have the gifts required for public office.
- People of color are inherently inferior.
- In all important ways, Western civilization is superior to African and Eastern cultures.

Erosion of the modern metanarrative and the Judeo-Christian metanarrative has also opened space for alternative stories, particularly the marginalized voices of women, people of color, non-Western cultures, and formerly colonized people in third world countries. As Christians we rejoice that oppression has lifted, but we also question how to press on in a multistoried world.

What will be required of the Church if it is to faithfully and effectively tell the story of God in a postmodern and pluralistic world? What kind of Christian foundations will prepare us? What manner of people should we be, and what should be our witness? Wrestling with and answering these questions is the purpose of this book. As we move forward, we will see how the Wesleyan tradition is excellently positioned to respect the postmodern rejection of oppression in all its forms, while at the same time affirming the universal Lordship of Jesus Christ. I believe that postmodernity sets the stage for the Wesleyan way of telling and living the gospel.

For Reflection and Discussion

1. Identify the marks and results of modernity with which you are most familiar.
2. In what ways do you believe modernity has contributed to the spread of the gospel?
3. In what ways do you think modernity has been an obstruction to religious belief?
4. What indicators, if any, have you observed that point to a transition from modernity to postmodernity? Are there evidences or characteristics of popular culture that you identify as postmodern?
5. Is the world in which you live more open to religious belief than it was 20 to 25 years ago or less open? With what attitude should Christians greet postmodernity?

4
RESPONSES TO RELIGIOUS PLURALISM WITHIN CHRISTIANITY

◆

"The basic problem with which the Scripture faces us [with] respect [to] revelation is that the revelation attested in it refuses to be understood as any sort of revelation alongside which there are, or may be, others. It insists absolutely on being understood in its uniqueness, [and] insists absolutely on being understood in terms of its object, God."[160]

The Dalai Lama, exiled Tibetan spiritual leader, visited Bloomington, Indiana, in September 2003. He made the trip to dedicate an interfaith temple, a new addition to the Tibetan Cultural Center. Representatives of 15 faiths attended the ceremony and recited prayers in their own languages. The Muslim representative presented the temple with a small book titled *The Meaning of the Qur'an*. A rabbi offered a ram's horn. A Navajo religious leader gave a seashell filled with sage, representing land and water. The Dalai Lama urged his audience of several thousand people to be religious and choose a faith.

Muhammad Ali, a Muslim, also attended the dedication ceremony. After the temple had been consecrated, Ali, who suffers from Parkinson's disease, offered written comments. Hana, his daughter, read her father's statement: "Rivers, ponds, lakes and streams all have different names, but they all contain water. So, too, different religions all contain truth."[161]

This story represents a common response to religious diversity, even for many Christians, and plunges us into a discussion of additional options. Within the Christian faith we find three dominant approaches to the plethora of religions in our world—pluralism, inclusivism, and exclusivism—as well as two more that are less prominent. More may exist, but Christians in various parts of the Church embrace at least these five. Exploring these responses will provide the basis for understanding a distinctive Wesleyan approach to religious diversity.

PLURALISM

Eminent historian Arnold Toynbee championed the pluralist response to religious diversity, stating that Jesus is just one of the many paths to the one

God. For Toynbee, the spiritual presence manifested in the universe and encountered in all the major religions is the common core. Religions should subordinate their differences and recognize the essence that unites them.[162] The children of this response to religious diversity are legion. Some of its more recent and prominent representatives are John Hick, Wilfred Cantwell Smith, Stanley Samartha, and Paul Knitter, with whom we've already become acquainted. Pluralists believe that God is a God of love, working within historical, cultural, and religious settings to give all people a capacity "to relate to him in such a way that salvation is possible for them."[163]

The pluralist assessment of religious diversity takes at least two forms:

Veiled Monotheism

According to the first form, the different understandings of "God" for Christians, Jews, Muslims, Hindus, Sikhs, and other religions are simply different expressions of the same God. Religions are different faces or masks by which God shows His many personality traits. All religions are different paths to, and accounts of, one divine reality.

"How could you possibly be so narrow and uninformed as to believe that Jesus is the only Savior of the world? He is just one among many. Jesus happens to be the Savior of Christians. That's all." That was the contemptuous response I received from a Christian minister in a mainline denomination right after I made a statement identifying Christ as the universal Redeemer. He and I were paired off as roommates at a conference for Christian ministers, and during a late-night conversation, I stated my belief that Jesus Christ is "the way, and the truth, and the life" (John 14:6) for all people everywhere. The minister quickly sized me up as unschooled in my behavior toward religious diversity. My statement had exposed me as someone who lacks cross-cultural awareness, is ignorant of other religions, and is oppressive toward others.

My roommate's rebuke would have earned applause from other Christians in the pluralist camp. Rev. Dr. George Regas, rector emeritus of All Saints Church in Pasadena, California, would have given it a hearty, "Amen!" During his aforementioned sermon preached in the Washington National Cathedral, Regas said, "I can no longer think about Jesus as the only way to God and to a saving faith . . . I personally reject the claim that Christianity has the truth and all other religions are in error . . . I think it is a mistaken view to say Christianity is superior to Hinduism, Buddhism, Islam, and Judaism and that Christ is the only way to God and salvation."[164]

A few winters ago some Episcopalians from Charleston, South Carolina, came face-to-face with the pluralist approach when they attended a church service in New York City. They visited the Episcopal Cathedral of St. John the Divine and were shocked to find a Shinto altar. When they voiced their objections to the bishop of New York, he dismissed them as narrow-minded people who couldn't appreciate the many paths to God.[165]

The pluralist response dates back at least a century and has various supporters. Swami Vivekenanda embraced the "many paths, one God" estimate of religious diversity when he addressed the World's Parliament of Religions in Chicago in 1893. Mahatma Gandhi also embraced this form of pluralism. Today's best-known representative of this position in the Christian setting is probably John Hick, a major philosopher of religion.[166]

Hick says that first-century Christians had a provincial outlook regarding religion and culture, and this viewpoint is what gave birth to the orthodox claims about Jesus contained in the New Testament and the creeds. The traditional Christian affirmations regarding Jesus developed through a mythmaking process. The Gentile church gradually elevated Him to divine status and then promoted Him to Trinitarian status. In their minds He developed into "God the Son," before whom all people must one day bow. But, Hick says, the human Jesus who taught in Galilee operated under no such illusions and made no such claims. Far from being the "Son of God," Jesus was in fact a quite parochial and time-bound figure. He mistakenly thought the kingdom of God would come in the near future and that He was God's last messenger. This, of course, did not happen. Jesus' followers were left with the problem of what to make of Him, and the elaborate affirmations about Jesus that eventually emerged reflected the disciples' efforts to process all that had happened. Jesus had exemplified the divine presence so intensely that His words and life continued "to make God real to those who [were] inspired by his life."[167] So orthodox beliefs regarding Jesus sprang from the meaning Christians attributed to Him based on their own hopes and dreams.

If people are informed, Hick believes, they can see why we should attribute the notion that Jesus Christ is the Savior of world to imagination and zeal. The apostolic belief that "God the Redeemer" was somehow incarnate in Jesus should be chalked up to ignorance about other equally legitimate paths to salvation. Such ignorance may have been excusable in the past, but not now, not among world citizens who are alert to the validity of religions other than Christianity. Our greatly expanded knowledge of the world—what Hick describes as "multiple changes in human awareness"—has made the former ignorance and Christian arrogance unacceptable.[168] Hick would have found a colleague in Guru Nanak who founded the Sikhs in the 15th century. A monotheistic religion, the Sikhs teach that the *True Name* (God, the Kindly) manifests himself in many ways and by many names. But He is One—eternal, transcendent, and ever-present.

The changed situation calls for new thinking on the Church's part regarding what it believes about Jesus. Hick claims that we are "on the moving hinge between the structure of Christian belief that dominated Western civilization for many centuries, and the still forming new structure of a Christianity that is aware of itself as one valid response [to God] among others."[169] This new reality is so sweeping that it requires a revolution in how Christians think about themselves and others.[170] The revolution will be on the scale of the Copernican revolution, during which the sun replaced the earth as the center of the solar system. In the new religious revolution, Hick says, God alone, not Christ or the Christian Church, should occupy the center of religious interest. Christian exclusivism—the belief that Christ and the Christian faith are the ultimate center of all knowledge about God—must cease.[171]

Hick thinks Christians are caught in a contradiction. On one hand, they extol the infinite mercy of God and His universal will to redeem all people. On the other hand, they have traditionally insisted that faith in one particular, historically located person—Jesus Christ—is necessary for salvation. These two beliefs, Hick says, are an oxymoron. To resolve the problem, Christians should not take the incarnation of God in Jesus literally.

The "incarnation" is a fitting way for Christians to express their experience of being redeemed by a divine power, Hick says. But that power is also at work in other religions. If taken literally, the idea of incarnation leads Christians to devalue the ways other religions encounter the divine. In *The Metaphor of God Incarnate,* Hick says that "incarnation" entered into the language of early Christians as no more than a figure of speech.[172] As the term became more common, it developed into a myth, "a powerful complex of ideas."[173] Hick doesn't think belief in the Incarnation should be abandoned. Instead, it should be seen as a powerful symbol for Christians, a meaningful story through which they encounter the divine.

Some Christians try to resolve the dilemma Hick has pinpointed by calling adherents of other religions anonymous Christians. He rejects this tactic because it perpetuates the old notion the revolution intends to correct. Other world religions don't await completion in Christianity; they are in themselves complete faces of God without needing to borrow anything from Christianity or receive the Christian gospel.

If Christ is not the final criterion of all religions, what is? Hick answers that, together, the religions show a human goodness "that reflects a right relationship to God." This uniting, universal goodness consists of "concern for others, kindness, love, compassion, honesty, and truthfulness."[174]

Should Christians continue to embrace Jesus as their Savior? Yes, because Jesus makes God real to all who are inspired by the Christian story.[175] But they should recognize that other stories do the same for people of other religions. Can Christians share the Jesus story with Hindus, for example? Again, the answer is yes, but not if they want to proselytize, and only if they are willing to listen with equal attentiveness to the Hindu stories.

Author Harold Netland summarizes Hick's position in three points. First, the great religions are various legitimate responses to one ultimate reality. Second, the great religions, including Christianity, are historically and culturally conditioned interpretations of this one transcendent reality. And finally, salvation is effectively occurring through all the great religions.[176]

Unveiled "Polytheism"

A second form of *pluralism* maintains that Hick has not yet embraced pluralism in the true sense of the word. It rejects his position for two reasons:

First, Hick assumes too much; his language is still too Western. According to Hick, behind the world's religions stands a unitary, single deity who manifests himself in many religious forms. The problem with this way of defining *pluralism* is that it implicitly imposes monotheism on all other religions. So it turns out that what initially seems to be an attitude of acceptance toward other religions actually places them in the framework of Hick's own religious tradition.[177]

Second, to have true pluralism, this second form of pluralism insists, we can't begin with a preconceived notion of ultimate reality and fit the other religions into that neat little box. Each religion must be free to articulate its own concept(s) of what it considers ultimate. No common or universal concepts regarding salvation or anything else should be sought because a common definition of religion may not exist.

Another objection to Hick's form of pluralism relies upon an understanding of religious language held by many postmodern thinkers. When Hick says religions are different faces or masks through which God reveals himself, he shows that he doesn't understand religious language. The language he uses is restrictive, not affirmative, because the concept of the "God" behind the monotheistic religions doesn't translate across cultures. When Hick speaks of "God," he makes the mistake of using that language to speak about Hinduism, for example. You can't even talk about Hinduism without stepping into its very different view of reality, its complex culture, and its language. Once you do, you realize the "gods" and the ultimate reality the Hindus are talking about are simply not the God Hick is talking about. Some Hindu gods, such as Shiva and his consorts, are thought to be authors of both good and evil, both construction and destruction, and Hindus who worship Shiva see no contradiction in this. Without intending to, Hick runs roughshod over religious diversity. He does not seem to recognize that language and religion are culture specific; we can't have or understand one without the other. We can't separate "god" from the language a culture produces or from the culture a language expresses.

So there is no single, overarching divine reality that the religions hold in common. For Hick's form of pluralism to succeed, he has to force the various religions to say things they don't intend to say. Since the meaning of "god" is indexed to a culture and its language, the concept makes no sense across cultures. This second form of pluralism insists that it represents true pluralism. We have to recognize it, respect it, and try not to make it all fit together.[178]

INCLUSIVISM

As with the pluralist position, there are at least two forms of *inclusivism*. Clark H. Pinnock, systematic theologian at McMaster Divinity College, and theologian John Sanders, formerly of Huntington College in Indiana, represent one form.[179] Roman Catholic theologian Karl Rahner represents another. Paul Tillich and C. S. Lewis were also eminent inclusivists.

Unlike what we observed in John Hick, the *inclusivist* response declares that "there is only one mediator between God and man, the man Christ Jesus." He is the High Priest in all things pertaining to God; He alone makes reconciliation for humanity's sins (Heb. 2:17). Only through Jesus Christ can we receive the gift of eternal life (Rom. 6:23). None of this is in question for inclusivists. At question in the two forms, however, is the *way* Christ relates to non-Christian religions.[180]

Inclusivism shares one thing in common with *pluralism:* Both give a positive appraisal of religions other than Christianity. However, the positive appraisal inclusivism offers is highly restricted. Building upon the conviction that God is actively present everywhere, inclusivism infers that God's saving grace is also active in some way among all people. According to Clark Pinnock and other inclusivists, it is quite possible that religions other than Christianity are in some way vehicles through which God's grace reaches people. Even so, inclusivists insist that only through Jesus Christ can we experience a full saving encounter with God. Any role that other religions might play is but anticipatory and preparatory.

Unlike pluralism, inclusivism rejects the notion that one religion is just as effective as any other for encountering God, nor does inclusivism diminish the urgency of evangelism. Rather, it affirms the universal activity of God's grace. He is working to draw all people to himself. The religions can play a preliminary role in God's plan.[181]

Cautious Inclusivism

Clark Pinnock represents this form of inclusivism.[182] He believes a wideness is present in God's mercy enabling it to reach all people.[183] He dismisses "the abhorrent notion of a secret election to salvation of a specific number of sinners."[184] Christ died and rose again for all. God is preveniently, or anticipatorily, active through His Son in all parts of the world. The Holy Spirit is active everywhere as the Agent of divine grace, bearing witness to Christ and drawing all people to Him. A Buddhist in Japan who trusts in Jizo—a divine-like helper who can descend into hell, deliver its sufferers, and transport them to heaven—would illustrate the Spirit's prior presence without "baptizing" the particular belief. "I believe," Pinnock says, "that the Spirit is present in advance of missions, preparing the way of the Lord."[185]

Pinnock and those who share his position think that through the Spirit's prevenient work, He *may* even be active in other religions. They *may* become "one of God's options for evoking faith and communicating grace." This is possible because of prevenient grace. "Non-Christian religions may be not only the means of a natural knowledge of God, but also the locale of God's grace given to the world because of Christ."[186] If a person responds positively to prevenient grace through another religion, he or she *may* be "saved" without ever hearing the gospel, and without ever explicitly confessing faith in Christ.[187]

Inclusivists holding to this form attach some important qualifiers:

- Cautious inclusivism recognizes that, in varying measures, there are depths of darkness, deception, and bondage in religions. Cautious inclusivism "avoids being rosy-eyed about religions that can be wicked as well as noble." Consequently, a given religion might not be at all serviceable to prevenient grace.[188]

- While the Holy Spirit may use the world religions as vehicles for divine grace, they are not *by themselves* vehicles of salvation. They don't independently mediate God's grace.

In chapter 9 we will observe similarities between cautious inclusivism and John Wesley's appraisal of non-Christian religions.

Less Cautious Inclusivism

Karl Rahner (1904-84) was one of the most influential Roman Catholic theologians of the 20th century. He represents a less cautious inclusivism, which assigns a role to other religions that cautious inclusivism does not. Rahner's explanations of God's grace distinguished his work.[189] Clark Pinnock called him "the most famous inclusivist."

Rahner believed that Jesus Christ is necessary for salvation. The Christian faith "understands itself as the absolute religion, intended for all men, which cannot recognize any other religion beside itself as of equal right."[190] Only in God's self-revelation in Christ does He communicate himself to us. The incarnation, death, and resurrection of the Word of God become flesh mean the same for all people and are meant for all people.[191]

However, while it is true that the one Word of God who became flesh reaches all people, He does so at different times and under different circumstances. Until the moment the gospel actually enters a person's historical situation, a non-Christian religion may serve in some way to prepare for the gospel's coming. Non-Christian religions show the marks of original sin and bear the weight of error regarding God. But non-Christian religions also contain "supernatural elements arising out of the grace which is given to men as a gratuitous gift on account of Christ." For this reason, in varying degrees, they can be recognized as *lawful religions,* or bearers of God's grace that anticipate the arrival of the Christian gospel.[192] Until the gospel enters the historical situation of another religion and encounters its adherents, the other religion, as a temporary stand-in for Christ, is a valid means to salvation. Because God extends the possibility of salvation to all, we have every reason to "suppose that grace has not only been offered even outside the Christian Church, but also that, in a great many cases at least, grace gains the victory in man's free acceptance of it."[193]

After the gospel of Jesus Christ encounters a person of another religion, his or her old, temporary religion ceases to be valid. Christ encounters him or her with the offer of salvation, and he or she must decide for or against God's truth. But until the encounter occurs, the candidate for Christian faith ought not be seen as a non-Christian. Rather, if he or she has responded faithfully and positively to prevenient grace, he or she should be regarded as an anonymous Christian. The salvation that has reached the person is Christ's salvation.[194] For an anonymous Christian, Christian conversion involves *consciously* embracing Christ in the depths of his or her being.[195] A missionary should view the world as needing to explicitly embrace the divine offer of grace that already belongs to it through the Holy Spirit.[196]

EXCLUSIVISM (PARTICULARISM)

The third response to religious pluralism is a polar opposite of pluralism known as either *exclusivism* or *particularism*.[197] Among the best-known exclusivists are John Piper, Ronald Nash, R. C. Sproul, and Carl F. H. Henry.

Like inclusivism, exclusivism affirms that people can know God only through Jesus Christ and that salvation comes through Him alone. Both positions would agree with Hendrik Kraemer, Dutch Reformed theologian and missionary to Indonesia, that, "the biblical, and thus the Christian, criterion of religious truth . . . is the Person of Jesus Christ who is the Truth."[198] In Him and in Him alone, the Father has acted to redeem "by the blood of the eternal covenant" (Heb. 13:20-21).

After this, the two positions diverge sharply. Inclusivists believe they can affirm Jesus Christ as the only Redeemer and still adopt a somewhat positive assessment of other religions. Exclusivists sharply disagree. Based on how they read the New Testament, exclusivists believe that the only way to salvation is through an explicit knowledge of and belief in Jesus Christ. The following text is pivotal: "If you confess with your lips that Jesus is Lord and believe in your heart that God raised him from the dead, you will be saved. For one believes with the heart and so is justified, and one confesses with the mouth and so is saved . . . But how are they to call on one in whom they have not believed? And how are they to believe in one of whom they have never heard? And how are they to hear without someone to proclaim him? And how are they to proclaim him unless they are sent?" (Rom. 10:9-10, 14-15).

In light of such texts, exclusivists reject the notion that other religions can act as vehicles for God's saving grace.[199] Except perhaps under very special circumstances, only those who in this life hear the gospel and explicitly respond in faith to Jesus can be saved. There is no hope for those who pass from this life without having heard and responded to the gospel of Jesus Christ.[200] This applies equally to Pinnock's and Rahner's versions of inclusivism.

R. Douglas Geivett and W. Gary Phillips cite numerous biblical themes they believe support an exclusivist evaluation of religious pluralism:

- Both Testaments assess other religions as nonredemptive at best and absorbed in the kingdom of darkness at worst.[201] The first chapter of Romans teaches that the wrath of God comes upon those who are alienated from God as He has revealed himself in Christ. And doesn't the New Testament declare that redemption comes only through Christ Jesus? (Rom. 3:23).

- The Scriptures consistently set forth a pattern of fewness in redemption and wideness in judgment. In the great Flood (Gen. 6—8) only eight people were saved. At the close of Jesus' parable of the Great Banquet (Matt. 22:1-14), He declared, "For many are called, but few are chosen" (v. 14).

- The New Testament records instances in which, even after people had received some special revelation, they "were required to believe further redemptive truth in order to be saved" (John 4:9, 24; Acts 2:5, 38; 9:2; Rom. 10:1-3).[202]

What are we to make of the Great Commission (Matt. 28:16-20), exclusivists ask, if inclusivists are correct? If people who have not heard the gospel can be saved without hearing it, why should missionaries and evangelists suffer persecution to spread the gospel of Jesus Christ? Dutch missiologist Johannes Verkuyl believes inclusivism threatens to produce a "subversion of the missionary mandate" and candidly calls this a "betrayal of Jesus Christ."[203]

So exclusivists believe that for people to be reconciled to God, they must make a specific confession of faith in Jesus as the Redeemer. To make this confession of faith, they must first hear the gospel faithfully proclaimed. Only the Holy Spirit can convince, grant, and empower a person's confession of faith, and this happens when Christ transforms the sinner, *not before*. Salvation comes through "knowledge of the truth" (1 Tim. 2:4), which means knowledge of "the man Christ Jesus" (v. 5, NIV).

Clearly, according to the exclusivist position, the majority of humankind will forever be lost because they will never hear the gospel.[204]

A MODERATING POSITION

Harold Netland offers a moderating response to religious diversity among evangelicals that rejects both inclusivism and exclusivism. He says that both approaches stretch what the Bible clearly supports. He—along with other evangelicals such as J. I. Packer, John Stott, Chris Wright, and Millard Erickson—recommends that we "adopt a modest agnosticism [lack of certainty] regarding the unevangelized."[205] We should not speculate about how God will choose to deal with those who have not heard the gospel but leave that to God's care. In principle we can say that God might indeed save some people who have not explicitly heard the gospel. But to move beyond this, to begin speculating, "is to move beyond what the Scriptures allow."[206] We can be certain only that "Jesus Christ is the only Savior, and that salvation is by God's grace alone, on the ground of Christ's cross alone, and by faith alone."[207]

AN EVOLUTIONARY ASSESSMENT

Although not currently prominent in Christian settings, an evolutionary evaluation of all religions is still championed by some. It is based on an evolutionary view of human life and social structures. Although many religions exist, all of them are undergoing historical evolution. They are evolving toward a common truth. At this point, no one can know for certain what the outcome will be. But we can be certain the process is moving along a path that leads away from isolation and toward increasing dialogue, interchange, and harmony. Eventually the process will deliver a harmonized world religion that will surpass the current diversity and conflict. Representatives of this position include R. C. Zaehner, Wilfred Cantwell Smith, Ninian Smart, and Steven Konstantine.[208]

COUNSEL FROM KARL BARTH

In this chapter we have often spoken of religions. But it would be incorrect to assume that the debate regarding religious diversity can be settled by answering the question, "Which religion should we embrace?" To make sure we are proceeding along a Christian path, we should listen to Karl Barth, the great 20th-century Protestant theologian quoted in the introduction.[209] Barth recognized that, like all religions, Christianity can be distorted and abused. In recent centuries evil men and women have made Christianity an ally of brutal military aggression, racism, hypocrisy, and thinly disguised greed. Barth knew that the marks of original sin are embedded in all institutions, Christianity included. When Christ calls someone to be His disciple, He calls him or her to follow Him, not the Christian religion. The gospel of Christ is not the gospel of Christianity. Promoting Christianity should not be a Christian's interest.

However, even though Christianity is subject to fault like other religions, it is still the only true religion. Its truth lies not in itself *as a religion,* but in its being the only religion that bears witness to Jesus as the Christ. Its truth is the grace of God's revelation. Its proclamation of the gospel, not its institutional structure, is its truthfulness. In this way alone, Christianity can be exalted in revelation, even though the judgment of grace stands against its misdeeds.[210]

The God who revealed himself in Christ is the free, sovereign God. He is faithful to His own nature, revealed in Christ, but in His free activity He is not limited to the boundaries of Christianity. Barth had no interest in promoting Christianity as a superior religion, and neither should we. Let us not equate religion with revelation. Proclaiming the gospel of the free and living God is our mission.[211]

For Reflection and Discussion

1. Why are there so many different responses to religious pluralism among Christians?

2. Select five to seven persons in your church, at work, and/or at play and ask them the question, "What should be the relationship between the Christian faith and other world religions?" Do some of their responses parallel some of the responses discussed in this chapter?

3. Which of the responses to religious pluralism discussed in this chapter seem to be most at odds with each other? Which ones seem to be most in harmony with each other?

4. Which of the responses to religious pluralism would be least likely to appeal to the New Testament for support? How would each one respond to the Great Commission of Matt. 28:16-20?

5. Is it legitimate to distinguish between Christianity and the Christian faith?

PART II

THE NEW TESTAMENT AND RELIGIOUS PLURALISM

5
WHAT IS THE
GOSPEL OF GOD?

The Book of Second Samuel records a humorous, albeit sad, story about a young man named Ahimaaz (2 Sam. 18:16-33). David's son Absalom had tried to seize the throne from his father. But David's army, led by Joab, defeated Absalom and put down the budding civil war. Absalom tried to escape on a mule, but the mule went under a tree, and Absalom's long hair got caught in the branches. He was still alive when Joab found him hanging there. Defying David's instructions, Joab killed Absalom and had his body thrown into a pit and piled over with stones.

Afterward, Ahimaaz, son of Zadok, asked permission to run to Jerusalem to carry the news to King David. Joab at first denied the request and sent a Cushite instead. But Ahimaaz kept pestering him. Finally, Joab changed his mind and let Ahimaaz run. Even with a late start he outran the Cushite. When Ahimaaz saw King David he cried out, "All is well!" David asked, "Is it well with the young man Absalom?" Lamely, Ahimaaz answered, "I saw a great tumult, but I do not know what it was" (vv. 28-29).

Think of that! Ahimaaz had insisted on running, had overtaken the Cushite, but didn't have anything worth saying when he arrived. His admirable speed was surpassed only by his lamentable ignorance. So the king ordered Ahimaaz to stand aside. In a few minutes the Cushite came roaring in, equipped with the message the king needed to hear.

The New Testament mentions people who seemed to have inherited Ahimaaz's deficiency. They went around preaching, but they either didn't understand the gospel or intentionally distorted it. They ran, but they didn't know what to say once they arrived.[212] The Epistle of Jude calls such people "waterless clouds carried along by the winds; autumn trees without fruit" (Jude 12). But that shortcoming need not befall any of us. The New Testament can equip Jesus' disciples for running and faithfully telling the story.

"Do you know why I am not a Christian?" a friend once asked. Her answer was shocking, not what I expected. "I am not a Christian because based on what I hear from many of you Christians, *the gospel is too small*. It isn't sufficiently challenging. It seems to be all about *you*—*your* subjective needs, *your* eternal salvation, *your* prayers for *yourself* and *your* immediate circle, and *your* eventual escape from a 'hopeless' world!" Wounded, my first impulse was to be defensive, to start reeling off excellent exceptions to refute the indictment. But my second impulse was more sober. I listened. What had she seen in us that caused her dire assessment, her rejection? Is it possible that some of us, at least, have so reduced the horizons of the gospel that her judgment is understandable?

At least this much is certain. If the gospel we embody and present to others doesn't have New Testament dimensions, then it will not adequately engage our broken world. And if we reduce it to our individual feelings, needs, and aspirations, then we should not be surprised if the gospel becomes indistinguishable and melts away into a pluralistic soup. The world has its share of religions that begin with self, one's own clannish worldview, and rarely extend much farther. This makes it easy to comfortably and neatly tuck them away into the folds of religious pluralism. If the gospel of Jesus Christ could not liberate people from their self-centered confines, then it would have to humbly take a seat at the pluralistic table.

But the gospel we encounter in the New Testament—the gospel that sent the Church running to the ends of the earth—is immensely larger. The term the New Testament uses for *gospel (euangelion)* means "a good message or good news." To preach the gospel is to announce good news, to declare glad tidings. New Testament writers tell us why the gospel of Jesus Christ is good news for all people and for God's creation and why it can never be successfully reconciled with the ideology of religious pluralism. Reading the New Testament afresh can equip us runners with a message worth telling when we arrive, worth giving to a friend for whom it is currently too small. Regardless of what is politically correct, and regardless of the pluralistic mood, God has spoken in His Son, and this is good news for the whole world. In this chapter we will reflect upon six big dimensions of the gospel:

- The gospel is the gospel *of* God (authored by Him) for us and for all creation.
- The gospel is good news *about* God.
- Jesus *is* the gospel (He is God's Good News).
- The gospel is good news *about* the kingdom of God.
- The gospel is good news *about* a new order that replaces the old.
- The gospel is for a pluralistic world.

THE GOSPEL IS THE "GOSPEL" OF GOD FOR US AND FOR ALL CREATION

The New Testament tells us the gospel is the good news of Jesus Christ. This is true, but it doesn't mean that the gospel is a story about a once-upon-a-time parochial Jewish rabbi limited to a certain time period and a particular culture. The gospel to which the New Testament witnesses is the gospel of God (Rom. 1:1; 15:16; 2 Cor. 11:7; 1 Thess. 2:8). It is news that comes *from* the Triune God, and it is news *about* what He has done and is doing in the world (Rom. 1:1-6; 2 Cor. 11:7). It is news *for* us and *for* all creation.

After John the Baptist was arrested, Mark tells us, "Jesus came to Galilee, proclaiming the good news of God, and saying, 'The time is fulfilled, and the kingdom of God has come near; repent, and believe in the good news'" (Mark 1:14-15). Matthew says that after having called Simon Peter, Andrew, James, and John, "Jesus went throughout Galilee, teaching in their synagogues and proclaiming the good news of the kingdom and curing every disease and every sickness among the people" (Matt. 4:23). In His first public sermon, Jesus said, "The Spirit of the Lord is upon me, because he has anointed me to bring good news to the poor" (Luke 4:18).

Though the ideology of religious pluralism disagrees, God is the gospel's point of origin. When Christians proclaim the gospel, they do so in response to God's initiative and commission. The Book of Revelation speaks of the gospel as "an eternal gospel" of God, and its goal is to bring all those who dwell on earth—every nation and tribe and tongue and people—to "fear God and give him glory." But who is this God? He is the Creator and Redeemer—the One "who made heaven and earth, and the sea and the springs of water" (Rev. 14:6-7).

THE GOSPEL IS GOOD NEWS ABOUT GOD

The gospel tells us what God is like, what is true regarding His character. It tells us that God who is the mighty Creator has also definitively acted in Christ as the gracious Redeemer (John 3:16). The gospel tells us what God *has done, is doing, and will do* on behalf of humankind and the creation to reconcile us to himself.

The gospel also emphasizes that we find this redemption only in the one, true God. When we encounter Him, we meet the "I AM" who graciously called the worlds into existence (6:41-59) and delivered the Hebrews from Egyptian bondage. When Jesus says, "I am the way, and the truth, and the life.

No one comes to the Father except through me" (14:6), the incarnate God is speaking.

Some postmodern thinkers claim that all religious stories are creations of the communities that embrace them, that the stories they tell are of their own making, limited to particular cultures and conceptions. But the New Testament says just the opposite regarding the gospel. It declares that in Jesus of Nazareth, the God who created the heavens and the earth and who spoke through Moses and the prophets, completes and tells the Story, *His own* Story. He gives us opportunity through the Spirit to receive His Story, to be transformed by it, and to become a part of it (Acts 4:12).

JESUS IS THE GOSPEL

Jesus didn't just preach the gospel; He *is* the gospel, the Father's self-disclosure. In Him the gospel of the kingdom of God is enfleshed. He is the unique and unsubstitutable person who, through His unbroken obedience to and faith in His Heavenly Father, defines and accomplishes redemption for the world. The apostle Paul said the "gospel of God" is the "gospel concerning his Son" (Rom. 1:1, 3). All that Jesus *is, said,* and *did* reveals His Heavenly Father. Others can preach the gospel; Christ *is* the gospel.

The New Testament's overarching message is that through Jesus' faithfulness and obedience—even to death on the Cross—something of cosmic importance happened. Even as He was the Author of the first creation (John 1:1-5; Col. 1:15-20), the Mighty Redeemer has become the Author of new creation (2 Cor. 5:17; Rev. 21:1-4). The Early Church believed that those who viewed the Lord as anyone less had not understood Him at all. Not only is our Lord the Alpha, but He is also the Omega. Through His Son and by the Spirit's power, the Father has "set the cosmos aright and delivered it from the powers under which it [was] enslaved, in order that humans might obey God freely."[213] Jesus the Messiah suffered and was rejected, crucified, and buried. But the Father vindicated His witness and faithfulness by raising Him from the dead (Rom. 1:1-6). God calls all people into the new creation and freedom Christ has won.

THE GOSPEL OF THE KINGDOM

In Jesus the long-anticipated universal reign of God ("the hope of Israel" [Acts 28:20; 15:13-18]) has been *inaugurated.* When Jesus said, "The kingdom of heaven has come near" (Matt. 3:2; 4:17; Mark 1:14) or "the kingdom of God has come to you" (Luke 11:20), He meant that He believed God had planned from the beginning to address and deal with problems in His creation through Israel. Its history would reach a great moment of climax. The "creator God, the covenant God, would at last bring his love and justice, his mercy and truth, to bear upon the whole world." He would bring renewal and healing to all creation.[214] The New Testament exults that God accomplished all of this in His Son (Luke 10:21-22; 2 Cor. 1:19-22).[215]

Properly receiving the gospel of God means doing so according to the full magnitude of Jesus' proclamation and accomplishment. One's entire disposition and existence in the world must be realigned and redirected to receive, proclaim, and rejoice in this good news. The kingdom of evil that stood against the will and reign of God has been decisively defeated. "By the finger of God" Jesus cast out demons and demonstrated that the kingdom of God had come (Luke 11:20; see Matt. 4:23-25). Such good news is reason for the whole world to rejoice.

Often when we speak of the gospel, we immediately think of personal salvation. Indeed, the gospel does include setting individuals free from the tyranny of sin and restoring them to covenantal relationship with God. We rejoice in the Lord for our salvation, for the Father has chosen us in love to be His children through Jesus Christ. The personal dimension of salvation must never be in question, but it is part of a larger picture—the kingdom of God.

So often, many of us who faithfully fill church pews each Sunday have taken the New Testament and reversed this order. Today's average evangelical Christian speaks boldly about the gospel, usually explaining it as being forgiven for *my* sins and entering into a *personal* relationship with Jesus Christ. But if you were to ask many of them about the significance of the kingdom of God, they might mumble something about the Second Coming. This order—the gospel first, then the Kingdom—is unheard of in the New Testament, where there is no gospel without the kingdom of God (Matt. 4:23; Luke 16:16). The gospel is the good news that the kingdom of God has come (10:8-9), a kingdom characterized by grace and love into which all are called. Christ inaugurates and embodies this kingdom, this universal reign of God, and offers forgiveness and redemption, new creation and new community, to all people. Let all creation exult!

If we reverse the New Testament order—I can get saved and go to heaven while the rest of the world goes to hell, and there's no loss—then we actually betray the gospel. If the gospel is all about *my* salvation apart from God's plan to unite all things in heaven and earth in Christ (Eph. 1:9-10), then the gospel has shriveled like a rotting orange. If I say that I am saved, but don't give a rip about ecology or the creation's transformation, if I make the kingdom of God a second-rate consideration, then I shouldn't be surprised if outsiders looking in believe the gospel is myopic. If a person views the gospel in purely individual and private dimensions, he or she is passing up a sumptuous banquet and settling for morsels—just like the invited guests who didn't show up at the banquet in Jesus' parable about the kingdom of God (Matt. 22:1-10; Luke 14:12-24). We have been offered the opportunity to become part of the new Kingdom order, the new reality established by Jesus Christ—a global, cosmic, socially as well as personally transforming order. To receive the gospel is to embrace the Kingdom (10:8-12).

THE OLD AND THE NEW ORDER

The old religious order that tried to close the doors of the Kingdom to sinners and the unlearned has had to yield (chap. 15). In the crucified and risen Christ, the old order of powers and principalities that claimed deity and authority over the world's affairs has been overthrown (1 Cor. 15:20-28; Eph. 1:15-23). That's good news for all who want to be rid of sin's tyranny and who will radically embrace the reign and ways of God. The new order, the order of the Kingdom, is good news for the whole creation, for God is now reconciling the world to himself (Rom. 8:18-25; Eph. 1:8-10). Good news! Jesus' resurrection meant not just the promise but the actual inauguration of the world's salvation, redemption, and justification.

People who had never before heard good news received Jesus gladly (Luke 7:36-38; 15:1-2; 19:2-8) because He dispelled their darkness, set them free, and gave them eternal life. People publicly written off as hopeless were marvelously transformed by the good news of God's gracious reign. Creation rejoiced to hear that its liberation had come.

The apostle Paul speaks of the gospel of the Kingdom as a divine rescue and transfer: God "rescued" sinners who were in bondage to "the power of darkness." He "transferred" them "into the kingdom of his beloved Son, in whom we have redemption, the forgiveness of sins" (Col. 1:13-14). This great "doing" of God is good news to all who will become a part of His Story, regardless of how extensively sin, guilt, fear, and despair have characterized their stories up until now.

A remarkable illustration of the Kingdom's new order and the good news that accompanies it has recently emerged from Colombia, a South American country plagued by cocaine-related violence. Near Medellin, Colombia's most violent city, stands Bellavista prison, whose occupants are terrorists, guerrillas, paramilitaries, bad cops and soldiers, narco-traffickers, common criminals, and sicarios (killers for hire).

Fifteen years ago, violence reigned in Bellavista. Behind its high walls, inmates once played soccer with a decapitated human head. The prison's death toll ran as high as 60 per month. Rival groups brought warfare into the prison. Hopelessness seemed to have sealed Bellavista's future.

But today, thanks to the transforming power of the gospel, Bellavista is a place where many Colombians, deeply divided by religion, economics, and politics, are reconciling their differences. Each Thursday in Bellavista's chapel, small-group leaders from each cellblock fast, pray, and study Scripture. Eyes closed, hands clasped, arms raised, the inmates pray for the redemption of Colombia. "We repent. We exalt Your name. Heal our land."

How did the change occur? In January 1990, Bellavista inmates rioted. Days into the standoff, Oscar Osorio, a Bellavista convict who had become the prison chaplain, brought together a handful of Christian volunteers associated with Prison Fellowship. Singing hymns and carrying white flags, Osorio and his volunteers marched through the prison gates, fearing they might be shot. Osorio commandeered the prison's public address system, boldly calling prisoners to repent. Stunning the prison authorities, inmates laid down their weapons. The riot was over. And the killing stopped.

In 1991 chaplain Osorio invited Jeannine Brabon, an Old Testament scholar, to preach during a Bellavista worship service. At the end of her sermon, 23 terrorists and killers for hire accepted Christ. Brabon began to disciple converts and conduct Bible studies inside the prison. The gospel swept through Bellavista like holy fire. Today, prisoners awaken to sounds of singing in the cellblocks, where each Christian aims to share his faith twice a day. Though less than 10 percent of the inmates are Christians, it's enough salt and light to bring peace. "Today, the presence of God is in that prison," says Brabon. "There can be hope for Colombia."[216] This is the work of the risen, triumphant Christ who is making all things new.

THE GOSPEL FOR A PLURALISTIC WORLD

The gospel is good news because it is for all people. Paul told the Roman Christians: "Just as one man's trespasses led to condemnation for all, so one man's act of righteousness leads to justification and life for all. For just as by one man's disobedience the many were made sinners, so by the one man's obedience the many will be made righteous" (Rom. 5:18-19). The Greek word meaning "many" is used both times. On the Day of Pentecost the apostle Peter cited the prophet Joel and proclaimed that God is *now* "pour[ing] out his Spirit upon all flesh [people]" (Acts 2:17). Moreover, the apostle Paul desired that, through the proclamation of Jesus Christ, "all the Gentiles, according to the command of the eternal God" might come to "the obedience of faith" (Rom. 16:26).

For the gospel of Jesus Christ to command the attention of a pluralistic and postmodern world, it will have to be proclaimed according to its full magnitude. If the gospel is God's Story for all people, then those who now live by other stories will need to hear the gospel as a Story whose splendor outshines their own. Just as was true for the woman "who was a sinner" (Luke 7:37) and Zacchaeus (19:2-10), the gospel will need to arrive as liberation, not as a new oppression. The gospel won the hearts of people in the first century because it was a story of liberation and promise, unlike the old stories by which they had lived.

All across the Greco-Roman world the young Church proclaimed that in the death and resurrection of Jesus Christ, the old structures of sin and death had been judged and sent packing. In Jesus the new age of new creation and reconciliation had begun. Christians have been swept up in a grand drama of redemption that radically reverses self-centeredness and ends isolation. The drama of transformation will conclude when the Son "hands over the kingdom to God the Father, after he has destroyed every ruler and every authority and power" (1 Cor. 15:24) that stands against God's righteous, life-giving reign.

Far from being one small story in an ocean of other equally valid religious stories, the gospel is all about the definitive revelatory and redemptive deed executed by the eternal God. Jesus Christ is God's and the world's metanarrative. God, not the Church, says so. The Church has no other justification for being than to tell God's Story far and wide. The finality and authority of the gospel doesn't depend upon human arbitration and consensus. In power, the Spirit will enlighten those who hear, so that they may embrace the Story as their own good news (2:3-14).

As this chapter has shown us, the New Testament is unwavering in its affirmation that, in Jesus Christ alone, God has acted definitively to redeem the world. In all instances, the New Testament writers trust the Holy Spirit to present the gospel's merit to their hearers. In not a single instance do they resort to coercion, appeal to political authorities for enforcement, promise social perks, or resort to trickery. They are confident that, in Christ, the God who created the heavens and the earth is fulfilling His promises to His people and to all creation. For them, the gospel can carry its own weight.

Making the whole gospel the defining reality of Christian existence and witness is our charge too. It alone is the Church's constitution and mission, the only Story we have to tell. The Good News, and nothing else the Church possesses, is the hope of the world. It will win the hearts and minds of people to whom it is addressed because it is the work of the eternal God.

As Karl Barth reminded us in the previous chapter, the gospel, not Christianity, is the Church's principal cause and joy. It calls the Church to its own constant Spirit-led conversion. In a pluralistic world, the gospel will have to be as big and inclusive as Jesus. Through the Church, the world will have to see that the gospel offers freedom from the tyrannies that set people and nations against themselves and their neighbors. The gospel will have to tell of a God whose good news answers our need for living in harmony with the world's ecosystem. Our lives must demonstrate how the gospel turns the old order's system of power, privilege, and exploitation upside down and inside out, by proclaiming good news for the poor, release to the captives, sight for the blind, and liberation for the oppressed (Luke 4:18).

For Reflection and Discussion

1. In what ways can Christians commit the error of making the gospel unattractive by making it "too small"?
2. By surveying two of the four Gospels, observe ways in which Jesus' actions announce the arrival of the kingdom of God. What does each instance seem to say about the nature of the Kingdom?
3. Examine how the gospel and the kingdom of God are linked in the four Gospels.
4. Select five to seven Christians and ask them to identify the relationship between the kingdom of God and the gospel.
5. Why is it important to say that the gospel is first good news *about* God, and then good news *for* humankind?
6. How would you answer the assertion that the Christian gospel is just one more religious story human cultures generate and offer to the world? Why must we both qualify and affirm the statement that "the gospel is the Church's story"?

6

A MISSIONAL PEOPLE:
THE NEW TESTAMENT CHURCH IN A PLURALISTIC CONTEXT

The New Testament announces "the desire of the unique God to summon from out of the human mass a unique community established in his name, and the desire of that community to serve God in love and obedience by responding to his call."[217]

In 204 B.C. the Romans visited a shrine in Asia Minor and brought back the silver statue of Cybele, the Great Mother of the Gods.[218] They also brought her sacred symbol, a small black stone that had "fallen from heaven." After consulting Cybele's sacred books the Romans had concluded that having her statue in Rome would rid Italy of Hannibal, who had invaded during the Second Punic War (218-201 B.C.).[219] Cybele's introduction marked the beginning of a slow ascent of diverse religious practices from the Middle East. Before this, the Romans had respected the deities of their former enemies, but Roman custom encouraged Romans not to participate in foreign religions.[220] For a long time no temples to foreign deities were permitted in the Roman Forum, the city's religious center.

But within 250 years after Cybele's arrival, when the young Church began preaching the gospel in the Greco-Roman world, foreign deities of almost every description were being permitted and honored in the heart of Rome.[221] The relatively simple picture that marked Cybele's arrival had changed dramatically. The religious landscape in Rome as well as elsewhere in the empire was saturated with polytheism (many gods, none of which were absolute) and syncretism (the blending of parts of various religions). Having surveyed this crowded scene, Paul observed that there are many "so-called gods in heaven or on earth" and many such "lords" (1 Cor. 8:5).

Problems in the young Christian community in Colossae illustrate the religious ferment of the Greco-Roman world. False teachers who wanted to blend Jesus into a pluralistic froth were bombarding the Colossae Christians. These teachers had caught the ear of the new converts and were telling them that, for their worship of God to be complete, they should recognize and worship the additional divine beings that fill the heavens. Jesus is just one among many, they said. God in His fullness is not completely revealed in Jesus. The people were also being told they would have to adopt a string of regulations regarding seasons, worship of angels, and so on. Paul heard about all this and exploded. He rebuked the false teachers. He declared that no *extras* are needed. In Christ *alone* God in His fullness *(pleroma)* has become incarnate, and Christians are made complete *(pleroma)* in Christ (Col. 1:15-20; 2:8-15).

Christians today can't point fingers at the false teachers in Colossae without turning those fingers back on themselves. Consider, for example, the kinds of hard-and-fast expectations certain speculators want to impose on Christians concerning the Second Coming. They say Jesus is coming back according to a strictly prescribed order of events on a strictly prescribed schedule, and you're fooling yourself if you don't accept this. Or think of people who want to impose the old Jewish dietary restrictions on Christians and argue about which day you worship. Or what about those who tell us that unless we possess certain privileged gifts we aren't filled with the Spirit of God? This same spirit of imposing "more than Jesus" was plaguing the church in Colossae, and it made Paul indignant. With some of the strongest language in the New Testament, he wiped the slate clean of any competing religions and all suffocating clutter.

We believe the New Testament to be authoritative for Christian faith and practice, so let's examine how the expanding Church told the Story of God in its pluralistic world. We will look at the Church's *missional* character as well as three New Testament case studies to observe how God's *mission* was implemented. This will help us answer the question, "How should *we* tell the Story in a pluralistic world?"

A Missional Church

The Church we meet in the New Testament is defined as *mission,* not as a static institution.[222] The Old and New Testaments show that God is a missionary God. Instead of remaining aloof, He acts as Creator and Redeemer. He delivered a bunch of slaves from Pharaoh's grip and transformed them into a people whose singular reason for existence was to declare God's name among the nations. He loves the world and gives His only begotten Son who gives birth to the Church—the new and true Israel. The gospel that created the Church, the gospel that it embodies and proclaims, is not its own. The Church is a divine instrument, not a hawker of its own inventions. To be God's people is to be defined, filled, and directed by this missionary God. Being engaged *in* mission proceeds from *being* a missional people.

Theologian Douglas Harink says that, collectively, the Church *is a missionary*. God's missionary aim from the foundation of the world has been "to bring about the obedience of faith among all the Gentiles" (Rom. 1:5). Now, in Christ, the God of Israel has called a people, the Church, from among the nations. By serving God in love and obedience, its form of life will bear "witnesses to . . . God's will for all humanity and all creation." Through its witness to the nations, God will call others into His mission.[223]

Robert Webber, a well-known teacher of early Christian worship and practice, says that God's mission is nothing less than to rescue the world from the powers of evil through the work of Jesus Christ (John 3:16).[224] As we meet young Christians in the New Testament who have been transformed by the Holy Spirit, this becomes abundantly clear. Most of the early Gentile converts had spent years immersed in pagan practices. No wonder the Epistles give so much attention to teaching disciples how to be God's missionary people, instructing them in the difference between pagan practices (sexual promiscuity, covetousness, repaying evil with evil) and holiness (loving one another with brotherly affection, holding fast to what is good, blessing those who persecute you). Paul addresses 1 Corinthians to "those who are sanctified" and then says they are "called to be saints" (1 Cor. 1:2). Much of the letter is spent correcting problems and instructing the saints (those who belong to Christ) in elementary Christian doctrine and practice. The Corinthian Christians had indeed become new creations in Christ, but a lifetime of growth and change lay ahead.

The apostles' letters to the young churches vigorously rejected any compromise between the missionary people and the pagan beliefs and practices that surrounded them. Peter said Christians are no longer to live in obedience to human passions, but by the will of God in the Spirit's power (1 Pet. 4:1-6). Paul told the Christians in Thessalonica that their conversion meant turning completely from idols to serve the true and living God (1 Thess. 1:9; 5:23). He instructed the Roman Christians that just as they had once completely served wickedness, they were now to become instruments of righteousness (Rom. 6:12-23). In these ways, God's mission would be fulfilled.

Humanly speaking, the obstacles the Church faced in fulfilling its calling were daunting. The abundance and apparent strength of its religious competitors alone would have been intimidating. But the Church was able to face the Greco-Roman world with boldness because in its risen Lord it had encountered and been redeemed, commissioned, and empowered by the *missional* God. It's that simple and that astounding. In the Spirit's power the Church was actually participating in God's work. The kingdom of God was advancing over all the earth, and Christians were its emissaries. Stephen's sermon just before his death recounted the history of Israel—how God had reached out in His missionary character time and again, culminating in Jesus' betrayal and cruci-fixion. Stephen chastised the Jewish leaders for rejecting the Righteous One and declared that because of their colossal failure, God's mission had now been transferred to the Church (the true Israel), as validated by the Holy Spirit. By faithfully proclaiming the gospel of the Righteous One, the Church was continuing the Story of the *missional* God. More accurately, through the Spirit, the risen and ascended Lord was speaking and acting through the Church (Acts 7:1-53).

Because Christ is the *missional* God incarnate (Col. 1:15-20; 2:9), at the name of Jesus "every knee should bend, in heaven and on earth and under the earth, and every tongue should confess that Jesus Christ is Lord, to the glo-ry of God the Father" (Phil. 2:10-11). All humankind can now set its hope on Jesus Christ. Through Him they can "live for the praise of [God's] glory" (Eph. 1:12).[225] This is the Story God's *missional* people tell.

If all of this was true for the young Church, then adjusting the gospel to the existing plurality of religions was not an option. God had decisively re-vealed himself as the Redeemer. He called a people into existence and had commissioned them to tell His Story without modification.

The homes of Christians within Thailand's Lahu tribe demonstrate mod-ern-day missional faithfulness to God's Story. Traditional beliefs of the tribe point to the Creator God, but they cannot find Him, so they empower *sha-mans,* or witchdoctors, to act as mediums between the tribe and the spirit world. The Lahu are animists and see their world as a balance of the spiritual and the physical. When things go wrong in the village or with the harvest, the shaman is called upon to find out what or who the problem is and correct it.

In each traditional Lahu home there is a spirit shelf containing some spe-cial string, small objects, and a candle that burns each night to ward off evil spirits. The shaman helps the families keep these supplies up to date so that harmony and peace reign in the village. But when Lahu families come to Christ, the Christian pastor collects spirit shelves from each home and burns the shelves in the center of the village on the day the families are baptized. This gives witness to non-Christians that these new Christians are choosing to depend upon Jesus alone to keep them safe, not upon the old ways of the Lahu shamans. For the first few nights after baptism, the Christian pastor visits each home and prays for the families who now go to sleep in the dark but with the light of Christ now shining in their homes. They sleep in peace and without fear of the evil spirits.

As the number of Christian families increases in a village, the influence of the shaman decreases, often creating conflict. Sometimes the shaman blames the Christians for any problems that arise in the village or in the fields where their crops are located. Sometimes anger cannot be contained, and shootings take place. But in most cases, the power of Christ is peacefully transforming the Lahu people, who have found their Creator God.[226]

The Early Church, like these Lahu Christians, responded to religious pluralism with *missional* fidelity. No less is expected of us in the 21st century. Then and now the Church's mandate is to be faithful to the *missional* God—in worship, nurture, and evangelism. The Epistles of the New Testament show us that tending to fidelity was intentional and persistent. The apostles didn't leave missional fidelity to chance.

THREE NEW TESTAMENT CASE STUDIES

A similarity exists between the pluralist context of the New Testament Church and our current situation. It will help us to look at three examples of how the Early Church exercised its *missional* character: Paul's "sermon" at Lystra, which occurred during his first missionary journey (Acts 14:8-18); Paul before the Areopagus in Athens, during his second missionary journey (17:18-34); and the letter to the Ephesians. While Paul faithfully declared the revelation of God in Christ in these situations, he also looked for ways in which God had already acted to prepare the way for the gospel.

The Sermon at Lystra (Acts 14:6-20)

After opponents in Iconium tried to stone Paul and Barnabas, they fled to Lystra, a Roman colony in Asia Minor. There, a man crippled from birth listened to Paul speaking. Looking at the man intently, and realizing that he had faith to be made well, Paul spoke to him in a loud voice: "Stand upright on your feet" (v. 10). When people saw what Paul had done, they shouted, "The gods have come down to us in the likeness of men!" (v. 11, RSV). They branded Barnabas as Zeus, the chief god of the Greek pantheon. Because Paul was the chief speaker, the crowd identified him as Hermes, the messenger of Zeus (compare Gal. 4:14).

According to a popular myth, Zeus and Hermes had visited this region once before in the likeness of men to test the citizens' piety. A man named Philemon and his wife, Baucus, were the only ones to extend hospitality to the gods. Zeus and Hermes told the pair to climb a mountain because a flood was about to sweep over those who had acted impiously. To atone for this error, later citizens of Lystra built a temple to Zeus in front of the city (Acts 14:13).

Believing that Zeus and Hermes were once again visiting the city, and not wanting to repeat the first error, the priest of Zeus responded immediately to Paul and Barnabas. He brought oxen and garlands to the gates and prepared to lead the people in offering sacrifices.[227]

When Paul and Barnabas saw all this, they tore their clothes and rushed into the middle of the growing crowd. Having gotten their attention, Paul rejected the names that had been given to them. "We also are men, of like nature with you," he told the Lystrans (v. 15, RSV).

Then, rather than trying to identify Christ with a member of the Lystran pantheon, Paul proclaimed the good news of the Redeemer God. He implored the citizens to completely turn away from vainly worshiping a variety of deities. The risen Christ could set them free from idolatry and the bondage it generated. They could now serve the "living God, who made the heaven and the earth and the sea and all that is in them" (v. 15).

In this pluralistic setting, says author Bruce Winter, Paul told the Lystrans that God had in the past permitted them and other nations to walk in their own ways and follow their own religions. But even then, Paul told them, the true and living God had not remained a total stranger to the nations, leaving no witness of himself among them. God, not Zeus or any other deity, had shown His providence by sending rains and fruitful seasons. The living God had been present and active even though the people misidentified the source. God's goal in doing all of this, Paul continued, was to bring joy to their hearts—a joy that would be completed only by receiving the gospel.[228]

Paul Before the Areopagus[229]

Luke tells us that Paul arrived in Athens during his second missionary journey (17:16-34). As he awaited Silas's and Timothy's arrival, he grew deeply troubled over the city's many idols. Athens was a veritable catalog of religious and philosophical pluralism. Paul presented the gospel to the Jews and the devout people in the synagogue. But each day he also presented the gospel in the marketplace to anyone who happened to be there.

While in the marketplace, some Stoic and Epicurean philosophers heard

Paul preaching. To say the least, they were not favorably impressed. Some asked, "What does this babbler want to say?" (v. 18). (The Greek word for "babbler" literally means "cock-sparrow," one who picks up scraps of learning.) Others apparently mistook Paul's preaching on Jesus and *anastasin* (the Greek word for "resurrection," v. 18) as two new foreign deities.

Paul succeeded, however, in piquing their interest. So the Stoics and the Epicureans took hold of the apostle and brought him to the Areopagus. Having corralled him, they asked him to explain the strange new teachings he was presenting. Luke tells us that the Athenians and foreigners who dwelt there "spend their time in nothing but telling or hearing something new" (v. 21). The Athenians at this time were famous for their curiosity.

Paul stood in the middle of the Areopagus and began to speak, addressing the Stoics in their heartland. (Zeno [335-263 B.C.], the founder of Stoic philosophy, had established his school nearby in the southwest stoa[230] of the ancient agoras, or places of assembly.)[231] Paul began to explain Christ and His resurrection by first identifying telltale markers of God's prior activity in His hearers, markers Paul could use as entryways for the gospel. He used his knowledge of the Hellenistic world to span the distance between God's preparation and the explicit proclamation they were now hearing. Paul could not have helped but notice the Athenians' religious hunger. They were addicted to religion, as evidenced by their many objects of worship. They had left nothing to chance. One altar was inscribed "to an unknown god," just in case a person was unsure of which deity to appease or thank. He or she could cover the bases by sacrificing at that altar. Paul took this mentality and ran with it: "What therefore you worship as unknown, this I proclaim to you" (v. 23). His sermon made known the otherwise unknown God.

The Stoics. During the era when Paul was in Athens, the chief characteristic of the Stoics was insistence on practical and moral principles that tended to take on a religious coloring. Among their central doctrines was belief in humankind's kinship with God, who is the ruler of the world (7:35).[232] Building upon this Stoic belief, Paul told them that the God who raised Jesus from the dead is the Creator of the world. He is the Lord of heaven and earth (17:24) and gives all people life, breath, and everything they have (v. 25). So He is not distanced from us. The Stoics thought that there was only one God, that He gave life to all, and that He should be sought, but that He is called by many names. They would have latched onto Paul's use of the term *God* (v. 27).[233] Both the Stoics and Paul stressed God's providence. If we will but open our eyes, the Stoics said, we will see how God bountifully cares for the world. Paul responded that humans actually live, move, and exist because of God's creative presence (v. 28). This God confirmed through Jesus' witness by raising Him from the dead (v. 31). This was probably Paul's most important bridge-building element.[234] The Stoics believed also in divine judgment (v. 31), and this, too, provided common ground between the Stoics and the gospel.

The Epicureans. Epicurus (341-270 B.C.), the founder of the Epicurean School, concentrated on ethics even more than the Stoics did. For him, sense-knowledge was the fundamental basis of knowledge. He wanted to free people from fear of the gods and the afterworld and to give them peace of soul. The gods don't interfere in human affairs, Epicurus said; true piety consists of right thought and action, not worshiping and sacrificing to the deities. In other words, true piety is a matter of ethics, not religion. Epicurus taught that the gods are alive, immortal, and blessed, and we should honor them. However, we should not seek to know them, pray to them, or ask them to become involved in our lives because they simply don't become involved in human affairs.

The Epicureans would have strongly agreed with Paul's statement that God doesn't live in man-made temples (v. 24) and that He cannot be captured in gold, silver, and stone (v. 29). (Practically, however, the Epicureans often tailored their teaching about the gods to accommodate popular religion. Offer sacrifices and seek divine favors if it makes you feel better, they said.)[235] The Epicureans also would have agreed with Paul's statement that God is not some petty deity that needs to be supported through human worship and sacrifices (v. 25). He is fully God no matter what humans do or do not offer Him.[236] But since the Epicureans believed God is far removed from daily human affairs, they would have disagreed with Paul's claims that God "gives to all mortals life and breath and all things" (v. 25) and that "in him we live and move and have our being" (v. 28).

Though the Stoics and Epicureans held significantly different ideas about God, Paul believed that the God of the gospel had been active in adherents of both philosophies, and he built upon this in his proclamation. But as important as beliefs were for building bridges to the Stoics and Epicureans, Paul didn't settle for pluralism and didn't refrain from challenging their beliefs. He forth-rightly called upon them to recognize that their beliefs were far from complete. They awaited true fulfillment in the risen Christ. Now that Christ had come, the time of anticipation was over, and the time had arrived for repentance and re-ceiving the risen Christ (v. 31). Whatever the religious panorama might have been in the past, the situation had radically changed. The future, Paul told them, belongs to the risen Lord. All religions, all cults, and all practices of popular piety have reached their end in Him.

The Letter to the Ephesians

This letter[237] fairly sings the authority of Christ over all so-called divine powers, exalting His power to break the hold of evil and reconcile people to God. The letter is heavy with allusions to the religious and cultural context in which the Christians in Asia Minor lived. Ephesians helps us understand the challenges the young Church faced when declaring its faith and offers important guidance for us today.

An astonishing array of religious options existed in Asia Minor:

- The cult of the goddess Artemis (Diana to the Romans) strongly influenced religious life in western Asia Minor. Artemis was the virgin goddess of the moon and twin sister of Apollo. Her most noted temple was at Ephesus. Built outside the city walls, it was one of the seven wonders of the ancient world. The influence of the Artemis cult on the lives of its devotees extended to matters of culture, family life, economics, education, and most areas of local government. It demanded strict loyalty.[238] This cult could easily absorb elements from other religions (syncretism).
- Mysteries and sacred prostitution figured prominently. They were often associated with the cult of Artemis and other goddesses.
- Hellenistic magic was prominent, and visionary-mystical cults attracted many.
- A major Jewish presence was also in the area. Jewish magic, characterized by an emphasis on Hebrew phrases, names, angels, and demons was one component of Jewish life in Ephesus.

Given this bazaar of religious options, the temptations to become syncretistic are not surprising. The Artemis cult and others would have easily reduced Christ to a much lesser role than the one in whom "all the fullness of God was pleased to dwell" (Col. 1:19), and through whom God had reconciled to himself "all things" (v. 20). The cults would have seen Christ as just one more divine power among many, gladly blending Him into the pluralistic mix. In some cases He would have become one more tool for manipulating the powers of the heavenly realms.[239]

To all of this, add another powerful opponent of the gospel. When Paul engaged the religions of his day, he had to confront not only the characteristically religious cults but also the Roman imperial cult, the closest thing to a world religion at that time. It dominated the Roman Empire from one end of the social order to the other. Emperor veneration could generate either enthusiastic affection or chilling fear for failing to participate.

All of this, says Douglas Harink, "had to be countered by another power, the Wholly Other power of God's imperial rule."[240] Against all these options and temptations, the Epistle to the Ephesians uncompromisingly declares that Christ stands high above all the gods, above all the powers. In the past they have used "the rituals, habits, customs, and social and political practices" of the Gentiles as their instruments.[241] But now in Christ, God has mounted a successful attack on all the powers that enslave.[242]

Who is this Christ? Paul told the Ephesians that He is the One in whom God is drawing together all things. When the time is fulfilled, God will unite "all things in him, things in heaven and things on earth" (Eph. 1:10; see vv. 3-10). There is one Lord, not an amalgam of deities who have independent legitimacy. Nothing compromises the uniqueness and finality of Jesus Christ.[243] For the Father has put "all things under [Christ's] feet and has made him the head over all things for the church" (v. 22).

The good news for all people, including those under the dominance of today's cults, is that Christ is the Victor, Lord over all. God, rich in mercy, sets captives absolutely free. He can transform them into His sons and daughters, making them part of His *missional* people, all to the "praise of his glorious grace" (v. 6).

For Reflection and Discussion

1. The first-century world was polytheistic. The many gods took many different cultural forms or faces. Identify some of the gods your culture has created and now worships (e.g., in the entertainment industry). Do these gods permit syncretism and polytheism?

2. If God is a missionary God, and if the Church justifies its existence in faithful service to this God, what other definitions and justifications for the Church's existence will be ruled out?

3. In Lystra Paul refused to obstruct the gospel by making himself the center of attention. In what ways do contemporary witnesses for Christ face the same challenge? In what ways do Christian denominations face this threat?

4. What conviction or belief would have led Paul to look for bridges between the people to whom he preached and the gospel he preached?

5. What could have made Paul so confident regarding the power of the gospel in the religiously pluralistic Greco-Roman context?

PART III

PLURALISM AND REDEMPTION FROM A WESLEYAN PERSPECTIVE

7

WHY OUR HISTORY MATTERS

The roots of my grandmother, Cattie Priester, were deeply planted in the old South with its sense of identity and manners. Newcomers to the farm on the Big Salkehatchie River in South Carolina could expect to hear the question, "Who's your people?" That translates into, "What are your family connections, your roots?" A person's identity was incomplete until he or she could answer Cattie Priester's question. For her, the deeper the roots, the better the person.

This sentiment propelled the 1977 television miniseries *Roots,* which traced the journey of Kunta Kinte and his descendants through 150 years of slavery in America and into eventual freedom.[244] More than 130 million viewers watched at least part of the 12-hour series.

Roots triggered an interest in genealogy that sent millions of people in search of their family histories and identities. Alvin Poussaint, a professor of psychiatry at Harvard Medical School, says *Roots* unleashed the "Who am I? Where did I come from?" phenomenon.[245] People saw how their own stories were incomplete in the absence of knowledge about their roots, and they went searching for ways to complete them.

What is true of human roots is also applicable to us as Christians. Our identity is incomplete unless we are informed by the rich Christian heritage that shapes the whole Church. Christians whose roots reach no deeper than their own subjective experiences and homespun ideas are sitting ducks for deception and error. They fit the description in Jesus' parable of the seed that sprang up quickly and then withered because there was no root system (Mark 4:3-9). This shallowness is not necessary. Christians can become deeply rooted in the Christian faith, and congregations are responsible for this planting. The New Testament urges us to drink deeply of Christ's riches, to become mature in Him, and so produce a "harvest of righteousness" (Phil. 1:11). This requires that we explore our spiritual roots and draw our nourishment and identity from them.

The whole of Christian history forms the larger Christian root system.

This is as true for those in the Wesleyan doctrinal tradition as it is for any other part of Christ's Church. Our *primary identity* is with historic Christianity, not with the Wesleyan tradition. Along with all orthodox Christians, we confess "one Lord, one faith, one baptism, one God and Father of all, who is above all and through all and in all" (Eph. 4:5-6). In the Nicene Creed we affirm one holy catholic (universal) and apostolic Church. What unites Wesleyans with their sisters and brothers in other parts of the Church is far more important than what distinguishes them. Sectarianism isn't in the Wesleyan tradition's defining spirit.[246]

But just as all denominations have characteristics that mark them, so in the Wesleyan tradition we understand some features of the Christian faith in ways that mark us. These result from our understanding of both the Story of God and how the grace of God has encountered us. Without infringing on Christian unity, in this book we are interested in responding to religious pluralism in ways that are molded by the Wesleyan doctrinal tradition. Our purpose is to lay a foundation on which to build our response.[247]

SOME HISTORICAL PERSPECTIVE

The Wesleyan heritage and the family of denominations identified with it arose in the 18th-century Evangelical Revival that swept Great Britain (its counterpart occurred in America, especially in New England where Jonathan Edwards was a towering leader). John Wesley (1703-91) and his brother, Charles (1707-88), were two of the major figures in the revival. They were well educated, and each experienced an evangelical conversion that changed their lives. Both became Anglican priests, John best known as a preacher, theologian, and organizer, and Charles best known for the rich hymns he gave to the Church.[248]

Ministry to the poor, social reform, and confidence in the transforming grace of God marked the Evangelical Revival. The Wesley brothers held strong convictions that the power of the gospel could change lives and communities without respect to social status, and this propelled them to proclaim the gospel of hope to many people whom the established church had often ignored.[249] They believed that Christian discipleship must take concrete, practical form in love for one's neighbor, taking seriously the New Testament call to holy living. They believed that through the transforming presence of the Holy Spirit, Christians can do what their Lord commanded—love God with all their heart, soul, strength, and mind, and their neighbors as themselves (Luke

10:27). They did not minimize the effects of sin on individuals and societies, but they believed the transforming grace of God was greater. An optimism regarding grace peppers their sermons, hymns, and writings. How could they have otherwise remained faithful to the gospel? They were simply echoing Paul's joyous announcement in Romans: "The abundance of grace and the free gift of righteousness" (5:17) are more powerful than sin's dominion. The kingdom of grace has eclipsed the kingdom of sin (vv. 15-21).

In the 19th century a renewed emphasis on Christian holiness began in the eastern United States and spread throughout the country. The revival affected numerous denominations, including Methodists, Quakers, Presbyterians, and Baptists. Portions of the revival stressed the doctrine and life of Christian holiness as people believed the early Methodists had taught. Central were the Wesleys' emphasis upon Christian holiness as both thorough transformation and works of love and mercy that impact individuals and society. The renewal contributed to the formation of the Wesleyan Methodist Church (1843), the Free Methodist Church (1860), and the Salvation Army in England (1865). In the 1880s the Church of God (Anderson, Indiana) and the Church of God (Holiness) were formed. In 1908 a merger of other various Holiness groups brought the Church of the Nazarene into existence. Because of their association with the 19th-century revival, these denominations are identified as part of the Wesleyan-Holiness tradition.[250]

A Brief Doctrinal Overview

The Triune God

Along with all orthodox Christians, Wesleyans affirm the reality of the one, eternal, and triune God who is Father, Son, and Holy Spirit. There is no other. For Christians, speaking of God means speaking of the Trinity. Put differently, we don't begin by describing God's characteristics and then add the Trinity as an afterthought. To speak of Him accurately, we must begin by speaking of the Trinity because this is the way He reveals himself to be—He *is* the Triune God. The doctrine of the Trinity is what distinguishes the Christian doctrine of God as *Christian,* rather than as Jewish, Muslim, or Sikh.

Christians believe that God is *One,* that His being One is not simply a number but a *unity,* and that His *unity* resides in His being essentially Triune in nature. This is most clearly manifest in God's love. He is love, and His love is first of all expressed in a mutual indwelling and self-giving between Father, Son, and Holy Spirit. Theologians use the Greek word *perichoresis* (mutual indwelling) to describe how, in love, each person of the Trinity indwells the other, without ceasing to be distinct in their personhood. The love that characterizes the Triune life is the love with which God gives himself to the world and in which He invites us to live. So, when God expresses His love to us He is actually *doing* what He *is*. He is expressing the character of His own life.

The meaning and importance of the Trinity can be difficult to wrap our minds around. Thankfully, our redemption doesn't depend on how completely we understand the Trinity. The Church's language regarding the Trinity results from its desire to be faithful to God's self-disclosure and activity and to the witness of the Scriptures. Consequently, we affirm that God's creativity, His self-giving love, His faithfulness, and His acts of redemption are all thoroughly Triune and one in character.

All aspects of Christian faith, salvation, worship, piety, hope, and service are grounded in the life of the Triune God. Wherever God acts, it is the action of the Trinity, whether in moments of creation or re-creation. That is why every prayer, all acts of worship, enactment of the sacraments, all confessions of sin, and every expression of hope occurs in the name of the Father, Son, and Holy Spirit.

God Incarnate

We believe that in Jesus of Nazareth the Triune God became incarnate and acted to redeem the world. This is the uniform witness of the New Testament and of apostolic faith. In Jesus, God *revealed His glory* and *declared His name* in all the earth. In Him all the promises of God find their fulfillment (2 Cor. 1:18-22). Jesus is God's good news for all creation. To this the Holy Spirit, the Scriptures, and the Body of Christ bear witness.

Christ is God's good news of forgiveness and reconciliation, community and hope, and holiness and fulfillment *for all humankind*. In His life, death, and resurrection, Christ was victorious over death, hell, sin, and the grave *for all*. He is Christ the Victor. We believe that His victory was on all humankind's behalf. By setting prisoners free from sin's tyranny, by transferring them into His kingdom, Christ shows that God is indeed the Savior of the world.

Contrary to what John Hick and others believe, God did not choose to reveal himself in many religious and cultural forms, any one of which would successfully extend access to God. That philosophy is at odds with the Word of God. The one eternal God acted definitively to redeem through the life, death, resurrection, and ascension of Jesus Christ. The New Testament tells us that God put His great power "to work in Christ when he raised him from the dead and seated him at his right hand in the heavenly places, far above all rule and authority and power and dominion, and above every name that is named, not only in this age but also in the age to come" (Eph. 1:20-21). The action of the Father himself will forever frustrate those who, in the interest of religious pluralism, try to put distance between the Father and the Son. The Epistle of First John serves as a sentinel: "No one who denies the Son has the Father; everyone who confesses the Son has the Father also" (1 John 2:23).

The Scriptures

The Old and New Testaments, Wesleyans believe, bear inspired, full, and faithful witness to the Story of God, and therein resides their importance. They comprise the Scriptures of the Church and are the normative witness to the work of God in the world through Jesus Christ. Together, the Old and New Testaments tell the story of God's "mercy in calling out and sustaining a people who are to live in obedience to him and to be a servant of divine mercy to all the nations and the world."[251] They are united by one God and one Story that reached its climax in Jesus Christ (Eph. 1:7, 18-23). As the Book of Acts declares, the Story continues in the risen and ascended Lord who is made present in the Church and in the world through the Holy Spirit (Acts 2:14-26).

All other texts, traditions, people, ideas, and institutions stand under the primacy of the Scriptures. The Holy Spirit breathes life into the Scriptures and bears witness that they sufficiently and unerringly reveal the will of God in all things necessary to our salvation. Any doctrine missing from the Scriptures should never join the ranks of necessary Christian faith and practice.[252]

Wesleyans believe that the Church of Jesus Christ is the proper home of the Scriptures and that only in the context of a confessing and faithful community of Christians can the Bible be properly received and understood. The Scriptures tell the Story of God for the people of God. They were written "from faith, for faith."[253]

Consistent with the 16th-century Protestant Reformers, Wesleyans insist on *sola scriptura* (Scripture alone). This means that all other sources of Christian knowledge (such as Church tradition, doctrine, reason, experience, and great Church leaders) must submit to the Scriptures—in theory and in practice. But we also recognize that faithful interpretation of Scripture never happens in a vacuum. It occurs under the formative influence of subsidiary sources of authority such as the great creeds of the Church (e.g., the Apostles' Creed, the Nicene Creed, and the Creed of Chalcedon). We recognize that the Scriptures are read and understood in particular ecclesial (denominational) communities or doctrinal traditions. Such influences affect how we read and understand the Bible, even though some Christians like to think this isn't true for them. They claim to understand the Bible without any reference to prior doctrinal, historical, or social perspectives. But as soon as they begin to speak, they reveal their predispositions and presuppositions and demonstrate that "the Bible alone" is "both conceptually and practically untenable."[254] This reality should keep all Christians humble before Christ, the Scriptures, and each other.

Tradition, Reason, and Experience

In the Wesleyan tradition we identify four sources that shape and govern our understanding of the Christian faith. The Scriptures are the principal source and have unchallenged primacy. The remaining three sources of authority for understanding our faith are *tradition, reason,* and *experience.*

Tradition

When speaking of *tradition* as a source of authority for our faith, we mean "the Church's time-honored practices of worship, service, and critical reflection."[255] We don't mean general cultural customs. Tradition includes hymnody, the seven ancient catholic (ecumenical) creeds,[256] the history of the Church, the writings of formative and honored theologians (e.g., the early Church Fathers, Luther, Calvin, Wesley) and, for us, formative theological voices in the Wesleyan tradition.

Reason

By *reason* we mean the human capacity to reason and reflect. It includes responsible thinking and "understandings of the world gained through systematic philosophical reflection and through scientific investigation."[257] We do not mean autonomous reason as advanced by many Enlightenment figures. For us, reason, like all other human capacities, must stand in God's service. As it was for Athanasius in the 4th century and Anselm in the 11th, reason is "faith seeking understanding." To serve the Church well, reason must have as its home the wisdom that comes from above (James 3:17). We place a premium on education, not as an end in itself, but as a vehicle through which to worship and serve God in the Church and in the world.

Like all of God's gifts, reason submits to Christian formation through prayer and Christian instruction. Under the Spirit's and the Church's guidance, we use reason to understand the Scriptures. It is a necessary tool for understanding biblical texts and how to apply them to life in the world.[258] However, use of reason never occurs in the absence of historical and cultural influences. We all reason from somewhere. So we would be wise to always reason humbly and to submit the results to critique by our sisters and brothers in Christ, both past and present.

Experience

Usually when we speak of *experience,* we are referring to things that have specifically happened to us or to others. Experience in the Christian sense does include our own experiences of grace and new creation in Jesus Christ, such as the Spirit witnessing[259] to our individual spirits that we are the children of God.[260] This is what John Wesley meant by "experimental religion."[261]

But experience extends much further than our personal encounters with the Redeemer. It includes the rich history and wisdom of the people of God who have gone before us—those in whose debt and under whose instruction we stand. Experience includes our joyful memories of the Church's successes as well as our painful memories of its failures to understand and faithfully live the gospel. Experience also includes sisters and brothers learning from one another as we exercise our Spirit-given gifts in Christ's Body.

Another aspect of experience is the life of God in the collective community of faith. The experience of God in all parts of the Church, such as the intense suffering for Christ now being endured in some parts of the world, should inform and guide us. The historic and collective experience illumines the meaning of Scripture and also "confirms the testimony of scripture in the hearts and lives of the community."[262]

Grace Freely Extended to All

Foundational to our understanding of God and the salvation He provides, we believe that God freely extends His grace to all people. He does this without reference to time, location, or any other finite element. His sovereignty is chiefly manifest in His love for the world. He reveals himself not as raw, threatening, and excluding power but as the Creator-Redeemer who actively seeks to reconcile all people, regardless of how hopeless their conditions in life may seem to be (John 3:15; Rom. 5:18-19). God is like a shepherd who places himself at risk to find one lost sheep. He is like a poor woman who diligently looks for a lost coin. He is like a father who in vulnerable love forgives a prodigal but penitent son (Luke 15).

Whoever will confess that Jesus is the Christ will be saved. This was true for Muhammad, a 50-year-old man reared in Pakistan. As a child, Muhammad memorized the Koran and read many books on religion, but none of them satisfied his hunger for God. He came to believe there "was no reality in any religion; all of them are false." He recalled that his "soul was losing composure day by day." Muhammad heard from Christians that Jesus Christ died for the sins of all people, that He is the Redeemer. He thought all of this to be empty fantasy. "No one," he said, "would sacrifice his life for strangers."

Then one day Muhammad saw the *JESUS* film. What he learned about Jesus was completely different from what he had previously understood. He came to know that Jesus died on the Cross for our sins, that He was buried and raised to new life by the power of God. Muhammad knew that his torturous search had ended at the Cross and empty tomb. "My spiritual blindness was removed. Jesus opened my eyes," he said. "My search for truth is now over. Jesus Christ is the Savior, the Son of God."[263]

The Wesleyan conviction regarding the universal range of Christ's atonement establishes both our vision of the world and our disposition toward it. Philip Meadows, Methodist theologian, summarizes our conviction. As opposed to a "theological pessimism, which considers the bulk of humankind to be reprobates, on their way to damnation," we affirm "an optimism of grace which makes all people candidates for heaven."[264] If we trust Paul's words in Rom. 5, how could we believe otherwise? He clearly tells us that just as sin and death have spread to all persons ("the many"), "much more surely have the grace of God and the free gift in the grace of the one man, Jesus Christ, abounded for the many" (v. 15).

Salvation by Grace Through Faith Alone

Along with the 16th-century Reformers, Wesleyans believe that sinners are reconciled to God by grace through faith alone. We cannot leverage God with our own righteousness because we do not have a righteousness of our own "that comes from the law, but one that comes through faith in Christ, the righteousness from God based on faith" (Phil. 3:9). "While we were still sinners, Christ died for us" (Rom. 5:8, NIV). Apart from Christ Jesus we are hopelessly enslaved to sin. We believe that if we rely upon ourselves, we cannot successfully take a single step toward God. Only through the Son's faithful obedience to the Father—even unto death on the Cross—is there hope for salvation. As the apostle Paul put it, we are benefactors of "the righteousness of God through faith in Jesus Christ" (3:22). For him, "the righteousness of God" meant first God's own creative and saving activity (vv. 23-26), and also the grace gift of righteousness in which those who trust in Jesus Christ share (Rom. 3:22; 2 Cor. 5:21).[265]

For Wesleyans, being reconciled to God and becoming righteous by faith does not mean God forgives sins and then merely covers the sinner with the garment of Christ's righteousness without affecting the body underneath.[266] God doesn't just look at the same old people in a new way because He now sees them through Christ. Reconciliation includes transformation by the Holy Spirit, a real change, a new creation. By the Spirit, the risen Christ actually takes up residence in the believer and initiates a comprehensive renewal of God's image. This is what I remember most about the little flock that welcomed my mother and father. A cotton sharecropper and his family, for example, could boast of no worldly standing and certainly could not boast about their formerly chaotic lives. But they could testify with confidence—with an identifiable before and after—that Jesus Christ had transformed their lives, had freed them from the demons that had enslaved them. And so they loved to sing and tell about it, even if sometimes in some unlettered ways.

I like George Foreman's description—yes, the same George Foreman who was not once but twice the heavyweight boxing champion of the world. In a major upset, on March 17, 1977, Foreman lost to Jimmy Young, putting a temporary end to his effort to regain the title lost in 1974. Foreman was a leading contender for the heavyweight title and was expected to win easily. Young was only a light-hitting fringe contender from Philadelphia. Before the fight, Foreman felt empty. For some reason, while standing on the balcony of his hotel room, he prayed to a God he wasn't sure existed: "God, maybe you can take my life and use it. Maybe you can use me as something more than a boxer."

After the loss to Young, Foreman fell into what he described as a hellish, frightening place of nothingness and despair. Then, he says, he felt a giant hand carrying him out of the emptiness that surrounded him. He began to cry out, "Jesus Christ is coming alive in me!" Having frightened his handlers half to death, Foreman ran to the shower, shouting, "Hallelujah, I'm clean! Hallelujah, I've been born again!" A strange story? Not for those acquainted with the "amazing grace" by which God leads people to new life in Christ.

Where is George Foreman today? In Houston, Texas, pastoring a small Baptist congregation that meets in a metal building in a run-down part of town.[267]

Christian Transformation

Wesleyans believe that internal convictions or assurances may testify to the transforming work of the Holy Spirit but that the most important evidence of the new birth is a changed life that actively expresses love toward God and one's neighbor (1 John 5:1-2). Wesleyans are more impressed by the power of transforming grace than by the power of sin in a Christian's life. We believe very strongly in the sanctifying power of the Holy Spirit in lives fully yielded to His reign. Our confidence is in the victorious Christ.

Not all doctrinal traditions agree with this. For some the hold of sin and the old identity as a sinner dominate, and real transformation that radically changes the Christian's disposition toward God and one's neighbor seems to hope for too much. Wesleyan confidence in God's transforming grace is echoed in Dietrich Bonhoeffer's distinction in *The Cost of Discipleship* between cheap grace and costly grace. Cheap grace, Bonhoeffer said, is "the grace which amounts to the justification of sin without the justification of the repentant sinner who departs from sin and from whom sin departs. Cheap grace is not the kind of forgiveness of sin which frees us from the toils of sin. Cheap grace is the grace we bestow on ourselves."[268] Costly grace, on the other hand, "is *costly* because it calls us to follow, and it is *grace* because it calls us to follow *Jesus Christ*. It is costly because it costs a man his life. It is costly because it condemns sin, and grace because it justifies the sinner."[269]

On May 10, 1775, Ethan Allen, Benedict Arnold, and the Green Mountain Boys from upstate New York crossed Lake Champlain from Vermont. At dawn they overwhelmed the sleeping British garrison at Fort Ticonderoga, winning the first battle of the American Revolution. But in July 1777 the British commander, General John Burgoyne, managed to take back the fort for the Red Coats by hauling a cannon to the top of Mount Defiance, towering above Fort Ticonderoga. The Americans said it couldn't be done, a cannon couldn't make it up that slope, but General Burgoyne insisted, "Where a goat can go, a man can go. Where a man can go, a cannon can go." He was right. One glimpse of the exposed fort below makes clear Burgoyne's strategic advantage. On July 6, with exploding cannon balls raining down, American commander General Arthur St. Clair evacuated the fort.

More than two centuries later, in the summer of 2001, two Asian visitors to Fort Ticonderoga sat atop Mount Defiance, holding laptop computers. E. T. Morrel, an area resident, struck up a conversation with them. They confidently told him the British had not successfully driven the Americans out of Fort Ticonderoga. Astonished by this revision of history, Morrel asked, "Why not?" With an air of triumph, the two visitors pointed to their computer screens and answered, "Because our computer models say it can't be done!"[270]

Wesleyans have no limiting computer models. They rely on the expectant testimony of Easter and Pentecost. Christ has spoiled the enemy's stronghold and has put him to flight. New Testament scholar Richard B. Hays says that the gospel Paul preached dealt "not merely with forgiveness but with *transformation*."[271] Being baptized into Christ means passing from the kingdom of sin and death into the kingdom of righteousness and life. "The notion of effective transformation through union with Christ is fundamental" to Paul's theology, to his ethics, and to his understanding of normative Christian life.[272] Justification by faith alone should not be taken to mean that "those who put their faith in Jesus Christ will find mercy despite their inability to do what God's Law requires." Failure to recognize the importance of real participation in the effects of Christ's death and resurrection can underestimate "the transforming power of God's grace."[273] Hays' assessment of Paul's vision of transformation captures precisely what Wesleyans affirm. "When Paul breaks out into praise in Romans 7:25a—'Thanks be to God through Jesus Christ our Lord'—he is not merely offering thanks for forgiveness; he is celebrating liberation from the bondage and paralysis that formerly blocked obedience to God's will."[274]

Methodist theologian Theodore Runyon says that John Wesley's doctrine of universal depravity recognized abundant evidence of human fallenness everywhere. But Wesley believed the reign of sin can be rooted out. "The sanctifying grace of God is given in order that the devil and all his works might not only be renounced but actively opposed and even destroyed."[275]

The Church, the Sacraments, and the Redemption of Creation

The Church

Consistent with the New Testament, Wesleyans affirm that God's plan of redemption centers on the creation of a new people called the Church ("the Israel of God" [Gal. 6:16]), and redemption and nurture occur only in this context. "Christ loved the church and gave himself up for her, in order to make her holy by cleansing her with the washing of water by the word, so as to present the church to himself in splendor, without a spot or wrinkle or anything of the kind—yes, so that she may be holy and without blemish" (Eph. 5:25-27). Paul makes clear that we are *in* Christ only as we are members of His Body—not as disconnected parts. The Father has made Christ the Head of all things for the Church, "which is his body, the fullness of him who fills all in all" (1:23). Lest there be any doubt, Paul even refers to the Church as "our mother" (Gal. 4:26). Diminish the Church, and we diminish redemption altogether.

Wesley's ministry and writings abundantly demonstrate his love for the

Church and the instruction he received from the New Testament.[276] He believed that the Church is best "defined *in action,* in her witness and mission, rather than by her form of polity (structure and government)."[277] He recognized that the New Testament offers no form of authentic discipleship apart from the Church, for it is "the fullness of him who fills all in all" (Eph. 1:23). Theologian Henry H. Knight observes that for the early Methodists, gathering in community for instruction, prayer, and service were considered absolutely necessary for maintaining and increasing faith.[278]

The Sacraments (Baptism and the Lord's Supper)

The sacraments play a pivotal role in the Wesleyan understanding of how God's redeeming grace reaches us. Authors Rob L. Staples[279] and Henry H. Knight[280] have considered this topic carefully. John Wesley defined *sacrament* as "an outward sign of inward grace, and a means whereby we receive the same."[281] He adopted from Augustine this distinction between the outward sign (*signum,* the baptismal water, the bread, and the cup) of the sacrament and the inward grace (*res,* the thing signified).[282] Through the Holy Spirit, Christ is present and uses the sacraments as a means of grace.[283] "Grace gives life to the sign, while the sign points to Christ as the source of grace."[284] All this happens because of the "living, acting God."[285]

The foundation underlying all sacramental theology "is the fundamental insight that *God may accomplish spiritual ends through material means.*" Because God is the Creator and Sustainer and is present in His creation, He can work the spiritual through the material. The creation is His servant, not His enemy. Hence, the created order can become a carrier of divine grace. God extends His grace to us through the sacraments.[286]

For Wesley the sacraments are the ordinary means through which God accomplishes our salvation. But He did not make them absolutely necessary for salvation. The Wesleyan tradition doesn't embrace sacramentalism (the belief that salvation comes only through the sacraments), but it does "maintain the 'sacramentalist vision.'"[287] Redemption is not synonymous with the sacraments,[288] nor are they absolutely necessary as the sole means by which God conveys salvation. But they are ordained of Christ as real means of redeeming grace.

Baptism. Wesleyans understand baptism to be *the sacrament of initiation.* In keeping with the New Testament, Christian baptism signifies initiation into Christian faith and life. Wesley calls it "the initiatory sacrament, which enters us into covenant with God."[289] It stands at the beginning of the Christian life and is not to be repeated. Staples gives five interrelated, but distinguishable, meanings of baptism. It is:

- the mark of our inclusion in the new covenant that Christ established
- the symbol of our identification with the death of Christ
- the symbol of our participation in the resurrected life of Christ
- the symbol of our reception of the Holy Spirit (in regeneration)
- the action through which we are made part of Christ's body, the church[290]

The Lord's Supper (the Eucharist). The Lord's Supper is *the sacrament of sanctification.* In the Lord's Supper, the Christ who is changing His people into His own image is spiritually and beneficially present.[291] Staples asks whether it is legitimate to associate the Eucharist with sanctification, the process of redemptive transformation. He answers, "Wesley thought so." For him "The Lord's Supper was ordained by God to be a means of conveying to men either [prevenient], or justifying, or sanctifying grace, according to their several necessities."[292]

As the sacrament of sanctification, the Eucharist can be "understood as that means of grace, instituted by Jesus Christ, to which we are invited for repentance, for self-examination, for renewal, for anticipation of the heavenly kingdom, and for celebration in our pilgrimage toward perfection in the image of Christ. All of these are involved in our sanctification, and all of these are benefits available to us at the Lord's table."[293] This is made possible through the agency of the Holy Spirit.[294] More completely stated, in the Eucharist the whole Trinity is present to bestow the riches of Christ to the Church.[295]

Staples' summary bears repeating:

> God's Word is spoken in nature and in history, in creation and in redemption, in preaching and in sacraments. The supreme and final Word of God is Jesus Christ, the Word made flesh. If Jesus Christ is the Word of God, and if the Word is to speak to the whole person, Christian faith dare not lose the word that comes through sacrament, because human beings are not disembodied spirits of both body and spirit. We live by symbol and sacrament, as well as by the spoken word, and we need "every word that comes from the mouth of God" (Matt. 4:4).[296]

So far we have stressed the more personal dimensions of the sacraments, but there is a public dimension as well. The sacraments also openly declare that the universal reign of God has come in Jesus Christ and that the Church is formed in the power of God's reign. The Church is called to institute ministries (preaching, teaching, witnessing, praying, and bringing good news to those who are oppressed) that declare God's reign in liberation and reconciliation.

Redemption of Creation

The Gospel of John tells us that the Logos who became incarnate as the Redeemer is the same One through whom the Father created all things (John 1:1-5). Redemption is new creation; it is the Father creatively moving upon the chaos as He did so long ago. The close relationship between creation and redemption in the New Testament is intentional and astonishing (Rom. 8:18-25; Eph. 1:3-11; Col. 1:9-20). While many other religions in the first century and since viewed the world as inherently opposed to God and all goodness, the Scriptures speak of the world as having been lovingly created by God.

Like all humankind, the creation has been deeply scarred by sin. But certain that the Creator is also the Redeemer, the Old and New Testaments affirm that for redemption to succeed, God must act on behalf of all He has created, must accomplish the redemption of it all. Otherwise, salvation would have to be redefined as God picking through a trash pile. The New Testament confidently proclaims that God is the Redeemer, not the junk dealer. What He accomplished in Jesus of Nazareth is good news for the whole creation. For some reason, this understanding of salvation so essential to the Bible is easily neglected by many contemporary evangelical Christians.

But John Wesley did not neglect it. For him the span of redemption is holistic as the Bible is holistic; it includes God's creation. With John and the apostle Paul, Wesley believed that renewal would be partial and incomplete if the created order were left out of new creation. Wesleyan theologian Steve McCormick says that for John Wesley, in the new creation there was an indissoluble link between the human creation and the material creation. The physical creation itself will share in the redemption of the children of God. The anchor for this confidence is the Incarnation.

> It takes a material creation to receive grace and give grace. After all, the Word made flesh continuously mediates, by the Spirit, the grace and love of our Maker in and through the physical creation. This is why it is not possible to "know," "obey" and "love" the Triune Creator apart from the creation. And as the human creation begins to love, as God is love, the rest of the groaning creation rejoices! Then and only then will we know how to "serve" the creation and offer back to the praise of our Creator, maker of Heaven and Earth, a fully "restored" creation in the New Creation.[297]

We will return to this topic in the final chapter, "Anticipating the Story's End."

For Reflection and Discussion

1. What is the difference between denominational sectarianism and recognition of doctrinal distinctives? Does the distinction *necessarily* distract from the unity of Christ's Church and its witness?

2. We live in a time when many Christians want to minimize the importance of doctrine. Why is this true, and what dangers does it pose?

3. The four sources of doctrine in the Wesleyan tradition form an integrated unity. But one source is superior to them all. Reflect upon the unity of the sources and upon the importance of the Bible's superior position.

4. How would you identify the defining spirit of the Wesleyan tradition?

5. Many Christians do not embrace the importance of the Church as the Wesleyan tradition does. Survey what the New Testament says about the Church to learn whether the Wesleyan tradition is in line with the New Testament. You may be interested to know that *Strong's Exhaustive Concordance* is available on-line at <http://www.apostolicchurches.net/bible/strongs.html>.

8
AMAZING GRACE:
THE WESLEYAN WAY OF SALVATION

The paths to salvation established by the wisdom of God can be quite astonishing at times. Cheon-to Kim (Ben) was reared a Buddhist in South Korea. He had attended a Christian church a few times, but it didn't interest him. "I preferred a Buddhist temple because when I went there, I felt so peaceful, and I could relax easily. When I went to church, I felt a headache." Then one night, Ben experienced nightmares and awoke alarmed and frightened. For reasons he couldn't explain, he called out to Jesus, "continually and seriously." As he made his appeal, Ben experienced a peace he had never known. He confessed faith in Jesus as his Savior and was delivered from a life of fighting and alcohol. Later, God called him to prepare for the ordained Christian ministry, and he moved to Australia to begin his studies.[298]

By contrast, Stephane's story illustrates the reach of God's grace beyond the boundary of established religion. If being reared in an environment of atheism could isolate a person from Jesus Christ, Stephane Tibi[299] would be a candidate. Born in a Paris suburb in 1969, his father was a nonpracticing, atheistic Jew from Tunisia. His mother was an agnostic with a Catholic and Freemasonry background. Stephane spent his childhood in a religious vacuum lacking any instruction in the Christian faith. He could name almost all the gods of Greek mythology. But had he been asked, he would have identified the Trinity as "Jesus, Mary, and Joseph."

As a teenager Stephane was a functional atheist. Before adulthood he had never touched a Bible. When he was 18, his younger sister abruptly asked to be baptized, and Stephane tried to discourage her, telling her that she was just foolishly swallowing old wives' tales.

As a young adult, Stephane watched *The Mission,* a film about mid-19th-century Jesuit missionaries working in South America.[300] He watched for entertainment, not because of any religious motivation. In the film one of the missionaries reads a few lines about love. Unexpectedly, the words took hold of Stephane. He replayed the video to copy the words. Then he memorized them but still didn't know their source. Although the words didn't name

"God," they spoke of a love stronger than worldly power, selfishness, and prestige. Stephane reflects, "I longed to know that kind of love."

Because a Christian missionary had read the words, Stephane supposed the Bible might be their source. So into a bookstore he went, in search of "the words." Finding a Bible with a concordance, he searched until he located "the words" in 1 Cor. 13. He purchased the Bible and tried to read it. Although some of the stories in Genesis interested him, Stephane stumbled when trying to read the Gospels. So his Bible landed on a shelf, there to remain for years.

But the God of grace was not finished with Stephane. While studying to become a robotics engineer, he found himself impressed by the majesty and intricacy of the foundations of science. This showed him how humble a person should be in the presence of the creation, especially when the "new" is discovered.

During the final period of Stephane's university education,[301] he fell in love with a girl who, by contrast, showed no interest in him. But she did invite him to a meeting where psychology would be discussed. "I went, hoping to seduce her," he says. As it turned out, the girl was a Christian. She invited Stephane to attend more meetings.

Stephane began to see the futility of his ways. He had unsuccessfully sought peace through entertainment, love, and power. In despair over his emptiness, Stephane opened his life to the Christ who had been wooing him all along. He says, "In Christ I found the peace and grace of a loving God. Blessed be my Lord for this wonderful surprise, and for His patience and wisdom in bringing me to Him."

After having been a Christian for about 10 years, in 2003 Stephane became a master of divinity student at Nazarene Theological Seminary.[302] He reflects, "All along, God had been preparing me to hear and receive the gospel . . . Perhaps the greatest gift God has given is the grace of sanctification—this sweet and constant communion with my Lord."

Cheon-to Kim and Stephane's stories reveal the presence and activity of God engaged in the gracious work of awakening, transforming, and leading believers deeper into His will and way. We refer to this process as the way of salvation. This chapter discusses the "Wesleyan way (sometimes called 'order') of salvation."[303] Its purpose is to help us understand and appreciate the Wesleyan understanding of how God in Christ, through the Spirit, works to redeem. We will see just how extensive and persistent the creative love of God is. Wesleyans view the movements of grace in this manner because of how we understand the Scriptures, Christian tradition, and Christian experience.

Our understanding of the movements of grace should shape the way we live and tell the Story. It should be evident in all our evangelistic and missionary efforts. The hope is that understanding the Wesleyan way of salvation will help equip us more faithfully to "proclaim the mighty acts of him who called us out of darkness into his marvelous light" (1 Pet. 2:9). In addition, understanding the Wesleyan way of salvation provides the basis for our response to religious pluralism.

This way is not a rigid, lock-step path that discounts the varied stories Christians tell about how God led them to salvation. Noted Wesleyan theologian Rob Staples cautions against our "charting meticulously the order of salvation."[304] God doesn't use a cookie cutter when expressing His love for us. He takes our personal histories seriously. In the psalmist's prayer for deliverance, one reason for his trust was that God understood him completely: "O LORD, you have searched me and known me" (Ps. 139:1). God doesn't redeem as though He were herding cattle. John Wesley said that God's acts of salvation are not "riveted together like the links of a chain."[305] In Staples' colorful words, we should not "hold a stopwatch to the actions of grace."[306]

But what is grace? It is God acting in creative love. It is, Karl Barth said, the divine movement in which God freely "determines himself for sinful man and sinful man for himself." Grace is God taking upon himself "the rejection of man with all its consequences, and electing man to participate in His own glory."[307] Jesus Christ is the free grace of God incarnate.[308] Grace is God's own thorough self-giving, the goal of which is our movement toward God.[309]

Grace is the work of the Triune God. The New Testament helps us understand the offices of the Father, Son, and Holy Spirit. But underlying that, it announces the saving deeds of the One God. By the *will of the Father*, grace has come to us *through the faithfulness of Christ*—He is the *meritorious cause* of grace (Rom. 1:5; 3:24; 1 Pet. 4:10). Grace is mediated *through the Holy Spirit* who is the *effecting cause* of grace. The Holy Spirit administers the riches of redemption our Lord secured through His life, death, resurrection, and exaltation (Rom. 8:1-17; Phil. 2:13).

According to the Wesleyan vision of redemption, salvation doesn't dead-end in us. Salvation is about me, but it's certainly not all about me. The redemption that Christ extends to us is part of the comprehensive redemption God is achieving in His world (Eph. 1:3-10). A person's salvation is pointless unless the old enslavement to egocentrism is reversed, and he or she is reoriented to participate in the all-encompassing kingdom of God. In the crucified and risen Christ, the God of Israel has provisionally saved the nations from His wrath and freed them from bondage to false gods and powers. The Father has called all people everywhere to repent and to partake of Christ's victory by serving Him in holiness through the power of the Holy Spirit.[310] This breathtaking vision of the Kingdom indicates the magnitude of Christian redemption and provides the key for understanding the movements of grace in the Wesleyan "way of salvation."

PREVENIENT GRACE

So that Volodymyr (Vova) could be properly trained in atheism, at age 10 his father gave him *A Book for a Young Atheist*. His father, a member of the Ukrainian Communist party, raised his son to believe that science and religion have nothing in common, that religion oppresses people and suppresses the truth.

Looking back, Vova can trace the subtle and persistent movements of grace that brought him to faith in Jesus Christ. Slowly, God cracked the atheistic shell.

It began before Vova entered elementary school, when he met another child who had been baptized as a Christian. This made no sense to Vova, so he told the boy that nothing important had happened. At age 13, Vova and some friends harassed a woman leaving an Orthodox church. She rattled Vova's cocky atheism by warning, "Watch out! You may call down rocks from heaven on your heads!" Stunned, Vova asked himself, "Could God do that?"

As a rebellious teen in a Communist country, Vova thought it cool to listen to rock music. One day he listened to the music from *Jesus Christ Superstar*. He was astonished that young people in America could find Jesus attractive. About this time someone gave Vova a book about the historical Jesus. It presented Jesus as a real person. Vova told a well-educated family friend about the legends in the book. The friend responded, "Volodymyr, those stories are all true." For the first time, Vova had encountered a respected person who was also a disciple of Jesus Christ. He asked, "What should I do?" The friend answered, "Volodymyr, the law of God is written in your heart. There will be a day of judgment. You will have to account for what you have done with God's law!"

From 1985 until 1991, Mikhail Gorbachev was the general secretary of the Communist party. Under his leadership, a window opened for Christian evangelism, and an Episcopalian evangelist conducted services in Kiev. Out of curiosity Vova attended. During the sermon the Holy Spirit captured Vova's attention and clearly called him to become a disciple of Jesus Christ. He went forward as invited, prayed a prayer of confession and faith, and took his first step along the road to Christian discipleship. The journey from *A Book for a Young Atheist* to receiving Christ as his Savior had been a long one.

Today Vova pastors the First Church of the Nazarene in Kiev, Ukraine, and joyously traces the steps that led him to Christ. His story beautifully illustrates what Wesleyans, as well as other doctrinal traditions, mean by prevenient grace.[311] Wesley would have agreed with Roman Catholic theologian Karl Rahner that because of God's desire to redeem, the Holy Spirit graciously acts in all people whether or not they can understand the "ineradicable experience" of God.[312] The grace of God that brings about our salvation, Wesley echoes, is "FREE IN ALL, and FREE FOR ALL." True to the gospel message of the New Testament, he believed that God's grace depends not at all on human power or merit or good intentions or good desires, but solely upon the initiative of the free God.[313]

Apart from Christ, all people follow the "course of this world." They follow "the ruler of the power of the air," the spirit of disobedience (Eph. 2:2). Separated from the restorative grace of God, all people are and will remain dead in their trespasses and sins. Why? Because ours is a diseased relationship with God we cannot cure. Sin and its consequent alienation have enslaved the whole human race. All our members are sold into sin as "instruments of wickedness" (Rom. 6:13; cf. 7:14). But for the redeeming love and mercy of God, that fatal slavery and eternal death would never end.[314]

However, "to the praise of his glorious grace that he freely bestowed on us in the Beloved" (Eph. 1:6), He has not abandoned us to the alienation and death we brought upon ourselves. Rather, in Christ, God has graciously given himself to us—to all humankind—that He might reconcile everyone to himself (2 Pet. 3:9). As Wesleyans, we believe that the universal reach of God's grace makes it fictional and misleading to think of anyone as distanced from Him. No person anywhere, Wesley said, "is in a state of mere nature . . . wholly void of the grace of God. No man living is entirely destitute of what is vulgarly called 'natural conscience.' But this is not natural; it is more properly termed 'preventing [prevenient] grace.'"[315]

Prevenient grace is the grace that goes before to prepare people to hear and receive the gospel. It is the active presence of the Holy Spirit prior to conversion. Methodist theologian Philip Meadows explains, "No human being actually occupies the limiting condition of total depravity, for prevenient grace is at work in all people through the empowering presence of the Holy Spirit."[316] The first dawn of light regarding God's will, any initial sense of having sinned against Him, results from prevenient grace.[317] The Holy Spirit, not humankind, raises the question of God in us. "It is not nature," Wesley says, "but the Son of God that is 'the true light, which enlighteneth every man which cometh into the world.' So that we may say to every human creature, 'He,' not nature, 'hath shown thee O man, what is good.'"[318] Cheon-to Kim, Stephane, and Vova beautifully illustrate this.

In the Spirit's prevenient work, He restores a person's moral sense and freedom to respond to the offer of salvation.[319] Prevenient grace prompts "the first wish to please God." Wesley insisted that no one sins because God's grace is absent but because he or she doesn't act upon the grace God has given.[320]

There is a continuity of grace between the creation of the world and its redemption.[321] In line with the New Testament, Wesley believed that by grace God created the world and by grace He sustains it (Col. 1:15-17).[322] Were it not for God's grace, the world would sink into oblivion.[323] The same is true for us. We are totally dependent upon the gracious Creator (Acts 17:22-28; Col. 1:15-20). But the purpose of God's gracious presence is not just to sustain but to redeem as well. Prevenient grace prompts us toward the goal of faithful life in Christ.[324]

The short story *Revelation* by Southern writer Flannery O'Connor demonstrates the persistence and surprising character of God's grace. Ruby Turpin was a self-righteous, self-congratulatory hypocrite, hence a stranger to Christian salvation. She described herself as "a respectable, hardworking, churchgoing woman," anchoring her identity in her race and social class. Ruby seemed sealed in this cocoon until God used Mary Grace, a rude and "ugly" college student, to puncture it. In a turbulent scene, Mary Grace labeled Mrs. Turpin a "wart hog from hell!" Strong language, but exactly the judgment Ruby Turpin needed. In the midst of Ruby's bewildered condition, God called her to recognize the truth of Mary Grace's indictment, abandon her sinful pride of position and race, cling only to the grace of God, and be changed from a "wart hog from hell" to a child of God.[325]

Whatever form conversion takes, it is always preceded by the amazing work of prevenient grace. The Spirit will creatively use whatever vehicles He finds available—even people like Mary Grace, if necessary. A friend of mine, a Congregational minister in Massachusetts, told me that as an unconverted teen he knelt at the Communion rail to receive the Lord's Supper. He had heard the liturgy time and again. On this day, rather than reflecting on the meaning of the sacred event, he was eyeing a young woman assisting in administering the Eucharist and thinking, "She's pretty. How can I get a date with her?" Then, as though lightning had suddenly fallen from the sky, God convicted him of his carelessness and riveted his attention on the body and blood of our Lord. The presence of Christ overwhelmed him. He confessed his sins on the spot, became a new creation, and moved forward in faith.

Admittedly, it is easy to affirm the universality and persistence of prevenient grace when discussing doctrine or while joyously worshiping God alongside other Christians. It becomes more difficult while watching the people of the nations inundate busy crossroads of the world, such as Los Angeles International Airport. And it is harder still to believe the Spirit is working as we anguish over a wayward child or while absorbing the trauma of spousal infidelity. Nevertheless, our confidence is anchored in the God of steadfast love who is not willing that any should perish but that everyone should come to eternal life.

Nothing in Wesleyan doctrine better equips us for effective Christian witness in a pluralistic and postmodern world than our understanding of prevenient grace.

THE PARDON OF THE SPIRIT: JUSTIFICATION BY GRACE THROUGH FAITH

There are two great branches of salvation: justification (what God does for us through His Son) and sanctification (what God does in us by His Spirit on the basis of Christ's atonement), the two being inseparable.[326] While justification restores us to a right covenantal relationship with God and with others, sanctification changes *us*. In the broader sense, sanctification includes both regeneration (the "immediate fruit of justification")[327] and our lifelong journey with God in which He molds us into the image of Christ. The breadth of God's saving work in us can be stated with one hyphenated word: "justification-regeneration-sanctification."[328] Transformation of the whole person is God's intention, and justification provides the foundation.

In Paul's teaching regarding the death and resurrection of Christ, he brought together justification and regeneration, describing justification as being buried with Christ by baptism into a death like His, and regeneration as being united with Christ in a resurrection like His (Rom. 6:4-5). This is what it means to be born anew by the Spirit and walk "in newness of life" (v. 4). The major dimensions of justification are:

Repentance

Jesus began His public ministry by calling people to repentance (Mark 1:15; Matt. 4:17). Mark's Gospel connects repentance with "hearing the good news," and Matthew's with the nearness of the Kingdom. After Jesus' resurrection He told His disciples: "Repentance and forgiveness of sins is to be proclaimed in [Christ's] name to all nations" (Luke 24:47). On Paul's way to Jerusalem and to his eventual imprisonment, he said that he had faithfully "testified to both Jews and to Greeks about repentance toward God and toward our Lord Jesus" (Acts 20:21). Repentance in the New Testament is tied to hearing and believing (receiving) the gospel. The two go together. But what does *repentance* mean?

The most common New Testament word for repentance is *metanoia,* usually meaning a "change of mind" or "regret/remorse." *Repentance* also means "turning away from" (Mark 1:4). More correctly, it means an "about-face." By the power of the Holy Spirit, a repentant sinner confesses his or her sins against God and against others. He or she rejects and *turns away from* allegiance to the old order of sin, death, and hostility toward God and *turns to embrace* the new reality—the kingdom of God. Repentance involves a readiness to abandon rebellious opposition to what God wants and a determination to enter a positive relationship in which we seek to follow His will alone. So a readiness to obey—what Bonhoeffer called the first concrete step of obedience[329]—must be connected to repentance.

One of Wesley's descriptions of repentance appears in his sermon "The Marks of the New Birth." He says that renouncing oneself before God precedes the "true, living Christian faith." To be "found in Christ," a person must confess to God that he or she is a "lost, miserable, self-destroyed, self-condemned, undone, helpless sinner . . . one whose mouth is utterly stopped, and who is altogether 'guilty before God.'" The repentant sinner must be convinced that "of Christ only cometh our salvation."[330] If a person thinks more highly of himself or herself than that, then for him or her, the gospel will not be good news.

Reconciliation (justification) with the Father comes through faith (trust) in His obedient and faithful Son (Rom. 5:15-21; Heb. 10:7-10).

By the power of the Spirit, Jesus Christ—the New Adam—lived in unbroken fidelity to His Heavenly Father in all things, even death on the Cross. He is the faithful and righteous one (1 John 2:1), "the pioneer and perfecter of our faith, who for the joy that was set before him endured the cross, despising the shame, and is seated at the right hand of the throne of God" (Heb. 12:1-2, RSV). His pioneering faithfulness is the meritorious basis of salvation. Our faith is in Him. Because of His faithfulness in all things, we call Him Savior, the Redeemer. God "justifies the one who has faith [trust] in Jesus" (Rom. 3:26).

Justification

Justification by Grace Through Faith Is the Manifestation and Work of the Righteousness of God

The God who is holy love freely *gives* what He commands—reconciliation, or our peace with Him. When we say Jesus is the righteousness of God, we mean that in Christ, the Father himself *freely offers* the forgiveness and restored relationship He desires but which we in our own efforts are powerless to achieve. God has made Christ "for us wisdom . . . righteousness and sanctification and redemption" (1 Cor. 1:30). The law of God commands that we love, worship, and obey Him and that we love our neighbor as ourselves. Sold into sin, dead in our trespasses, we can't do this. Every time we try to *do* our way into God's favor, we rely on our own strength and repeat the sinful attempt at independence that began in Adam. The only way to end our self-centeredness and rebellious refusal to worship and love God is if He freely gives what He commands, only if He sets us free. Through Christ, and in the power of the Holy Spirit, the Father reconciles all who will abandon their own righteousness and radically rely upon His grace. "Only God alone," Wesley said, "can raise those that are 'dead in trespasses and sins.'" Only God who created a person can create him or her anew. Only He can pardon us, remove our guilt, and reconcile us to himself. "No angel, much less any human spirit . . . can bring one soul 'from darkness to light, and from the power of Satan unto God.'"[331]

Justification Marks the Beginning of the Christian Life, Our Adoption by God as His Sons and Daughters

Justification "begins the process of restoring the image of God in us, for our lives are realigned for a purpose: not only to receive from God, but [also] to share what we have received with others."[332] Using a Wesleyan metaphor, Theodore Runyon says that when by grace we repent of our sins and respond positively to the gospel, we "advance from the *porch* of prevenient grace to the *door* of justification and new birth."[333] This is the powerful action of the Holy Spirit, who convinces us of the truth of the gospel. He calls us to repen-

tance and faith and sustains us "in communion with himself through participation in his people."[334]

THE SPIRIT'S GIFT OF FAITH AND HUMAN RESPONSE

The 16th-century Protestant Reformation recovered the New Testament
teaching that we are justified by grace through faith alone. John Wesley stood
in complete harmony with the Reformers on this score. The Spirit gives the
power to believe, Wesley said, for "no man is able to work such saving faith
in himself."[335] If saving faith were a human accomplishment offered to God for
salvation, then our salvation would be our own doing. But God offers the gift
of faith to us, allowing us to participate in His life, which is eternal life.[336]

Without qualification, Wesleyans believe that faith is a gift from God.
We contribute nothing to our salvation. But it is a gift that requires us to respond.[337] To be sure, active response occurs only through the Holy Spirit's em-
powerment. But by freeing and empowering the will, God enables people to
embrace the Redeemer (Phil. 2:12-13). Methodist theologian Lycurgus Starkey
says this Spirit-enabled "cooperation is characteristic of each phase of salvation."[338] Eminent Reformed theologian G. C. Berkouwer agrees and says that
in both the Old and New Testaments, God's people were instructed to always
be conscious of the fact that He is the One who sanctifies them. On the other
hand, they were to actively present themselves for sanctification and actively
walk and live according to the will of the sanctifying God.[339]

Evangelical synergism is one way Wesleyans speak of the relationship
between divine initiative and human response.[340] The phrase preserves the es-
sential point that salvation is God's work from beginning to end and that the
Holy Spirit makes possible our response to the overtures of redeeming grace.
Redemption is a divinely authored covenantal relationship in which both
God's sovereign initiative and empowered human response are active.[341]

The divine initiative in evangelical synergism defends the Wesleyan understanding of grace against those who say that the element of human response encourages righteousness by works. And it puts light-years of distance
between us and those who think people have a natural capacity to turn to
Christ in their own strength. This error is called Pelagianism, the early fifth-
century teaching that denied the reality of original sin and the bondage of the
will and held that persons are free to turn to God on their own.[342] The New
Testament emphasizes Spirit-empowered human response to the offer of salvation.[343] We do not believe that God takes one step, and I take one step.

When it comes to our being reconciled, God takes all the steps, so that salvation is totally God's doing. Our understanding of this is captured in the instruction Paul gave to the Christians in Philippi: "For it is God who is at work in you, enabling you both to will and to work for his good pleasure" (Phil. 2:13). We are enabled to participate not just passively but actively in God's grace. It is God's power that draws and turns, so that we may voluntarily and by our own decision choose that which God in His grace has already chosen for us.[344] Brian Wren has captured drawing and turning in poetic form:

> When Christ was lifted from the earth,
> His arms stretched out above
> Through every culture, every birth,
> To draw an answering love.[345]

The Power of the Spirit as It Relates to Sanctification

The New Birth (Regeneration)

Justification by grace involves a relational change between God and the penitent sinner. God removes the enmity (hostility) between himself and the penitent sinner and restores a right relationship. Reconciled, we are at "peace with God through our Lord Jesus Christ" (Rom. 5:1).

Regeneration and sanctification involve an internal change. Justification is theologically prior to regeneration, but they happen simultaneously.[346] In the new birth, God renews our fallen nature through the regenerating (re-creating, 2 Cor. 5:17) work of the Spirit. Justification secures real forgiveness, restored favor, and reconciliation with God. The new birth begins the process of restoring the believer to the image of God. While justification removes the guilt of sin, regeneration takes away the power of sin.[347] Both come through being "in Christ."

Jesus called regeneration being "born from above." He instructed Nicodemus, "Very truly, I tell you, no one can see the kingdom of God without being born from above . . . What is born of the flesh is flesh, and what is born of the Spirit is spirit" (John 3:3, 6).

Regeneration is also the gift of eternal life (Rom. 6:23). "For God so loved the world that he gave his only Son, that whoever believes in him should not perish but have eternal life" (John 3:16, RSV; cf. 10:28). Paul says that if anyone is in Christ "there is a new creation." The old passes away and all things become new (2 Cor. 5:17).

Sanctification

G. C. Berkouwer says: "Everywhere in the Scriptures one may hear the trumpet-sound of this clear and forceful imperative: 'For this is the will of God, even your sanctification'" (1 Thess. 4:3).[348] Wesleyans heartily agree. We believe that justification and regeneration inaugurate the comprehensive inward and outward change of heart and life the New Testament calls sanctification (Rom. 6:19b-22). "At the same time that we are justified, yea, in that very moment, sanctification begins."[349] We are inwardly renewed by the power of God, a renewal Berkouwer calls "evangelical sanctification" because it is completely the work of God's grace.[350] He changes "the earthly, sensual, devilish mind into 'the mind which was in Christ Jesus.'" Theologian H. Ray Dunning says: "The essence of sanctification is the renewal of humankind in the image of God."[351]

For Wesleyans, sanctification in the broad sense involves the entire span of God's work—transforming disciples into the image of Christ and bringing them to final salvation at Christ's return. After the new birth, sanctification continues as we grow in grace, and, so far as this life is concerned, it concludes in glorification (1 Cor. 15:51-54; 1 John 3:1-4). The span of sanctification has three dimensions: we *have been* redeemed; we *are being* redeemed; and we *will be* redeemed. It is a process, a becoming, that lasts until the Second Coming (1 Thess. 4:13-18; 1 Cor. 15:51-58). Paul says, "Through the Spirit, by faith, we eagerly wait for the hope of righteousness" (Gal. 5:5; cf. 2 Pet. 3:13). Our confidence is now, and always shall be, in the atoning work of Jesus Christ. He alone will be our plea, our righteousness, when we stand before His judgment seat to give account for our stewardship of His grace (2 Cor. 5:10; Rom. 14:10).

The Witness of the Holy Spirit

In 1968 student riots in Tokyo closed the universities. Hitoshi (Paul) Fukue,[352] a junior at Sophia University majoring in English literature, was one whose studies were interrupted. Uncertain about how to continue, Paul cast about for direction. At the time he was a skeptic regarding all things religious, seeing no good reason to believe in God. During his time of indecision, Paul met Helen Wilson, a professor at Northwest Nazarene College in Nampa, Idaho, while she was visiting Japan. She encouraged him to continue his studies at NNC.

Paul responded to the invitation and moved from Tokyo to the small town of Nampa, Idaho. We probably couldn't imagine his culture shock. But something astonishing happened. "Never had I been in a setting where people cared so much for each other. In Tokyo, people had one interest—to take care of themselves." Repeatedly, NNC faculty and students went out of their way to welcome and assist this recently arrived Japanese student. "What," Paul asked himself, "do these people have that I don't have?"

Paul began to attend services in the college church. Again, the same spirit of love greeted him. But he grew more and more consumed with doubts regarding God's existence. "If God doesn't exist," Paul reasoned, "then nothing I see in these Christians really matters." One Sunday evening, driven almost to despair by his inner turmoil, Paul prepared to leave his room for the evening church service. He vowed, "If I can't answer the question regarding God's existence tonight, I will absolutely end this quest and terminate my interest!"

That evening, a missionary spoke. As he concluded, the speaker invited college students to come forward and commit themselves to God's will for their lives. Paul watched, wondering what they were doing. "Then, all of sudden, I found myself standing before the altar! I have no idea why or how I got there." Paul closed his eyes. Suddenly a bright light shone above him, brighter, he recalls, than the light of the sun. "At that moment I saw my heart as it truly was. I saw that my life had been one of self-seeking and self-interest alone. Even though I thought I was living an honest life compared to some others, I had never seen myself as in that moment of illumination. My heart was dirty." Paul felt that the judgment of God had settled upon him, had completely exposed him, and that he must surely die. He recalls, "God crushed me. I gasped for breath."

Almost simultaneously, Paul experienced indescribable love flooding over him. "I felt that I was being forgiven for my wretched condition. The same light that had revealed my sinfulness now embraced me with a healing I had never known. Tears of extreme joy and thankfulness poured down." In that moment Paul distinctly heard a call: "From now on, follow Me!"

He says that when he "came to himself," he didn't fully comprehend what had happened. "When I left the church, I walked back into the scenery to which I had grown accustomed. But now, everything had changed! The trees, the buildings, the skies, the stars—all looked differently."

Upon returning to his room, Paul remembered his earlier vow and clearly realized that God, who knew his heart, had convincingly revealed himself. Paul could never forget. "Then and there my questions about the existence of God disappeared. Later I came to see that the one who had revealed himself to me was the Christ who died on the Cross for my salvation. He had met me in transforming grace. Christ was the one who had instructed me to 'follow Him.' This I have done, by His grace, from that day to this."

Paul Fukue's experience on that Sunday evening beautifully illustrates being born anew by the Holy Spirit (John 3:5-9), becoming "a new creation" in Christ Jesus (2 Cor. 5:17), and being raised to life in Christ (Rom. 6:4-8). It also powerfully illustrates what the New Testament calls the witness of the Spirit (John 14:16; 16:13; Rom. 5:5; 8:1; 14:17). Paul's account is in harmony with 1 John's explanation that the Spirit's witness *to* us is first a truthful witness *about* Jesus Christ—that He is indeed the Son of God. The eternal life the Spirit imparts is Christ himself. "And this is the testimony: God gave us eternal life, and this life is in his Son" (1 John 5:11). The Spirit witnesses *to* the children of God that Christ has come to dwell *in* them (v. 20). While salvation is the work of the triune God, assurance of redemption is a distinctive role of the Spirit.[353] He is the Spirit of adoption, testifying to new Christians that they have indeed been adopted into the family of God and are now reconciled to God. By the atoning deed of Christ, they have become new creatures through grace. The New Testament attaches considerable importance to the Spirit's internal assurance. It should, because the Spirit's witness in believers was an important promise Jesus made to the disciples. He said the Holy Spirit would come to be in them (John 14:16-17).

Jesus' promise was inaugurally fulfilled on the Day of Pentecost. From that day forward, the promise has been the heritage of believers. Christians who were not present on the Day of Pentecost may know that they truly are the children of God and joint heirs with Christ because of the Spirit who now abides in them (Rom. 8:15-17; 1 John 3:23-24). In a soaring statement regarding the Spirit's work in believers, the apostle Paul says, "Anyone who does not have the Spirit of Christ does not belong to him. But if Christ is in you, though the body is dead because of sin, the Spirit is life because of righteousness. If the Spirit of him who raised Jesus from the dead dwells in you, he who raised Christ from the dead will give life to your mortal bodies also through his Spirit that dwells in you" (Rom. 8:9-11).

Not surprisingly, the witness of the Spirit plays an important role in the Wesleyan understanding of salvation. John Wesley defended its legitimacy against those who discounted its divine origin, while also confronting the error of placing one's trust in subjective emotions rather than in the Redeemer's faithfulness. Relying principally upon the New Testament, and secondarily upon the testimonies of many Christians, Wesley believed that a person who is converted to Christ may, by the Spirit, be immediately conscious that he or she has been "made alive unto God." The love of God is shed abroad in our hearts by the Holy Spirit, who bears witness that God has adopted us as His children.

But what is this witness or testimony of the Spirit? It is an "inward impression on the soul, whereby the Spirit of God directly witnesses to my spirit, that I am a child of God; that Jesus Christ hath loved me, and given himself for me; and that all my sins are blotted out, and I, even I, am reconciled to God."[354] Clearly, it precedes and authors our own human response. The enlivening Spirit *"inspires,* breathes into our soul, what of ourselves we could not have." The Holy Spirit has effected in us the reconciling work of God in Christ. This is the peace of God, and its result is joy. "Faith, peace, joy, [and] love, are all his fruits."[355] When does this happen? Wesley answers that the Spirit bears witness *in* us when He enables us to cry "Abba, Father!"[356]

But Wesley also knew that if there is an internal witness of the Holy Spirit, there is likewise an external one—the witness of a life being transformed in the image of Christ. The first witness is a direct witness to our spirit. The second is an indirect witness, but no less important. ("Now by this we may be sure that we know him, if we obey his commandments" [1 John 2:3; cf. v. 5].) When the redeeming Spirit is present and working *in us,* we will know it because He will produce the fruit of Christ *through us.* Wesley discounted those who confuse the "voice of their own imagination" with the Spirit of God, and then idly presume they are the children of God, even while "doing the works of the devil."[357] Being made alive to God in Christ by the Spirit (1 John 5:6-12) is inseparable from loving God with all of your heart, mind, soul, and strength, and loving your neighbor as yourself.[358] This is the evidence that cannot be brushed aside.

The assuring witness of the Spirit, both internally and externally, is thoroughly anchored in the divine mercy manifest in Jesus Christ. The New Testament promises that "if you confess with your lips that Jesus is Lord and believe in your heart that God raised him from the dead, you will be saved" (Rom. 10:9). Theodore Runyon explains, "The divine promises declared in Christ Jesus are more sure and more dependable than human feelings, and the promises must be allowed to instruct and correct our emotions."[359] Neither internal feelings nor external works form the basis for our justification, but Christ alone.[360] We must guard against reducing the witness of the Spirit to our shifting subjective emotions, but bearing this caution in mind, we should also boldly affirm our real participation in the redeeming life of God, which the Holy Spirit is achieving in us.[361]

THE LIFE OF GOD IN CHRISTIANS

At the heart of the Wesleyan understanding of salvation is a conviction that because the Spirit of Christ now dwells in us, we are no longer slaves to the flesh. We believe the atonement of Christ, the Holy Spirit, and the message of the New Testament establish the priority of transforming grace over the priority of sin's power in Christians. We are convinced that, through the Spirit, this victory is Christ's gift for all His sisters and brothers. This conviction has everything to do with God-given grace and faith and nothing to do with human achievement or sinless perfection.

Theologian Douglas Harink's comment on Paul's instructions to the Thessalonian Christians accurately describes what Wesleyans believe regarding Christian holiness. Not only did Paul condemn the Thessalonians' former idolatry, but he also called them to serve the one God of Israel in holiness as they conducted themselves "in their activities and relationships."[362] While the Thessalonian Christians' walk in holiness was "always genuinely their own," it was also "wholly the work of God." Put differently, their walk was 100 percent free response—they weren't puppets—but what made it possible was God working in them. From God, through the Spirit, they received "freedom from bondage to the powers of sin and death, power for a holy life, and confidence in the love of God (Rom. 8)."[363] Their participation in God's gracious work was to be "spread over the whole range of human life, active and passive, attitudinal and bodily, inner and outer, personal, social, and political." The holy life was to be a labor of love by which the Thessalonians participated in the work of God.[364] Not only had the gospel delivered the Thessalonians from the coming wrath of God and reconciled them to Him, but "through the Holy Spirit and baptism, they [were] made sharers in Jesus' death and resurrection life and members of a new people, the *ekklesia*." In Jesus Christ the Thessalonian Christians were given a new identity and a pattern of new obedience.[365] The sacrament of Christian baptism seals and bears witness to this grand work of God (Acts 2:38; 8:36-39; 10:44-48; Rom. 6:1-4).

THE GRACE OF ENTIRE SANCTIFICATION, OR CHRISTIAN PERFECTION

Sanctification is an important aspect of the Christian life for all orthodox

Christian denominations, teaching growth in the image of Christ in all of life's dimensions. Sanctification occurs through the work of the Holy Spirit in prayer, programmatic spiritual formation, the sacraments, Bible study, love for one's neighbor, public worship, and more. The 1646 Westminster Confession of Faith, so formative for Christians in the Reformed tradition, says: "They who are effectually called and regenerated, having a new heart and a new spirit created in them, are further sanctified, really and personally, through the virtue of Christ's death and resurrection, by his Word and Spirit dwelling in them."[366]

But in some denominational traditions, the emphasis on sanctification is accompanied by a parallel belief that, throughout this life, Christians should think of themselves principally as *sinners* who have been saved by grace. In these traditions, a person's sinfulness plays a central role in his or her identity as a Christian. Because the righteousness of God continues to be an *alien righteousness,* there is a sense in which the Christian's identity doesn't change. "Alien" means that the only righteousness we have is Christ's righteousness. This is certainly correct, for we have no righteousness of our own—ever. But saying no more than this fails to appropriately acknowledge the transforming Pentecostal Spirit who comes to cleanse, empower, sanctify, and give us victory over the power of sin. Without the Cross, the Resurrection, *and* Pentecost, Christian life would be no more than conflicted life. If it were not for "the Spirit of him who raised Jesus from the dead" dwelling in us (Rom. 8:11), then we could expect that, throughout this life, sin would exert a powerful counterbalance to the grace of reconciliation. The guilt of sin would still be removed, we would still be adopted as children into the family of God, but the enemy would continue to claim a major portion of our real estate.

But such a minimalist understanding of grace could never account for the gospel of transformation that propelled the New Testament Church into a pagan world mired in sin's enslaving power. Instead, the Good News included the promise of being "led by the Spirit," set free from the bondage of fear, and having the righteous will of God fulfilled in us through the indwelling and reigning Spirit (vv. 14-15). I once heard an eloquent Black pastor preaching an Easter sunrise service say, "Too many Christians are living on the right side of Easter, but on the wrong side of Pentecost."

Distinctive of the Wesleyan tradition is a conviction that the Spirit of God can decisively "incline our hearts" to love Him and our neighbor as ourselves. We accept the New Testament call and promise that Christians are to "live a godly life in Christ Jesus" (2 Tim. 3:12). Theodore Runyon's summary of the

Wesleyan vision makes clear the reason for this confidence. Created in the image of God, humans have been uniquely called to a life of communion with God, to receive the gift of himself and to faithfully reflect Him in the world, even as a mirror reflects a human image. God's great calling for us is not in vain. Through a relationship with Him made possible through Jesus Christ, and empowered and carried forward by the transforming Spirit, we can now faithfully live out that calling in the world.[367] The supporting New Testament mandate is clear. Whereas we once yielded ourselves without reservation to sin, now that we have been raised to new life in Christ, we must present our whole selves "to righteousness for sanctification" (Rom. 6:19). We believe that God can work in the regenerate heart, to satisfy the hunger for the holy life.[368] The Spirit's promise is that the God of peace, through Jesus Christ, will comprehensively sanctify the child of God—spirit, soul, and body (1 Thess. 5:23-24).

Entire sanctification simply means that what the Father has designed and promised to do *in* His children *through* Christ and *by* the Spirit, He can and will accomplish. It speaks of Christians living out of the new reality of transforming divine love, and that love being reciprocated toward God and our neighbor ("Love for God is perfected" [1 John 2:5, RSV], that is, brought to its intended goal or purpose). Entire sanctification speaks of divine transformation extending into every dimension of individual and social existence. It does not purport that this sweeping process is complete or that it guarantees against failures and subsequent needs for confession. Instead, its entirety denotes the free range in which God's transforming grace can proceed, and our Spirit-empowered compliance with it. Runyon asks: If the aim of God's transforming love (Rom. 5:5) is to produce a new creation in us, can our loving response be anything less?[369]

This is the confident Wesleyan hope of entire sanctification to which we believe all Christians are called. While *sanctification* describes the entire Christian journey toward full restoration of Christ's image in us, *entire sanctification* describes that formative, definitive event in a Christian's life that compels him or her to come to grips with what it means for Christ to be Lord of all. The full meaning of Christ's reign will unfold daily as it takes feet in the midst of temptations as well as victories, failures as well as successes—all in the power of the Spirit. Intentionally decisive in character, marked by a qualitative *before and after,* the event of entire sanctification is placed within the comprehensive sanctifying process by which God renews His people in His image, empowering us to love Him as we have been loved and our neighbor as ourselves. It is requisite preparation for living the life of holiness according to the riches of God's grace.

Wesleyans believe the resurrection of Christ and the gift of the Holy Spirit promise more than a constant struggle with the old nature. We believe and proclaim that the gospel of Jesus Christ is good news about victory *now* over that form of life inclined to the flesh. We believe that through the Holy Spirit "dwelling in us richly" (Col. 3:16), disciples can now fulfill "the just requirements of the law" (Rom. 8:4). We believe that the "Spirit of him who raised Jesus from the dead" (v. 11) can now reign in the children of God. Far from living in a twilight zone where one can never be quite sure whether the mind is set on the flesh or on the Spirit, Wesleyans believe we can have confidence— Christians can "live according to the Spirit" (v. 5). Normal Christian life involves exploring "the immeasurable greatness of his power for us who believe" (Eph. 1:19).

Christ who is rich in mercy will not disappoint the longing of His brothers and sisters to be possessed by Him and fully yielded to His reign and designs for His world. The Holy Spirit will hear the prayer of Christians who appeal for cleansing from any remaining challenge to Christ's Lordship. The Father of our Lord would not command His children to love Him with all their hearts, souls, minds, and strength, and then leave them hopelessly suspended between defeat and victory (1 Thess. 5:23-24). By grace, love for God and for one's neighbor can become the defining disposition of our lives. That which the Father designs by His will and grace, He can accomplish through His Son and by the Spirit.

REPENTANCE AND THE HOLY LIFE

The Wesleyan vision of Christian holiness becomes a reality by grace through faith alone. This means that at every moment we are radically dependent upon God's grace, not upon our own accomplishments or righteousness. Theodore Runyon says that what makes John Wesley's theology distinctive is his ability to integrate the renewal of the relationship between God and people (justification) and living out the relationship (sanctification). A Christian does not leave justification behind and move on to sanctification. We continue to be reconciled to God by grace and faith alone.

Runyon notes that Christians often have difficulty maintaining a proper balance between justification and sanctification, tending to emphasize one at the expense of the other. This has been true among parts of the Wesleyan tradition that stress entire sanctification as though it somehow supersedes justification. Wesley saw that neither justification nor sanctification ever fulfill their purpose apart from each other. The grace of God continues to transform us into the image of Christ as long as we live. Sanctification endlessly unfolds in a process by which more and more of life is practically and concretely defined by the reign of God. What is provisionally established in entire sanctification becomes ever more explicit in the obedience of faith and love. But the possibilities for the advancing sanctification of life always build upon the foundation of justification.[370]

"Every day, every hour," Fanny Crosby prayed, "Let me feel Thy cleansing power."[371] This should be the daily prayer of all Christians. Those who love God most dearly and who are most open to His grace are also most sensitive to their need for God's, and their neighbors', forgiveness. A paradox of the Christian life is that the more attentive we become to the Spirit of God, the more attentive we become to the many points at which we need the grace of forgiveness. Those who think otherwise set themselves up as candidates for self-deception and graceless perfectionism. Increased reliance upon the grace of God, increased Christian maturity and wisdom, and increased love for God and one's neighbor set the child of God free to confess when he or she has neither loved God nor neighbor as he or she ought. Every infraction against the law of love, John Wesley said, whether voluntary or involuntary, whether conscious or unconscious, continually needs the merits of the atoning blood of Christ.[372] Justification and sanctification make confession possible, not unnecessary. Moment by moment, grace alone is the basis of our relationship with God. We are always *being redeemed* by Him.[373]

Thanks in part to modern psychology, today we recognize that none of us know ourselves perfectly. Honest reflection alerts us to the fact that our motives are more complex and less well-defined than we often realize. Careful examination also reveals that we participate in social structures that show their fallenness, as illustrated by the gods of advertising and consumption that lure many of us in developed countries to use the earth's resources in intemperate, unstewardly ways. These gods would not hesitate to enslave us in greed. Or consider the demonic, lucrative, and pervasive structures that reduce the value of women to their sexual prowess. We could go on to detail structures fostered by racism, class privilege, and nationalism. We could also examine the activities of corporations in which our retirement funds are invested. The grace of God calls for honesty in all things, including our failures to be agents of grace, peace, and new creation.

As children of grace, we live between the "already" and the "not yet" of the kingdom of God ("The darkness is passing away and the true light is already shining" [1 John 2:8]). The inaugurated Kingdom awaits its consummation in the world, in the Church, and in us. Paul's writings show that he certainly understood this. After celebrating what God had already accomplished in him, Paul stated that he had not yet achieved the perfect image of Christ (Phil. 3:12-16). On the way to complete maturity, children of grace will be anxious to discover and confess the times they offend God and others. The Lord's prayer, "Forgive us our debts, as we also have forgiven our debtors" (Matt. 6:12), is a prayer for Jesus' disciples. At all times, pilgrims should be quick to confess where the image of Christ has yet to achieve its "full stature."

For John Wesley, Randy Maddox says, Christian repentance rests upon the fact that we rely constantly and completely upon God's pardoning love, a pardon that is graciously renewed moment by moment, and the importance of which never fades. It is always the basis for our standing before God.[374] Christian repentance "revitalizes our continuing *responsible* growth in holiness."[375] Such repentance is called evangelical repentance because it involves Christians hearing and responding to the gospel of grace over and over. This is the confession about which the Epistle of 1 John speaks: "But if anyone does sin, we have an advocate with the Father, Jesus Christ the righteous; and he is the atoning sacrifice for our sins, and not for ours only but also for the sins of the whole world" (2:1-2).

GROWTH IN CHRISTIAN HOLINESS

The new birth and entire sanctification are essential punctuation points in a continuum of transforming grace. Rob Staples tells us, "Wesley did not believe in a static state of perfection."[376] For him, Christian holiness "admit[s] of a continual increase."[377] The Spirit constantly renews the image of God in us. Wesley says that whatever a person's Christian progress, "he hath still need to 'grow in grace,' and daily to advance in the knowledge and love of God his Saviour."[378]

The New Testament regularly calls the Church onward. Christians live in the peace and rest of Christ, but there is no place for aimlessness or laziness. "The only man who has the right to say that he is justified by grace alone," Bonhoeffer said, "is the man who has left all to follow Christ. Such a man knows that the call to discipleship is a gift of grace, and that the call is inseparable from the grace."[379] The author of the Book of Hebrews said, "Let us also lay aside every weight and the sin that clings so closely, and let us run with perseverance the race that is set before us, looking to Jesus the pioneer and perfecter of our faith" (12:1-2). Let us steer clear of any idea about Christian holiness that undercuts this norm, such as the subtle notion that it depends upon our own achievements.[380]

Daniel Migliore identifies five marks of growth in Christian holiness:

- Maturing as hearers and doers of the Word of God.
- Maturing in prayer.
- Maturing in Christian freedom (freedom *from* all that obstructs the image of Christ in us, and freedom *for* the will of God and one's neighbor).
- Maturing in solidarity with those who suffer the many oppressions of sin, injustice, fear, and so forth.
- Maturing in thankfulness and joy.*

Roman Catholic theologian Karl Rahner asks: To what extent may we hope to grow in Christian holiness? He grandly answers: To the extent that we "unreservedly and unconditionally" set no bounds on the Holy Spirit, but allow Him "to move right out, in His own boundlessness, and up to the [presence] of God himself."[381]

In the sacrament of the Lord's Supper (the Eucharist) we Christians regularly partake of the broken body and shed blood of our Lord. Through this sacred, festive meal, the risen Christ becomes present anew in and among the Church by the Spirit—just as present as He was during the first post-Resurrection breaking of the bread (Luke 24:36-43). He of pierced hands and side comes to the Church to nourish its members in the way of holiness, to energize them for witness in the world, and to fortify their hope for His return.

The apostle Paul summarizes all of this beautifully. As we walk with the Lord in Christian freedom, and behold His glory, the Holy Spirit changes us into Christ's likeness "from one degree of glory to another" (2 Cor. 3:18).

THE NEW CREATION

Among Christian theologians, few have been more expansive, hopeful, and confident regarding the grace of God than John and Charles Wesley. Their thirst for the holy life did not waste itself on narcissistic introspection. Christ

*Daniel Migliore, *Faith Seeking Understanding: An Introduction to Christian Theology* (Grand Rapids: William B. Eerdmans Publishing Co., 1991), 178-82.

the Victor had captured them with His big plans for creation. They were caught up in the immense range of redemption (1 Cor. 15:20-28; Eph. 1:7-10; Col. 1:15-20). The God who wants all people to come to repentance and life (2 Pet. 3:9), and who includes the creation in the economy of redemption (Rom. 8:18-25), fueled their preaching and hymn writing. Only a vision of comprehensive salvation can account for their attacks on the entrenched sources of poverty and their tireless efforts to promote social and economic reform. The God who is reconciling all things to himself inspired them to expose the injustices of the British Enclosure Acts that, in the interest of increased agricultural efficiency and profits, denied peasants access to traditional gleaning rights and common grazing lands.[382] The enclosure laws drove peasants to the cities where their poverty usually became more desperate. Maybe the powerful had forgotten the poor subsistence farmers, but God had not. The God who is renewing creation also inspired in the Wesleys a love for justice that fired their opposition to the slave trade. "New creation" explains the literacy classes, credit unions, medical clinics, and self-help projects for the poor the early Methodists initiated.

Runyon observes:

> There is a peculiar affinity between Wesleyan theology—especially Wesley's doctrine of sanctification—and movements for social change. When *Christian Perfection* becomes the goal of the individual, a fundamental hope is engendered that the future can surpass the present. [At the same time], a holy dissatisfaction is aroused with regard to any present state of affairs—a dissatisfaction that supplies the critical edge necessary to keep the process of individual transformation moving. Moreover, this holy dissatisfaction is readily transferable from the realm of the individual to that of society—as was evident in Wesley's own time—where it provides a persistent motivation for reform in the light of a "more perfect way" that transcends any status quo.[383]

So liberation and new creation are at the heart of the Wesleyan vision of the gospel. "Creation" and "new creation" are the bookends of his doctrine of salvation.[384] Sanctification, which as we have seen includes the whole process of restoration, is both initially and finally expressed as "new creation." The Redeemer, through whom the worlds were created, acts again and again in the same magnitude to restore His creation. Renewal of creation will, in part, occur through Christians who are being renewed in Christ's image.[385] The Father is already renewing the face of the earth, Wesley believed, and He will carry on that work until He has "put a period to sin and misery, and infirmity, and death; and re-established universal holiness and happiness, and caused all the inhabitants of the earth to sing together, 'Hallelujah! The Lord God omnipotent reigneth!'"[386]

For Reflection and Discussion

1. Why is it important that our practice of missions and evangelism be guided by our theology?

2. Survey the New Testament's treatment of salvation as a creative act of God and of its relationship to the first creation. Reflect upon the love and power of God at work in both.

3. What is there about the Wesleyan doctrine of sanctification that calls for decisiveness and a holy life, without supporting the notion of perfectionism, of having arrived?

4. Why does the Wesleyan understanding of God's grace insist upon the priority of transformation over the priority of the power of sin in the Christian life? Does this priority still retain an essential place for confession of sin? If so, how?

5. Reflect upon the way God's prevenient grace worked in your life to draw you to Christ. Talk with other Christians to learn their stories. What is most common in their accounts?

6. How would leaving God's creation out of redemption affect the doctrine of God as Creator, and the meaning of salvation?

7. How should the reality and work of prevenient grace affect Christian witness, including missions?

9
A WESLEYAN RESPONSE TO RELIGIOUS PLURALISM

We have now reached the point where we can put the pieces together and specifically answer the question that has been simmering in earlier chapters: What is the Wesleyan response to religious pluralism? In answering this question, we could easily drift off into the remote and esoteric unless we connect it to an actual person. Numerous persons come to my mind when addressing this question. Among them are two rabbis and a friend who leads the Sikh Dharma community in Kansas City.

And then there is Ahmed El-Sherif, a devout Muslim who serves as head of Kansas City's American Muslim Council. Ahmed, a biochemist who heads his own firm, is a most gracious person who represents Islam admirably. He respects other people regardless of their religious affiliations. Ahmed particularly appreciates Judaism and Christianity and prays that Muslims, Jews, and Christians will work together to promote peace and justice. Each time Ahmed pronounces the name Jesus, he pauses to say: "Peace be upon Him."

Ahmed is heavily involved in Kansas City's humanitarian efforts. He has been a strong supporter of Heart to Heart International, an organization founded by Dr. Gary Morsch. Heart to Heart is a grassroots partnership that provides medical relief to distressed nations and peoples around the world. During the mid-1990s, Ahmed played a strategic role in helping bring together leaders from various Kansas City communities—Croatians, Jews, Muslims, Christians—to airlift medical assistance to Bosnia. Gary Morsch says that in Bosnia, Ahmed "became the onsite organizer of the project, effectively moving the shipment of medical supplies through the front lines." Rather than letting fear cripple him, Ahmed told Gary, "God will be with us." This hope has carried over into subsequent projects. "Ahmed," Gary says, "believes that if people will work together, the pain of wounded nations can be relieved."

Keep Ahmed or someone else you know who practices another religion in mind as we examine the Wesleyan response to religious pluralism.

As we have seen, assessments of other religions differ widely among Christians. The Wesleyan tradition has a distinctive way of responding to adherents of non-Christian religions. Our position isn't unique, but it does have our doctrine of grace stamped on it.[387] What we believe should guide the way we speak to the Ahmeds of the world and the way we engage in evangelism and missions.

In a time when religious extremists seem bent on treating as bitter enemies those who do not adopt their views, the Wesleyan tradition instructs us on how to live with respect for people of other religions, while remaining faithful to the New Testament's witness to Jesus Christ.

Without compromise, John Wesley affirmed the incarnation of God in Jesus of Nazareth; in Him alone is salvation found. So long as God gave him breath, Wesley preached the gospel in fields, streets, houses, chapels, ornate churches, and wherever else he could find hungry hearts. At the same time, he recognized that no one should try to instruct God in how to bring people to Christian faith. God is free to bear witness to His Son in any way He pleases. Wesley was optimistic regarding God's activity in people of other religions. In his sermon "A Caution Against Bigotry" based on Mark 9:38-39, he counseled Christians to "acknowledge the finger of God" wherever it appears. We should "rejoice in [God's] work, and praise his name with thanksgiving. Encourage whomsoever God is pleased to employ." Christians should avoid all bigotry toward people of other religions lest they obstruct the gracious work of God, Wesley said, and Christians should show kindness "in word and deed" to all.[388] At the same time, Wesley believed the non-Christian world is marked more by darkness than light. Philip Meadows says that at times Wesley even spoke harshly about the beliefs and practices of other religions. Yet he was consistent in his belief that God is graciously active in all people without regard to the religions they embrace.[389]

Consequently, when Wesleyans recognize the finger of God wherever it appears, they are expressing their confidence in God's prevenient grace. Their recognition has nothing to do with endorsing religious pluralism, with baptizing ways of salvation independent of Christ, or with saying that God's favor can be gained through good works and good intentions.[390] Protestant theologian Karl Barth said much the same. When people respond to grace, they will in some way lift up their voices in praise to God, and thereby bear witness that God's light, His grace, has fallen upon them.[391]

GRACE EXTENDED TO ALL

Its Universal Reach

The Wesleyan appraisal of the relationship between Christ and people of other religions rests squarely on the doctrine of prevenient grace.[392] It also rests on the universal provisions of Christ's atonement. We speak of the relationship between Christ and people of other religions, not Christ and other religions, because prevenient grace primarily reaches people, not religions. Other religions have secondary significance, and even then only as instruments of prevenient grace.

As we saw in the previous chapter, Wesley believed the gospel of Jesus Christ is meant for all people, not for an elect and predestined few. No one is excluded from God's rich provisions. The range of Christ's atonement can be seen in Paul's statement: "Just as one man's trespass led to condemnation for all, so one man's act of righteousness leads to justification and life for all" (Rom. 5:18). Christ has overcome death, hell, sin, and the grave on behalf of all people. Just as the Father took the initiative in sending His Son, He also takes the initiative in manifold efforts to lead all people to reconciliation. Because of the presence and persistence of grace, no one "is without some preventing grace; and every degree of [positive response to] grace is a degree of life," some degree of restoration.[393]

Prevenient grace goes forth without reference to the historical, cultural, or religious contexts in which persons are born.[394] It is the real presence of the Spirit of Christ in a person's soul, working to enlighten and draw him or her to repentance and regeneration and moving him or her toward new creation in the image of Christ.

Christological in Character

For Wesleyans, all grace is Christological in character. Only through the Son and by the Holy Spirit does the Father act to create and redeem. Philip Meadows says that for Wesley, while the scope of God's presence and activity extends to everyone, the possibility of salvation can be understood only with reference to the person of Christ.[395]

To speak of the Son—the Word of God—correctly, it must be with reference to the Incarnation, and this means with reference to the first-century Galilean called Jesus of Nazareth who was crucified under Pontius Pilate. Some theologians[396] want to talk about the universal and timeless activity of the Logos (the Word) without necessarily referring to the Incarnation, to this provincial Jesus who was raised in a backwater section of a backwater country. By avoiding Jesus, the "Logos" can be associated with any number of gods, making it intellectually and culturally acceptable in pluralistic settings where language about the Cross and the Resurrection is offensive. But the New Testament absolutely forbids this. According to the New Testament, if you want to speak truthfully about God, you had better be prepared to talk about Jesus of Nazareth in whom the Creator-Redeemer God became incarnate (John 1:1-5; Gal. 4:4). And you had better be prepared to talk about Jesus' crucifixion, resurrection, ascension, and return (6:12-14). The particularity of the Incarnation was as offensive in the first century as it is today. But the Church has no other word to speak but Jesus Christ and Him crucified (1 Cor. 1:18-31).

The coming of Christ is expectantly awaited in the Old Testament, and the New Testament often speaks of Christ's anticipatory presence and activity during the Old Covenant period. Only in Christ can we adequately understand God's redemptive actions in the Old Testament (see Jesus' own words, Luke 24:27, 44-47). The apostle Peter says, "Concerning this salvation, the prophets who prophesied of the grace that was to be yours made careful search and inquiry, inquiring about the person or time that the Spirit of Christ within them indicated when it testified in advance to the sufferings destined for Christ and the subsequent glory" (1 Pet. 1:10-11; cf. 1 Cor. 10:1-4). Paul tells us that Christ is the mystery of God "hidden throughout the ages and generations but has now been revealed to his saints" (Col. 1:26; cf. Matt. 2:23; Luke 1:70; 18:31; 24:44-48; John 1:45; 8:52; Acts 2:14-36).

People like John Hick and George Regas (chap. 4) who want to separate the salvation that comes through Jesus Christ that affects only Christians, and a far less provincial God who goes around freely revealing himself in other religions, will always find their efforts dashed on the rock-hard testimony of the New Testament. By the will of the Father (1 Cor. 2:6-8), the eternal second person of the Triune God became incarnate in Jesus of Nazareth; He *is the Gospel of God—no one else, and in no other way.*

In Jesus we encounter not one face of God among others but whole God incarnate. In Him the absolutely universal became absolutely concrete. God in His absolute fullness reveals everything about himself in Jesus of Nazareth, eliminating all wiggle room for other saviors and other revelations. According to the New Testament, one either embraces this scandal of particularity or walks away from God. No theological or social face lift can ever diminish its offensiveness (1 Cor. 1:18-25; Gal. 3:1-14).

The Possibilities of Prevenient Grace

No one can accurately predict how prevenient grace will begin to stir someone's hunger for God or anticipate the paths by which the Spirit will lead him or her toward an evangelical encounter with the Redeemer. But this much we do know: The Holy Spirit presses to awaken persons to their hope-lessness apart from God's mercy and to lead them to salvation. The redeeming work of the free God must be honored wherever it occurs, even if it occurs under circumstances we might not consider standard or orthodox. Confidence regarding the range of God's grace and love "made Wesley open to the possi-bility of eternal life for non-Christians."[397] A derivation of that not what Wesley actually said.

Through prevenient grace the conscience can become a vehicle of sen-sitivity and response to the prevenient Spirit whatever a person's religion might be. Paul says as much in Rom. 2:14-16, and my friend Ahmed is a good example. Recall Ahmed's tireless efforts in the early 1990s to organize relief efforts for people in Bosnia, without respect to their religious identity. Recall his confidence in God's protection under hostile conditions. For Wesley, our moral sense—our awareness of being morally responsible beings—is not sim-ply natural. It is the result of prevenient grace. "The existence of conscience, liberty and moral agency are all expressions of the Spirit's ameliorating pres-ence."[398] This doesn't mean, however, that everything in one's conscience complies with the Christian standard or that the conscience and the Holy Spirit are identical.[399]

In light of this, we shouldn't be surprised by the morality or virtue that may result from a person's positive response to prevenient grace. In a sermon titled "The Almost Christian," Wesley explained that through the workings of prevenient grace, a person could learn to show proper regard for truth and justice and to demonstrate a measure of love for and assistance to others. He or she may refuse to act unjustly or to steal from his or her neighbor. Preve-nient grace may produce a refusal to oppress the poor, to practice extortion, or to cheat either rich or poor in commerce. Obedience to prevenient grace may lead one to studiously avoid defrauding another of his or her rights, to feed the hungry, clothe the naked, and provide for those in need.[400] My friends who are leaders in the Kansas City Sikh community exhibit these characteris-tics in an exemplary manner.

Wesley's words should not strike anyone as strange. He is in harmony with the apostle Paul who recognized that there are "righteous Gentiles" who swim against the tide of Gentile wickedness.[401] Meadows observes that wher-ever there is moral truth and right action, grace is at work.[402]

While recognizing that prevenient grace may bear fruitful response in those who obey its prompting, we should be careful not to speak in generali-ties, as though prevenient grace somehow dismisses sin's darkness or that it easily overrides humankind's deadly servitude to sin. Wesley noted that "the generality of men stifle [the wooings of the Father] as soon as possible."[403] C. S. Lewis said that even as the Holy Spirit was drawing him toward faith he was looking for ways to escape. Far from searching for God, he knew himself to be a "zoo of lusts." He said that he was no more actively searching for God than a "mouse searches for a cat." Nevertheless, in retrospect he realized that all along, the Holy Spirit had been tracking him down.[404]

PREVENIENT GRACE AND EVANGELICAL CONVERSION

Positive moral response to prevenient grace as we have described it should not be confused with Christian salvation. It doesn't signal an explicit confession of faith in Jesus Christ. Wesley neither intended nor permitted that prevenient grace become a back door for reintroducing works righteousness, for baptizing non-Christian religions (he didn't baptize the Christian religion either), or for doing away with the need for a full revelatory and regenerating encounter with Jesus Christ. Salvation is not a matter of moral achievement and can even become its obstacle.

But Wesley did believe that when a person responds to prevenient grace, some form of positive renewal follows (what Maddox calls "a crucial degree of regeneration").[405] In fact, Wesley had a high estimate of what a positive response to prevenient grace can yield. In his *Explanatory Notes on the New Testament,* Wesley comments on Peter's conviction that "in every nation anyone who fears [God] and does what is right is acceptable to him" (Acts 10:35). Peter's statement is made in the house of Cornelius, a Gentile described as God-fearing but who had not been introduced to Jesus Christ until God sent Peter to him. Peter is aware that Cornelius's hunger for and worship of God, and God's acceptance of him, is true of some people in every nation. It would be true for people in religions other than the Christian faith. Wesley says that Peter's statement applies first to anyone who "reverences God, as great, wise, good, the cause, end, and governor of all things." Second, Peter's statement applies to anyone who not only has "an awe-full regard" for God, but who also "avoids all known evil." He endeavors, according to the best light he has, "to do all things well." Such a person is "accepted of God—through Christ, though he knows him not."

Wesley emphasized the general applicability of Peter's statement. It tells us that any person who fears God like Cornelius stands in His favor, whether or not he or she enjoys the benefit of God's Word and the sacraments.[406] Wesley would have agreed with Clark H. Pinnock that the Bible "recognizes faith [among the nations which is] neither Jewish nor Christian, [but] which is nonetheless noble, uplifting and sound." Abel, Enoch, Rahab, and Ruth are examples.[407]

Nevertheless, as Acts makes clear, even Cornelius's admirable fear of God awaited fulfillment in an explicit encounter with Jesus Christ. Peter had come to preach "peace by Jesus Christ" (Acts 10:36) who is Lord of all. He announced that everyone who believes "receives forgiveness of sins through his name" (v. 43). The addition of an explicit proclamation and evangelical encounter "is an unspeakable blessing to those who were before in some measure accepted. Otherwise God would never have sent an angel from heaven to direct Cornelius to St. Peter."[408]

So, the goal of prevenient grace for all people is an evangelical encounter with the crucified, risen, and exalted Christ. This means "a transforming personal and experimental [experienced] relationship with God."[409] Only God knows what form the encounter will assume. We should not miss the point in Acts that while Peter was still explaining the gospel to those gathered in the house of Cornelius and before any of them explicitly affirmed their faith in Christ, "the Holy Spirit fell on all who heard the word" (v. 44). They began "speaking in tongues and extolling God" (v. 46). Racing to keep up with what God was doing, Peter then declared that in light of the Holy Spirit's action, these folk were ready for water baptism. "So he ordered them to be baptized in the name of Jesus Christ" (v. 48).

Properly understood, prevenient grace anticipates our coming to know the excellence of Christ in His fullness; it doesn't replace this fullness. Understanding prevenient grace should make evangelism and missions more urgent, not less so. Only as the Holy Spirit opens the mind to hear and obey what the Scriptures say regarding our Lord can His prevenient work be brought to completion.[410]

When discussing what the Spirit can achieve through prevenient grace in devotees of other religions, let us note that Wesley made an important distinction between the "faith of a servant" based on "fearing God," and the "faith of a Son" marked by regeneration and the Spirit's indwelling witness.[411] Only as a son or daughter is someone able to exclaim in love and devotion, "Abba, Father!" The adopted sons and daughters of God are the true, real, inward, scriptural, or altogether Christians. This is the "more excellent way."[412] Nothing equals or takes the place of evangelical conversion.

However, for Wesley, "the faith of a servant" is a "faith that is properly saving." It "brings eternal salvation to all those that keep it to the end." But what characterizes such a faith? It is divinely inspired certainty regarding the reality of God and the ways of God to the extent that everyone who possesses it "fears God and does what is right" (v. 34). And whosoever, in every nation, believes thus far, Peter says, is "acceptable to him" (v. 35). But a person such as Cornelius who has not yet encountered the risen Christ, Wesley says, is only a *servant* of God, not yet properly a *son*. Nevertheless, let it be carefully noted that the servant is "acceptable to [God]." God's "wrath no longer abides on him."[413]

The "faith of a servant" marks the "almost Christian." The "faith of a son" marks an "altogether Christian." Wesley relies in part on 1 John: "Everyone who believes that Jesus is the Christ has been born of God" (5:1). He says that before his own evangelical conversion, he was "an almost Christian."[414] The marks of an "altogether Christian" are love for God, love for one's neighbor, and evangelical faith.[415]

Rob Staples says Wesley recognized degrees of faith, love, assurance, and holiness. His confidence rested solidly upon the Holy Spirit as operative in prevenient grace.[416] Nevertheless, even examples of embryonic faith (as evidenced in the disciples prior to Pentecost and Cornelius's story) do not displace the "faith through which we are saved," namely, evangelical conversion. This is full Christian faith. In his sermon "Salvation by Faith," Wesley says that evangelical conversion involves embracing "the whole gospel of Christ" and relying knowingly and completely upon the redeeming blood of the Mediator. It means trusting only in the risen Christ as our Atonement and Him living in us. In evangelical conversion the repentant sinner "closes" with Christ and "cleaves" to Him as "wisdom, righteousness, sanctification and redemption."[417] As important as the "faith of a servant" is, we don't collapse "the faith of a son" into it.

SALVATION FOR THOSE IN OTHER RELIGIONS?

As to the final salvation of those in other religions, Wesley thought we should leave the matter to God. We should not speak as though God has left such decisions to us. Wisdom will leave to God all assessments of what prevenient grace has accomplished. In harmony with the moderating position of Harold Netland, John Stott, and others we studied in chapter 4, Wesley said,

> I have no authority from the Word of God to judge those [outside the Christian faith]. Nor do I conceive that any man living has a right to sentence all the heathen and [Muslim] world to damnation. It is far better to leave them to him that made them, and [to him] who is "the Father

of the spirits of all flesh"; who is the God of the heathens as well as the Christians, and who hateth nothing that he hath made.[418]

The question arises, "When in response to the prevenient Christ, a person 'fears God and does what is right' (Acts 10:34), should we recognize the person as a Christian?" Normally, the answer is no. Prior to a transforming encounter with Christ, people do not know Christ revealed, the forgiveness of sins through the Spirit, or regeneration and adoption. Neither do they experience the indwelling witness of the Spirit that permits Christians to say, "Abba, Father!" The bridge between "the faith of a servant" and "the faith of a son" is, "How beautiful are the feet of those who bring good news!" (Rom. 10:15). Wesleyan theology views proclaiming and hearing the gospel as the goal of prevenient grace, not as being replaced by it. The need to be "born from above," "born anew" by the Spirit (John 3:1-16) is equally urgent for all people.

Nevertheless, wisdom will keep us from trying to foreclose on the options reserved for the free God. Steve Doerr, longtime missionary in Africa, recounts an incident told to him by a woman named Charlotte. She was raised a Muslim and affirmed and practiced Islam as an adult. But while still a young girl, Charlotte had a dream of a man in white that protected her from destructive, evil forces. The dream recurred, but she didn't understand its meaning.

Because she knew English, as a young adult Charlotte was hired to translate Christian literature in the country of Senegal. Not long after she started her job, she walked into the office of Danny Gomis, her Christian employer, in tears. While translating material that explained Jesus Christ, she had clearly recognized the man who had appeared in her dreams. Danny patiently explained what it means to place one's faith in Christ. Charlotte gladly confessed Jesus to be her Savior. But her newfound faith grew costly. For two years her Muslim father refused to recognize her.

Today, Charlotte is the office administrator for the French literature office of the Church of the Nazarene in Dakar, Senegal.

Another story—Fatima's—shows why we shouldn't try to establish any hard-and-fast rules about how God acts. Her story shows why the qualifier *normally* was used above. When Dr. Mark Quanstrom was pastor of a congregation in Belleville, Illinois, Fatima, a Nigerian, attended a Sunday morning service after being invited by neighbors. Fatima was in town to visit her daughter and son-in-law. Fatima continued to attend services for about six months. Mark made pastoral visits, during which he heard Fatima's amazing story.

Like Charlotte, Fatima was raised a Muslim. She had never been in a

Christian church, had never read the Bible, and had been taught to hate Christians. As an adult she lived for years in an abusive marriage. Her husband was cruel, and her children were disrespectful. Fatima's distress became so great she considered suicide. One afternoon at approximately 2 P.M. she was in her sitting room. Because of the heat, the doors and windows were open. All at once she noticed a light—brighter than the afternoon sun—shining on her face. The light came from the door. Fatima says that as she puzzled over the light, Jesus appeared to her. He bore some resemblance to pictures she had seen on television and church signs. Fatima rose to greet Him, and He immediately disappeared. "Am I dreaming?" she asked herself. No. She knew she was awake. All of a sudden, she was overwhelmed with joy and happiness. She began to repeat, "happiness, happiness, happiness!" Then she began to sing but had no knowledge of the music's source.

The next day, Christ appeared again. This time He spoke ("spoke right in my ears"). He told Fatima to rid her house of all of the charms, called ninjis, she had accumulated for warding off evil spirits (many Nigerian Muslims have retained animistic beliefs). Fatima obeyed. She put all of the ninjis in a bag and pitched them in the garbage.

Even though Fatima couldn't read very well, she purchased a children's Bible so she could learn more about her Redeemer. Then she found a Christian church that nurtured her faith. She attended church under the guise of going to market. Other women in the congregation were doing the same. But Fatima was disturbed by her deceit. She thought she should confess her faith to her family but was told by her friends to wait. Finally, after three years, she could no longer deceive her family. So on her wedding anniversary, Fatima told her family she had become a Christian.

Persecution began immediately, and continued. Her family would eat none of the food she prepared. Her parents disowned her. Her mother forbade Fatima's attendance at her funeral for fear Fatima might touch her and make her unfit for heaven. Fatima had a small food business. When the villagers learned she was a Christian they refused to make purchases. And her husband said that Allah would consider him virtuous if he were to kill her. To this day, her husband threatens death.

Fatima has been a Christian for about 12 years. Today, two of her seven children are Christians. A son is a Christian minister in South Africa, and a daughter is a layperson in Nigeria. And Fatima prays that her husband will also turn to Jesus.

THE CHRISTIAN GOSPEL
AND THE NON-CHRISTIAN RELIGIONS

So far we have spoken of the universality of prevenient grace as it relates to individuals who are devotees of non-Christian religions. We have not asked how prevenient grace relates to the non-Christian religions as such. Are the non-Christian religions grace-endowed paths to God that He somehow authors? Are they themselves products of prevenient grace, and are they thereby autonomously sufficient, at least in some measure?

Before answering directly, let's keep in mind that we can't neatly separate a person from his or her religion. The way a person responds to prevenient grace will likely be conditioned by the belief structure characteristic of his or her religion and by the patterns of life it produces. People and belief structures are to a large extent interdependent. At fundamental, even subconscious levels, religions form thought and practice. They largely form what it means to be a person. For example, what Buddhists and Christians teach regarding the self differs greatly. Buddhists, at least traditionally, say that belief in the reality of the self is an illusion that leads to constant suffering. This is the doctrine of nonself *(anatta)* and it forms the third Noble Truth. Believing the self to be real, we try to make it secure by satisfying our endless desires. But desire causes suffering and sorrow *(dukkha)*. The cessation of suffering begins by recognizing our fundamental error—that we have treated an illusion (the self) as though it were real—and by recognizing the impermanence of all things *(annica)*. By contrast, Christians believe the self is real, that God creates it, and that it is included in the goodness of God's creation. Salvation involves redeeming, purifying the self, and reforming it in Christ's image. And it includes redemption of God's creation. Think of the impact these differences will make on how Buddhists and Christians view human life and the world and upon how they define *salvation*. To take another example, a Hindu who believes strongly in the law of Karma (strict cause and effect—consequences —in all things, which extends into many future reincarnations) will explain catastrophic circumstances in a person's life quite different from a Methodist schooled to believe that the past doesn't have to dictate the future, that it may even to some extent be redeemed. These illustrations can help us see why we can't make sharp distinctions between a person's religion and the person a religion produces.

Let's also recall that when John Wesley spoke of "true religion," he did not equate it with the Christian religion. Like Martin Luther and Karl Barth,

Wesley had intense disregard for superficial Christianity. He recognized how easily this religion can be distorted. In the England of his day Christendom had become a haven for all kinds of religious frauds and scoundrels. Christendom can still become an instrument of evil powers and principalities and can in some of its forms end up opposing the gospel. Like Bonhoeffer who spoke of cheap grace, Wesley condemned a religion that is "lighter than vanity itself."[419]

"True religion," on the other hand, transforms the heart. It entails loving God with all our heart, and our neighbors as ourselves. It involves a heart made right "toward God and man."[420] Wesley would have agreed with Douglas Harink: Paul sought not to establish a religion, but a people of God distinguished by the power of God and the reality of the gospel working in them.[421] So, when the Spirit calls a person into Christ He is not calling them to embrace Christianity. Religion as such is not the critical issue.

With that distinction and warning in place, let's directly answer the question regarding Christ and other religions. Given the scandal of particularity (Jesus Christ is the Way, the Truth, and the Life) and the uncompromising importance of evangelical faith, is there a Wesleyan standard for assessing the role and importance of the non-Christian religions? Yes. The standard is expressed in the form of two questions: "To what extent does the religion in question serve the purposes of prevenient grace?" and "In what ways does it promote a 'righteousness' that approximates the 'faith of a servant'?" Some religions serve the aims of prevenient grace more effectively than do others. Take, for example, the Sikh teaching that true piety consists not in the exhibition of self-denial (making pilgrimages or smearing ashes over one's body), but in love for holy, pure motives, a love for virtue, sexual purity, and associating with both the elite and the outcasts without regard for caste. Contrast that with the worship of Kali, one spouse of the Hindu god Shiva, who when acting as the spreader of disease and misery evokes terror in the hearts of her worshipers and when acting as the enemy of demons fills her worshipers with gratitude. On the basis of distinctions such as these, we can make distinctions between religions. The value of a non-Christian religion rests upon its ability to serve as an instrument of prevenient grace. To that extent alone can its positive features be recognized, but even then only as a result of God's creativity in diverse cultures—not from some inherent and independent value in the religion itself. And even the most positive service to prevenient grace a religion provides is anticipatory and temporary. We can speak of other religions as providential only in a secondary and strictly instrumental sense. Never should we overlook the ways in which they are contrary to the gospel of God.

Some Sikhs, Buddhists, Jains, and others better serve prevenient grace than many superficial, egocentric, and semipagan Christians. Think for a moment of the greedy, showboating media healers and their devotees who reduce the whole Christian faith to one dimension—physical and monetary well-being. Reflect upon the corruption of Good Friday that permits men in Manila to whip their backs (flagellate) until they are ribbons of blood, all for the purpose of identifying with Christ and gaining release from their sins.[422] Or what about Christians who regularly overdose on a narrow understanding of the Second Coming, even while getting caught up in a narcissistic materialism that mocks the kingdom of God? Ahmed El-Sherif—who champions simplicity of life, who loves justice and mercy, and who champions a noble standard of monogamy and chastity—may be much closer to the kingdom of God.

In summary, it is altogether too general and indiscriminate to speak of how Wesleyans assess the relationship between the Christian faith and other world religions. No religion has saving merit of its own (including Christianity). No religion offers a path to God independent of Jesus Christ. John Wesley would have agreed with Clark Pinnock: "The idea that world religions ordinarily function as paths to salvation is dangerous nonsense and wishful thinking."[423] Of each religion the question must be asked, how well does it serve the purposes of prevenient grace? This places upon Wesleyans, in a pluralistic world, the responsibility to gain as much knowledge of the world's religions as we can and, where possible, to become acquainted with people in those religions. Doing so will help us sincerely understand them as people rather than as abstractions, recognize the convictions and hopes that shape them, and discern how the Spirit of God may already be drawing them to the Redeemer. Such knowledge serves the moves of the Spirit, not the ways of manipulation.

GOVERNED BY THE SCRIPTURES

Jesus said, "He whom God has sent speaks the words of God, for he gives the Spirit without measure. The Father loves the Son and has placed all things in his hands. Whoever believes in the Son has eternal life; whoever disobeys the Son will not see life, but must endure God's wrath" (John 3:34-36).

By Wesleyan standards, anything that John Wesley or we might believe regarding how Christians should view people in other religions, or the religions themselves, must stand under the New Testament's judgment. It must pass that test, and we believe that it does. The futures of people, nations, and religions converge in an eventual confession that "Jesus Christ is Lord, to the glory of God the Father" (Phil. 2:11). This affirmation is admittedly out of favor with the ideology of religious pluralism. But it is the affirmation of the New Testament, and to that we will be faithful. Here the Wesleyan tradition rests.

For Reflection and Discussion

1. At the end of 2 Corinthians Paul gives the following benediction: "The grace of the Lord Jesus Christ and the love of God and the fellowship of the Holy Spirit be with you all" (13:14, RSV). The order is important: the grace of Christ leads one to the love of God, and through the Holy Spirit produces fellowship with God and neighbor. Does the Wesleyan doctrine of prevenient grace protect the Christological character of God's grace? If so, how? If not, why not?

2. In this chapter we examined responses to religious pluralism. In what ways does the Wesleyan response to religious pluralism compare and contrast with those five responses?

3. Does the doctrine of prevenient grace necessarily undercut the importance of missions and evangelical conversion, or does it prepare the way for both? What are some of the risks associated with the Wesleyan understanding of the Spirit's work?

4. Does the possibility of a positive response to prevenient grace encourage the notion of works righteousness and a way of salvation independent of Christ?

5. Some people would say that it is unfair to other religions—and even oppressive—to identify their positive features as the fruit of prevenient grace. They would say that the religions themselves alone account for their content. How would you respond to these claims?

10
TELLING THE GOSPEL STORY IN A WESLEYAN WAY

We have reached the point where we need to ask, "How does being informed by Wesleyan theology, as well as the broader Christian heritage, affect the way we tell the gospel story in a religiously pluralistic world?" A person's orientation—historical, geographic, and social—will affect how he or she tells a story. It wouldn't work, for example, to try to tell a story about Cajun life in Louisiana by using a Vermont accent. Nor could stories about rural life in the majestic Green Mountains of Vermont be effectively told in a Cajun accent. A friend who lived for years in Maine masterfully tells stories about the Maine coast and the fishermen who work there. But when he moved to Ohio and told his stories, he was puzzled over why those Midwesterners sometimes had trouble getting the punch line.

The riveting southern writer Flannery O'Conner paints pictures of early 20th-century rural life in the southeastern United States that almost leap off the page. But she didn't begin this way. At first, after having finished her formal education as a writer, she sought success by writing about things "up North," things that were foreign to her soul. She failed. Then a trusted adviser told her to "go home"—both figuratively and literally. This she did, and subsequently succeeded in using the culture she knew best to draw unparalleled distinctions between what Bonhoeffer labeled "cheap grace" and "costly grace."

What is true of writers and storytellers is also true of doctrinal traditions. They tell the gospel story in different accents and from different perspectives. Just as the differences between a Louisiana Cajun and a Green Mountain Vermonter are understood as distinctions and not as a judgment against either background, so we recognize differences between the accents that distinguish a Wesleyan way of telling the gospel story from other doctrinal traditions. Just as a story misfires and loses its way if it is told out of context, so the Wesleyan way of salvation misfires and loses its way if we try to tell the gospel story in ways that are foreign to some of our essential doctrinal commitments. In this chapter we will examine how to tell the gospel story in ways that are faithful to the Wesleyan tradition's doctrinal commitments.

Before we consider a Wesleyan way of telling the gospel story, we need to be sure we are alert to the broader context in which the story is being told. Not only do we live and speak in the midst of accelerated religious pluralism, but we in the West also bear witness to the gospel in a post-Christian age. Drew University evangelism professor Leonard Sweet tells of a Columbus, Ohio, pastoral team who attended the NCAA March Madness basketball play-offs in Indianapolis. In the Hoosier Dome (now RCA Dome), they saw a man wearing an orange wig and holding a John 3:16 sign. He was seated opposite the pastoral team. Behind the pastors sat two well-dressed couples debating the meaning of John 3:16. One person thought the sign was an advertisement for a new restaurant. Another of the four thought the sign was signaling someone to meet the man in the restroom on the third floor, stall 16.[424]

Though humorous, the story illustrates the aspect of postmodernity spoken of as "the loss of Christian memory." It characterizes a "post-Christian" culture.[425] "Post-Christian" doesn't mean there was a time when the Western world was almost full of born-again Christians. And it doesn't claim there was a time when Western societies intentionally constructed their cultures along clear-cut Christian lines. Instead, it means that a Judeo-Christian understanding of moral foundations and conduct, of individual and communal life, is disappearing from our consciousness, language, and values. The Christian narrative plays a decreasing role in setting the standards that define values and govern discourse. A social fabric once largely woven according to Judeo-Christian themes is now badly frayed. It is being replaced by a tapestry of many stories, few of which name Christianity as their weavers and none of which provide meaning for society as a whole.

Brian McLaren, an insightful interpreter of postmodernity for Christians, notes that if a culture places the Bible in a position of authority, then a person can get away with appealing to the Bible to prove things. "But as the world changes and more and more people show themselves ignorant or skeptical of the Bible, saying 'The Bible says' doesn't prove anything."[426] Writer and pastor Bill Easum says that in 1983, the congregation he led began to notice that second grade children "didn't know anything" about Bible stories and personalities. And he cites a situation in which a public high school student who attended his church was forbidden to write an essay about Jesus because the teacher didn't consider Jesus a historical figure.[427]

When a story ceases to inform a culture, then its once familiar content becomes a stranger to the populace. A young man named Justin illustrates this.

Daniel Hill, pastor of River City Community Church in Chicago, engaged Justin in conversation at a Starbucks. Matter-of-factly, Justin informed Rev. Hill: "We all know that 'God' is out there at some level, but no one has a right to tell another person what 'God' looks like for them. Each person is free to express that however they want, but they should keep their opinions to themselves."[428] Perhaps the man with the orange wig in the Hoosier Dome holding the John 3:16 sign should have a conversation with Justin. Holding his sign, he had assumed incorrectly that the Christian narrative still plays a familiar and defining role in cultural memory. Just hold up the sign, he must have thought, and the audience would recall the reference. Just like that, Justin and others would give heed, the gospel would be proclaimed, and people would repent. Justin, and the two couples debating the meaning of the John 3:16 sign, demonstrated that the orange-haired evangelist had assumed too much.

But the loss of Christian culture isn't necessarily something to be mourned. Its existence may make Christian language and imagery publicly familiar, but in no way does it automatically pave the way for Christian holiness and witness. In fact, cultural Christianity can make the Christian faith so superficially accessible that it suffocates the way of the Cross. A man from my childhood illustrates this. Mr. Rivers was one of the recognized alcoholics in our town. On occasion, he would show up for one of our revival services and sometimes he would "get saved." But try as he might, he never succeeded in conquering the bottle. His relapses made him a perpetual candidate for the next revival.

If while Mr. Rivers was on one of his binges we had asked him, "Mr. Rivers, if you die today, will you go to heaven?" he probably would have answered no. Maybe he could have even provided a Bible reference to support his answer. But even though he didn't see himself as a Christian, Mr. Rivers was still living under a Christian umbrella, a Christian story. The language of heaven and hell, saved and lost, shaped the religious context in which he lived, but like many who are somewhat familiar with Christian talk, he remained a stranger to the gospel's power to transform his life.

As the loss of Christian memory expands, we will find ourselves turning more and more to the Early Church for guidance. Evangelism among Gentiles in the Early Church assumed no overarching Christian story in the Greco-Roman world. Rather, Paul had to preach and teach in words that a pagan world could comprehend, while not jeopardizing the power of the gospel. Brian McLaren thinks that is one reason why Paul didn't quote the Bible to the philosophers in Athens (Acts 17). "Paul knew that to persuade people, we have to start where they are and build the bridge from their side to ours. So he quoted their poets, not his prophets."[429]

The writer John Fischer understands this. He tells of attending a birthday bash at the Starplex amphitheater in Dallas. The partygoers were there to celebrate the anniversary of a local alternative rock station. On that summer night, the smoke from tobacco and some other leaves hung low. One band—Jars of Clay—was the only Christian group to appear. As Fischer looked out over the crowd, the six young men slipped onstage and began to sing, "Arms nailed down / are you telling me something?" Fischer told himself, "We've waited a long time for this."

A man standing next to Fischer had five earrings on his face, only two of which were on his ears. Noticing Fischer's backstage pass, the man with the facial jewelry asked, "Are you with Jars?" "Yes," Fischer answered. The man responded, "If you're going to see them afterwards, would you thank them for me? I became a Christian by listening to their CD. I played it over and over and figured out just about everything. I went and got a Christian friend of mine—pulled him out of a party—and told him I wanted to get saved right away. He didn't believe me. You wouldn't have either. I hated Christians."[430]

Many Wesleyan leaders believe this post-Christian context provides a golden opportunity for Christian witness. The primary reason is that Wesleyans have traditionally relied upon the power of the gospel itself, and upon the attraction of liberated and transformed lives, rather than upon being well-positioned socially and politically. But the opportunities provided can be seized only if we understand the pluralistic and post-Christian climate, and only if we understand the missionary promise of our heritage. The opportunities revolve around the Wesleyan vision of how God's grace operates, around His prevenient persistence even when human observers may not know the Spirit is working at all. It depends totally upon the power of the risen Christ to transform those who will receive Him, as well as the cultures in which they live.

As the Church's early witness in the Greco-Roman world demonstrates, the Holy Spirit doesn't depend upon the existence of an overarching cultural story. He certainly isn't thrown out of gear when one doesn't exist. He will slip right past ignorance of the Christian Story and will use the most unconventional devices to prompt hunger for salvation in the hearts of men and women. Openings for the Holy Spirit need not be explicitly religious. Aided by the Spirit, we who witness for Christ must learn to recognize and embrace the Spirit's moves. When telling the Story anywhere, missionary Floyd Cunningham says, "Christians must find how the light [of Christ] has already been shining. [They] must explain more perfectly the way of salvation through Jesus Christ so that, through grace, faith may arise."[431]

With this in mind, let's turn more directly to a Wesleyan way of telling the gospel story in a pluralistic and post-Christian world. There are at least *seven* distinct markers.

CONFIDENCE

Because of what Wesleyans believe regarding the Holy Spirit's universal and persistently gracious work, confidence (but not arrogance) should mark the way they tell the gospel story. No one should be more confident regarding the subtle creativity and inclusiveness of the Spirit's efforts. Consider for a moment some of the prominent moments in our history:

In 1739 George Whitefield asked John Wesley to come to Bristol to preach in the fields to the coal miners. The established church had largely ignored them. They were poor, uneducated, and lacking in social standing. From that sermon on, Wesley proclaimed and practiced the gospel of new creation and hope to the poor of England, Scotland, and Ireland. Though he was often attacked, especially in the early part of his ministry, and at times was in peril from mob violence, no danger could daunt Wesley or interruption restrain his preaching the grace of God.[432]

In 1787 a rising tide of racism in the American South was choking African-American participation in Methodist churches. Courageously, a Black Methodist minister—27-year-old Richard Allen—led in the formation of the African Methodist Episcopal Church. Allen and others had learned from their Methodist heritage how the gospel establishes the dignity and value of all people, without reference to race. They weren't about to let bigotry take that away. Richard Allen so highly valued God's children that he began to conduct night classes in Philadelphia to show his people how to help themselves in a hostile environment. The gospel of God's liberating love empowered both him and the targets of racial hatred to whom he ministered.

In 1843 the Wesleyan Methodist Church was formed in America. Its opposition to slavery was a major reason for its birth. In 1860 the Free Methodist Church was formed. The Free Methodists also opposed slavery and the widespread practice of parishioners either renting or buying the church pews they warmed on Sundays. This practice relegated the poor to benches in the back of the sanctuary. In defense of a gospel that ignores privilege and pushes aside exclusion, the "Free" Methodists called for "free seats for all." They announced that the riches of the gospel are intended for all, without regard for race or social standing. Defense of those who didn't have the social clout to speak for themselves was, the Free Methodists believed, just a part of being faithful to the gospel.

In 1865 William Booth, a former Methodist minister, recognized the need for a practical Christian ministry in the East End of London. By 1878 his East London Mission had grown considerably and had become the Salvation Army. Under Booth's leadership the Salvation Army became a major instrument through which the gospel of hope reached millions who would have otherwise been forgotten.

In 1895 Phineas Bresee's career as a minister in the Methodist Church seemed to be soaring. He led the First Methodist Church in Los Angeles and was also a presiding elder and prominent civic leader. But he abandoned it all to follow Christ's example by preaching the gospel to the poor in the center of Los Angeles. He and others formed the Church of the Nazarene in Los Angeles for this purpose. (1908 is the date for a merger of Holiness groups that gave birth to the continentwide Church of the Nazarene.)

These stories show that when faithful to its formative vision, the Wesleyan tradition has rejected despair, elitism, privilege, and human-constructed restrictions on the gospel. It has sought to follow the lowly Galilean who offered the riches of the Kingdom to those who had been forgotten and excluded. But the temptation to join the club of religious and social privilege, to forget that the grace of God eliminates all distance between "the righteous" and "the beggars," is as besetting for Wesleyans as for any others. We have sinned often in this regard. When this happens we must plead for God's forgiveness, pray for fortitude, and seek the Spirit's direction. The Wesleyan tradition is faithful to itself when, in the power of the Spirit, it continues to proclaim good news to the poor, release to the captives, recovery of sight to the blind, and announces to all the year of the Lord's favor (Luke 4:16-19).

What the apostle Paul said of himself is an accurate account of the Wesleyan understanding of God's grace: "From now on, therefore, we regard no one from a human point of view; even though we once knew Christ from a human point of view, we know him no longer in that way" (2 Cor. 5:16). Our defining confidence derives from our certainty that for all persons everywhere, to be "in Christ" is "new creation" (v. 17). The old order of slavery to sin and spiritual death passes away; everything becomes new!

Jesus inflamed His opponents because He indiscriminately extended God's love and forgiveness to all. As we have seen, He showed no respect for the established table practices that enforced rigid distinctions between the worthy and the unworthy. Tax collectors and sinners drew near to Him (Luke 15:1-2). He explained how a father still loved his prodigal son who had descended from "the big house" to the "pig house" (vv. 11-32). By doing these things, Jesus perfectly revealed the heart of His Father and perfectly exposed the sin of self-righteousness. We have a choice to make. We can grumble and gossip with the Pharisees, or we can be converted to the heart and mission of God.

The Wesleys and the early Methodists confidently modeled Jesus' inclusiveness. To justify our identity with the Wesleyan tradition, the breadth of the gospel that captured them and the confidence it inspired must capture and inspire us as well. We, too, must be found confidently declaring the gospel of transformation in "unpromising" places because there simply are no obstacles that can separate a thirsty sinner from the Water of Life.

THE SPIRIT WHO IS ALREADY THERE

Wesleyans believe that the Holy Spirit, not a human messenger, is the divine first responder. As we have seen, this confidence comes from what we believe regarding prevenient grace. We believe the gracious Spirit is closer to people than they are to themselves, yes, closer than their slavery to sin. In ways that only God will know, He is active in each person, seeking to draw them to eternal life and holiness.

"WITNESSING" AND "CONVINCING"

Wesleyans make a sharp distinction between witnessing and convincing. So does the New Testament (John 15:26-27; 16:8-11). Disciples witness. The Holy Spirit convinces. In the power of the Holy Spirit, disciples can bear witness to Jesus, but only the Holy Spirit can witness in a way that convinces. This distinction doesn't minimize the importance of our bearing witness; it just recognizes a work that only the Holy Spirit can perform. Convincing is not a matter of human words and action, no matter how true they may be. Rather, convincing involves a person being incontestably arrested by the Holy Spirit at the deepest levels of his or her existence. Through this a person knows that he or she not only has been confronted by Christ who is the Way, the Truth, and the Life but also has been confronted with the truth about himself or herself. Things can never quite be the same again.

The Great Commission calls all Christians to bear witness that Jesus is the Savior of the world. But there is only One who can bear the kind of witness that convinces, and that One is the Holy Spirit. Jesus told His disciples, "When the Spirit of truth comes, he will guide you into all the truth; for he will not speak on his own, but will speak whatever he hears, and he will declare to you the things that are to come. He will glorify me, because he will take what is mine and declare it to you" (John 16:13-14).

We might ask, "Why is this distinction so important?" For one thing, failure to observe the distinction inevitably introduces disorder. We are advised not to try to do God's work for Him by adopting strategies that bypass the Spirit's timing and subtlety. The witness trusts the Convincer, not his or her own impulsiveness. A second reason resides in what we believe regarding "coming to know Christian truth." The truth of the Christian faith is not first a body of divine information that needs to be transmitted or imposed on others through argumentation. It isn't carryout-boxed logic. If it were, then perhaps witnesses could convince by accurately conveying Christian information or through powerful argumentation. This is not the case. Instead, Jesus the Redeemer is the *truth* of the Christian faith. To know Him is to be transformed by Him, and only the Spirit can accomplish this. Knowledge and transformation inevitably intersect in the work of the Spirit.

It is true that giving an accurate, informed account of the gospel is a witness's responsibility, and that the Holy Spirit may use it. Disciples need to exercise every talent and opportunity they have to become versed in the Scriptures, conversant with their broader world and culture, and clothed with the Holy Spirit. But the critical point to consider is that Christ is encountered where the Spirit convinces and re-creates, not where someone is overwhelmed by information and argumentation—and certainly not by manipulation or coercion of any kind. Our alienation from God is principally in need of divine forgiveness and re-creation, not of having our information corrected. Sinners are convinced and Christ becomes known when the Creator-Redeemer God acts in sovereign grace to give eternal life to those who were before dead in their trespasses and sin.

For Wesleyans, Christian witnesses have three responsibilities: to demonstrate the reality of the gospel in their own lives, to present the gospel clearly, and to be sensitive to the Spirit's timing.

Brian McLaren tells of addressing a group of scholars from the People's Republic of China. They asked that he speak on the existence of God. But rather than argue with the scholars, he offered some questions a person would need to consider in any search for God. Then he simply shared his Christian faith. He told them how his faith in Christ helped him deal with the crisis of his son being diagnosed with leukemia. Then he opened the floor for questions. A distinguished gentleman stood and said, "Sir, I do not have a question, but I wish to thank you on behalf of all of us. You have helped us a great deal. Instead of telling us what to believe, you have told us how to believe, and that is very good."[433]

PATIENCE

Because Wesleyans believe that the all-knowing Spirit is the architect of evangelism, witnesses can be patient. Some people, including Matt, think Christians aren't patient. "Christianity is for simple-minded people," he told pastor Dan Hill. "When they talk to you, they act as if you are a robot. They have an agenda to promote, and if you don't agree with them, they're done with you."[434] Matt's indictment should remind us of the important difference between the urgency of the gospel and the impulsiveness of a human witness. There is indeed an urgency to the gospel, but the timing for response belongs to the Lord. Even Jesus came into the world at the right time ("the fullness of time" [Eph. 1:10]). According to "his counsel and will" (v. 11), God prepared the world for the birth of His Son in Bethlehem.

A faithful Christian witness is motivated by a desire to see others enter the kingdom of God. Love for the gospel and for people makes this urgent. But with urgency comes the risk of rushing ahead of the Holy Spirit. The Spirit patiently cultivates the many factors that lead to a person's redemption. In His own way, the Spirit will lead a person to repentance and regeneration. It may be through us, or it may be through the next witness that a person's fullness of time will come.

In my first pastoral assignment I fished with Bruce,[435] hunted with him in dismal weather, and ate a truckload of Chinese food with him. I preached Sunday after Sunday as Bruce sat attentively. But when Esther and I moved from that assignment, Bruce was still not a Christian. Within a few weeks after the new pastor arrived, I learned that Bruce had become a Christian. "What! Why not while I was his pastor?" Because when I left, the Holy Spirit still had more work to do, and He accomplished it through others.

The Spirit may even have to remove the clutter we Christians have unloaded on our friends, our children, and even whole cultures. Sometimes the Spirit has to engage in crisis management for people who have been hurt in church disputes or because of someone's hypocrisy. For others the Holy Spirit has to sort out childhood traumas. Only the Spirit can peel away the layers of hurt and accurately track the progress. Because of a raw memory of the many Christians who lent their support to the Holocaust, a rabbi friend told me, "When you tell me that Jesus loves me and wants to save me, I freeze. I hear Nazi jack-boots coming down the street."

How long will it take for the Holy Spirit to prepare a person to receive the gospel? As long as He needs. That should not be our concern. We are called to complement His work, not to do or obstruct it. Our hope and confidence is that when the crucified and risen One is revealed in the power of the Holy Spirit, people will receive Him gladly.

None of this is meant to discount carefully considered method in evangelism and mission. But it is meant to make absolutely clear that methods, theories, and strategies must be thoroughly governed by the nature of the gospel and by the Holy Spirit who is the Evangelizer of the Holy Trinity.

In the Absence of Coercion

If Wesleyans are faithful to their understanding of how God's grace proceeds, they will avoid all forms of religious persecution and coercion and will seek none of its bitter benefits. The gospel of grace and religious coercion are mutually exclusive concepts. We should firmly oppose using governmental, cultural, economic, and intellectual power to gain special privileges for Christians or to impose Christianity on anyone. All forms of coercion, whether subtle or overt, soil the gospel and betray the Holy Spirit. The man who heatedly told me, "If you aren't Christian, you aren't fully American" illustrates the point. Any such equation is rightly perceived as oppressive.

We Believe the Integrity of the Gospel Protects the Integrity of the Person

When meeting anyone, including adherents of other religions, we should recognize another whom God has created and loves and who is currently being attended by God's prevenient grace. Douglas Harink speaks of the gospel's vulnerability and says witnesses must not try to remove this aspect. That the call of the gospel may be refused is essential. "It is intrinsic to the vulnerability of the gospel and [the] commission of its messenger that this be the case. In fact, this, too, is the ministry of reconciliation, which is prepared to suffer such a refusal for the sake of honoring the other."[436]

A person should become a Christian only because he or she has freely embraced the gospel, founded upon internal conviction. Along with Karl Barth, we believe that God "leads by cords of love,"[437] not by coercing us or violating our consciences in any way. Wesleyans should be at the forefront of protecting religious freedom for all. Religious minorities should be confident that we will defend them if their freedoms are threatened. We should oppose all use of the powers of state to advance the interests of religion. Reliance on the power of the state, instead of the Holy Spirit, to win people to Christ or to advance the Church corrupts the Christian message. It is an admission of failure. What we object to in others we must not permit in ourselves.

DIALOGUE

What Wesleyans believe regarding prevenient grace creates an appropriate place for dialogue with people of other religions. This is one of the most troublesome topics associated with religious pluralism, a term that means different things for different people. For a Wesleyan, what would dialogue between Christians and people of other religions involve? We believe Jesus Christ to be God incarnate, the gospel of God for all people. So dialogue doesn't mean a conversation about equally adequate religious options. Nor is dialogue an opportunity for manipulation or oppression of any kind. That, too, violates our understanding of the gospel.

For Wesleyans, dialogue means placing ourselves in the service of prevenient grace. It should be marked by love, genuine respect, and sensitivity to how a person may already be responding to the prevenient Christ. Dialogue should evidence a total absence of coercion or rudeness. When invited to testify to our faith in Jesus Christ, we should do so in an informed manner. We should have confidence in the Spirit of the gentle Savior who "will not break a bruised reed or quench a smoldering wick" (Matt. 12:20). Douglas Harink says correctly that a Christian should enter into dialogue with a person of another religion only if he or she is living a "cruciform life," that is, steadfastly seeking to follow the suffering and rejected Messiah. Like Paul, we should seek only the persuasion that comes from "Christ crucified and the working of the Holy Spirit."[438]

Philip Meadows says that while dialogue should occur and should be sincere, it must not "detract from the task of evangelism, i.e., inviting persons to embark on the more excellent way and to become followers of Jesus Christ."[439] He concludes that it is the "prevenient purpose of the Spirit of Christ to direct all people to the person of Christ, and it is our responsibility as Christians to enable that to happen."[440]

Jeff Sellers tells a story that illustrates the challenge we face in telling the story, and why Wesleyans should confidently look to their heritage for guidance. In the spring of 2003, Robert Louis Wilkens was engaged in a conversation with a young woman in a hotel lounge in Erfurt, Germany. Erfurt is the medieval town in which Martin Luther was ordained a priest. The topic of religion arose. Wilkens asked the young woman if she was a member of a church. Without reluctance or embarrassment, she responded, "Ich bin Heide" ("I am a heathen"). The young lady telegraphed that she is "post-Christian." She is among the 80 percent of the town's population that has no identity with Christianity. And she is part of the decades-old decline in the number of Christians in Western Europe.[441]

In the presence of that young woman, and the pluralistic and post-Christian world she represents, Christians can either escape to a religious ghetto and wait for the next bullet train to heaven, or in the power of the Holy Spirit confidently and joyfully wade into that world to tell the Story. We can be sure of this: the Spirit—the First Responder, who has been on the scene long before we arrived—will be there to greet us.

For Reflection and Discussion

1. What are some of the most visible signs of a post-Christian West that you have observed?

2. How may we maintain a proper distance between the witnessing that we Christians are to do, and the convincing that only the Holy Spirit can do?

3. What are some of the ways in which Christians can misrepresent (and have misrepresented) the gospel in how they present it to others? What is there about the nature of the gospel that requires us to protect the integrity of all persons?

4. How is one to distinguish between patience and negligence, between urgency and impulsiveness, when bearing witness to Christ?

5. Reflect upon the meaning of dialogue as an instrument of prevenient grace. Should Christians await permission from a person of another religion before telling him or her about Christ the Redeemer? Explain your answer in light of Jesus' earthly ministry?

PART IV

STORYTELLERS:
CHRISTIAN LIFE AND WITNESS IN A RELIGIOUSLY PLURALISTIC WORLD

11
CHRISTIAN FORMATION:
SHAPED BY THE "REAL WORLD"

"Paul's aim was not to propose another religion to the nations, but to call out and build up a people in their midst, a people formed by allegiance to the one God of Israel and his Son, Jesus the Messiah."[442]

"Windy" was the nickname of one of my childhood friends. It seemed that Windy knew more about automobiles than Henry Ford. He could speak volumes on why Fords were superior to Chevrolets, Chevrolets to Chryslers, and on down the line. But when a car hood was lifted, Windy either fell silent or became confused. He had trouble distinguishing between the starter and the alternator, between spark plug wires and battery cables. Though he could talk about automobiles until he was blue in the face, he had not actually explored with tools in hand what makes them tick. And now you know how Windy got his name.

No such discrepancy can be attributed to Li Tianen, one of the patriarchs of the house church movement in China. His formation as a Christian was forged in the fires of persecution. In 1960 he was sentenced to 10 years in prison because of his Christian leadership. Assigned to a labor camp, he dug and moved iron ore. For praying in his cell, Li was often forced to stand against a wall for up to six hours—even in the freezing cold of winter. Wearing no shirt, he was forced to spread his arms wide. Still, he remained faithful to his Lord.

In 1975 Li was arrested again. This time he was sentenced to death. But on three separate occasions, unexpected circumstances caused the Communist authorities to postpone his execution. Fang Tianci, secretary of the Nanyang City Communist Party, pressed vigorously for Li's execution. Ironically, after China's Cultural Revolution collapsed in 1976, Fang himself landed in prison. He had been an ardent supporter of the Gang of Four[443] that led the Cultural Revolution. Even more amazing, Fang was assigned to Li Tianen's cell!

Arriving in the cell, Fang knelt before Li Tianen. Trembling, he addressed Li: "God in Heaven, you are an awesome power! I was ready to execute you three times, but the Jesus you believe in protected you. [Karl] Marx was not able to save me. Now I believe the gospel you believe is real."[444]

The record stands: Li Tianen has lived the Story. But think for a moment about some Christians who didn't. In 1933, through murder, deceit, intimidation, and popular support, Adolf Hitler became the dictator of Germany. On September 1, 1939, without provocation, his army invaded Poland. World War II had begun. By the time the Nazi attempt to enslave Europe collapsed in May 1945, millions of combatants and civilians had died. Among them were 7 million Jews, Jehovah's Witnesses, Gypsies, dissenting clergy, and homosexuals. They died in death camps such as Auschwitz-Birkenau, Dachau, and Treblinka.

Many forces conspired to make Hitler's reign of terror possible. Shamefully, one of those was the state-established Protestant Reich Church, also known as the German Christians.[445] One of the German Christians' six major themes was: "It is because of Hitler that Christ, God the helper and redeemer, has become effective among us."[446] The National Bishop of the German Christians, a Nazi sympathizer, was Ludwig Muller. He, along with most other clergy, willingly embraced the Aryan Clause that denied the pulpit to ordained ministers of Jewish ancestry. In 1933 Hitler gave Muller the title Reich Bishop (bishop of the kingdom, or empire). In Reich churches the Nazi swastika hung over the altar. The symbol of the cross was placed in the center of the swastika.

Only a minority of Protestants (and Roman Catholics) opposed Hitler. They formed the Confessing Church. The Rev. Martin Niemöller and Dietrich Bonhoeffer were some of its leaders. The Nazis arrested Niemöller for "malicious attacks against the state." He spent seven years in Dachau and Sachsenhausen. Dietrich Bonhoeffer spent years in prison and was finally executed by the Gestapo in 1945.

How could a majority of Christians in Germany have so readily and vigorously supported Hitler? How, without a whimper, could they have become complicit in a demonic enterprise that conquered and exterminated millions?

Dietrich Bonhoeffer cut straight to the bone in his answer to the question—an enemy of the gospel of Jesus Christ had shaped the Reich Church. It had, he said, bought into and then peddled cheap grace instead of proclaiming costly grace. Cheap grace justified the sinner without ever demanding that he or she confess his or her sins and be converted. The church had not prepared itself to recognize and do battle with the powers of hell, so it was a sitting duck when those powers came calling. The discernment and courage needed for forceful witness and resistance, much less martyrdom, didn't exist. Hell came armed to the teeth, but the Reich Church was a stranger to the weapons of the Holy Spirit. The German Christians had rejected the prophetic word of the gospel and had refused to be disciplined by the Scriptures. The times called for a church diligently and comprehensively formed by the gospel, ready to suffer for Christ, but the light in its lamp had gone out and no oil was in reserve. The sum of the story is that the German Christians tried to place the Son of God in the hire of hatred and aggression and predictably wound up enslaved to these powers.

The fundamental difference between Li Tianen and the German Christians is that even though both bore the name Christian, they belonged to two different worlds—one eternal and the other temporary. They walked by the light of two radically different visions of reality. For Li Tianen, the real world is the kingdom of God, and everything that challenges it—even if it is a brutal and powerful Communist state—is false. For the German Christians, the real world was identified with national power, military might, race, and economic success. The kingdom of God was forced to find its place amid all of that. As noted in chapter 1, a theme of the German Christians was "Germany the end, Christ the means."

Centuries ago Augustine talked about these two different worlds and spoke of them as two different cities.[447] One city is the City of God; it is eternal. The other is the city of man; it is built upon false foundations and is passing away. Jesus said the two worlds can't be reconciled and that no one can give allegiance to both (Matt. 6:24; Luke 16:13). Telling the gospel Story the way it deserves to be told simply cannot happen unless our allegiance to the real world is undivided, unless we are being formed by the Story of God. Believing and acting otherwise has often gotten the Church into trouble and has sometimes branded Christians with the nickname Windy. What are the features that distinguish between the real world and the false world, and what is required for becoming real-world people?

THE QUESTION

Will we be disciples of Jesus Christ? The question is that simple and that sweeping. Some of us have craftily tried to dodge the question by busying ourselves with secondary questions, and then fooling ourselves into thinking we have faced the big one head-on. We have worked ourselves into a lather over denominational squabbles, gossiped over who is in and who is out of religious structures, or exhibited holy zeal in support of Christian causes we want our political party to champion. The list of secondary pursuits is probably endless. But in the end, the fundamental question remains: "Am I a disciple of Jesus Christ?" By comparison, nothing else really matters, does it?

Today we are presented with grand opportunities for Christian witness. But capitalizing on these opportunities in a post-Christian, postmodern, and religiously pluralistic age will require a church and people steeped in both discipleship and discernment of the Spirit's work. Pluralistic, relativistic, and syncretistic forces will brush aside poorly formed Christians. However, because of what the Root and Offspring of David, the Bright and Morning Star, offers the Church, that doesn't need to happen. "Behold, I have set before you an open door, which no one is able to shut; I know that you have but little power, and yet you have kept my word and have not denied my name" (Rev. 3:8, RSV).

THE REAL WORLD

What does discipleship require? What is necessary for Christians to be fundamentally formed by the Story of God? Theologian Hans Frei has thought long and hard about this.[448] He has concluded that faithful discipleship rises or falls, depending upon which world we believe to be *most real*. He asks: Do we believe that the Bible's vision of what is truly real, valuable, and lasting is in fact the way things are and ought to be? Do we believe the Bible's "storied account" of the world and of God's people is the one that will not pass away?[449] Even more pointedly, do Kingdom values form the nerve center of our lives? Do we use those values to chip away at the "false world," and do we oppose what stands against the reign of God? Do the Scriptures direct our reading of the world, or does the world determine how we read the Scriptures? Christian discipleship, Frei says, boils down to placing oneself in the middle of the Story of God, making it the formative appraisal of everything, and being transformed by it.[450]

Those piercing questions lead to others. Like the pearl merchant in Jesus' parable who quickly recognized the "pearl of great price" (Matt. 13:46, KJV), do we recognize and value the kingdom of God when we see it, or are we duped by this present age with all its arrogant claims of being the real world? What do we make of Jesus' mandate, "Whoever would save his life will lose it; and whoever loses his life for my sake, he will save it. For what does it profit a man if he gains the whole world and loses or forfeits himself" (Luke 9:24-

25, RSV)? If Jesus' words open the door to the real world, then they close the door on another world, a world consumed by worship of self. The false world trumpets its claims through advertising and consumerism, glorification of violence and vengeance, idolatry of leisure and greed, and exaltation of state, money, and class. A thousand additional agents do its dark bidding. Theologian John Milbank says the picture is fairly simple: either the Christian story tells us how things really are, or it doesn't. And if it does, then the only access we have to how things really are is through Jesus Christ.[451]

Is it possible to follow Jesus around and still not be transformed by Kingdom values? Apparently so. The disciples were once bent out of shape over a foolish woman who acted as though Jesus was more valuable than a box of precious spices. Just think of what those ointments would have sold for! (Mark 14:3-11). On another occasion the disciples were clawing like cats over who would be the secretary of state, who would be the secretary of defense, and who would be the chairman of the board—this after Jesus had given them His "body and blood" and was about to lay down His life (Luke 22:24-27). Peter even rebuked Jesus for talking about the Cross (Mark 8:31-33). Not surprisingly, they were ill-prepared to hear, "The greatest among you must become like the youngest, and the leader like one who serves" (Luke 22:26). The truth is that living and learning in the school of Jesus, being conformed to the real world over which He is Master, will require a lifetime. No wonder He said, "If anyone would come after me, he must deny himself and take up his cross *daily* and follow me" (9:23, NIV, italics added).

Christians and Christian congregations have no more pressing assignment than to pursue Christian discipleship. Each church in the Book of Revelation that came under judgment had left off that pursuit and become occupied with lesser things.

Questions about the real world as the New Testament presents it come down to this: In all dimensions of life, what does it mean to concretely affirm that all so-called gods and lords, whatever their guise, are liars? How should we then live if in fact Christ has exposed this world's lies for what they are and has disarmed the powers and principalities of this age (Col. 2:15)? Douglas Harink says the question Paul asked the Galatian Christians is our question too. "Which power (or which god or lord)" will shape "the life of this new Jew-and-Gentile . . . community?"[452]

JUDGED BY THE REAL WORLD

The New Testament writers strive to help Christians distinguish between the truth about the world as revealed in the inaugurated kingdom of God and the old false order that the kingdom of darkness then and now supports. As we listen to the New Testament, we learn just how subtle and powerful the voices of that kingdom can be. Those young Christians in the first century struggled to solidify their allegiance to the real world and to live in the power of their risen Lord (2 Pet. 3:11-13). The apostles told them repeatedly that the real world is the world of hope. Their old world of pagan bondage is the world of despair, and it is passing away.[453]

Look around. Isn't our current situation much the same? The unrelenting pagan messages bombarding us from every which way threaten to eat like acid through Christian identity. Like a virus, the idea that "we are what we desire, what we own, and what we consume" tries to invade the cell wall of the church and sometimes manages to steal into the church's life. Ronald Sider, a contemporary Christian prophet, asks why it is that many evangelicals live "almost as sinfully as their pagan neighbors."[454] After considering survey data from the Gallup Organization and the Barna Group, and adding his own observations, Sider concludes it is because there is "widespread, blatant disobedience" to the gospel among us. There is, he says, a major crisis within evangelicalism—life not disciplined by the Holy Spirit. The data spells this out in five areas: divorce and its attending sources (such as placing self above covenant and lust above love), materialism and disregard for the poor, sexual disobedience, racism, and spousal abuse. In spite of our testimonies and songs, Sider charges, too many of us are being shaped by a world alien to the holiness of God. Many of us have embraced a cheap grace that leads to our being easily beguiled by a fallen world. Too often we have reduced the gospel to little more than forgiveness of sins and have neglected the holy life, life radically transformed in the image of Christ by the Holy Spirit.[455] We have not, he says, boldly announced the transforming power of the gospel as it applies to sin in both its individual and social, visible and sinister, forms.[456]

FORMED BY THE REAL WORLD

With Sider's analysis in mind, how might the gospel of God, the real world, become the control center for putting life's parts in order? How might it become the clearinghouse for our habits, leisure, homes, occupations, and aspirations? Robert Webber, whom we met earlier, answers that Christian congregations must become communities where people learn the habit of "living out the principles of the Kingdom" in all things. And they must be able to invite others to come and see what life formed by the gospel of God actually looks like. The postmodern world, Webber says, longs for this kind of community. "The disintegration of life has resulted in the loss of an integrating center . . . The church is not to be a mere ordinary community, but one of a special sort because it is God's second act of creation, that foretaste of the kingdom to come."[457]   *It is the only connection we have with the king to... that is here*

What would this require of congregations, individual disciples, and families? What would becoming "Story-formed people" indexed to the kingdom of God entail?[458] This question can be answered in three parts: living counterculturally, learning to speak the Christian language, and the resources that await us.

Living Counterculturally

Hans Frei and other Christian teachers say that becoming Story-formed, real-world people will require Jesus' disciples to live counterculturally and to form countercultural communities (not to be confused with isolationism, 1 Cor. 6:9-11). As were the early Christians, we are engaged on many fronts in a massive clash of worlds. Conformity with one world simply excludes conformity with the other (Luke 16:13; 1 John 3:11-18). Real-world living requires discernment, courage, and deep-seated convictions about what does and does not conform to righteousness. Christians should be alternative people who participate in an alternative world. Wesleyan theologian Henry Knight adds that, without diminishing the urgency of Christian witness in the world, congregations must be about the business of teaching Christians how to develop critical distance from the pagan culture that surrounds them. We need communities of Christians formed by the Story who can help one another live out the new life of Christ. "In a postmodern world," Knight says, "the persuasiveness of the truth claims of Christianity will depend on communities of persons whose characters reflect, and who struggle to enact, the love which was revealed in Christ."[459] For such living we may be assured that the Holy Spirit will equip us (Eph. 6:10-20).

Unless we understand Christian discipleship as living counterculturally, the New Testament will make no sense. How else are we to understand its repeated calls for holy living in the midst of a culture dominated by the powers and principalities of this age? See the two conflicting cultures in Peter's instructions: "Therefore gird up your minds, be sober, set your hope fully upon the grace that is coming to you at the revelation of Jesus Christ. As obedient children, do not be conformed to the passions of your former ignorance, but as he who called you is holy, be holy yourselves in all your conduct" (1 Pet. 1:13-15, RSV).

In the White House one day during the summer of 2003, the president of the United States walked up to a man named Robert Sutton and gave him a joyous bear hug. That would not have been noteworthy except that Robert Sutton is a convicted murderer—but that's not the end of the story. While in prison, the gospel of Jesus Christ had reached Robert. He had been radically transformed and had been introduced to a Prison Fellowship Ministries program (Inner Change Freedom Initiative) that prepares prisoners for life on the outside. Robert is now bearing witness to Christ on the outside.

The difference between Robert Sutton, the murderer, and Robert Sutton, the Christian, is Christ, the One who disarms the powers and principalities, the Author of the real world. The man who founded Prison Fellowship Ministries, Chuck Colson, is also an ex-con and looks at prisoners not through the old structures of sin and death but through the eyes of Jesus Christ who can make all things new. Colson is a counterculture person, an agent of God's alternative world.[460]

Learning to Speak the Christian Language

How did Colson and many others learn to live counterculturally? How did the real world become the beacon by which they navigate? Some have answered this question by comparing learning to be a disciple of Jesus with learning to speak and understand a language. A language can be spoken and used poorly, or it can be spoken and understood well. It all depends upon whether or not we learn and practice its rules of grammar. A friend once told me he was fluent in Spanish. I asked, "Can you read and write Spanish?" He answered, "Oh, no. I haven't bothered to learn the grammar, and I don't know the alphabet. I picked up some things from some dock workers, and then I just laced together other things on my own." My friend didn't understand that fluency requires submission to rules the speaker doesn't control and becoming versed in the vocabulary and culture with which the grammar is identified. This is best accomplished within a community that speaks the language and practices the form of life the language supports.

The Christian faith also has its rules of grammar (doctrine), vocabulary, and practice (ethics). To understand, digest, and communicate the Christian Story, the rules of Christian grammar must be learned—and learned in a community in which the language is well known. Some folk want to treat Christian discipleship as my "fluent" friend treated Spanish. They want to pick up a few words here and there, and then throw in a lot of other things on their own.

Congregations must provide rich opportunities—in worship, Bible study, study of the great Christian creeds and hymnody, evangelism, compassionate ministry, and so on—for learning Christian grammar and for practicing the form of life it supports. They must also teach the rules for reading the Bible. The idea that anyone can just pick up the Bible, read it, and interpret it according to the whims of his or her own subjective notions is nonsense. There are rules for reading the Scriptures correctly, and they are learned only in the bosom of an informed, Spirit-created, and Spirit-directed community. Apart from a community that confesses Jesus as Lord, the Bible loses its way. Christian formation, Robert Webber insists, is "ecclesial [churchly] spirituality." The Book of Acts tells us the Church is where the incarnation continues, the place where Christ is made near.[461]

Resources That Await Us

Let's face it. Christian discipleship is no cakewalk, and it isn't for the faint of heart. If success depends upon our wisdom and efforts, then we should quit now. I have listened to people who despair of living victoriously in Christ after having inventoried their own resources. "Human, all too human," they conclude. The problem is that their inventory was incomplete. Left to our own resources, none of us can be schooled by Jesus. The apostle Paul admitted this, but then said that the primary power for Christian discipleship belongs to God, not to us. Just as in the beginning, when God said, "Let light shine out of the darkness," and it did, so now by the Spirit He issues the same command in those who yield to His will. He has "shone in our hearts to give the light of the knowledge of the glory of God in the face of Christ" (2 Cor. 4:6). Augustine's prayer in the *Confessions* echoes Paul, "My whole hope is in thy exceeding great mercy and that alone. Give what thou commandest and command what thou wilt."[462]

So the good news is that all the resources necessary for Christian formation reside in the resurrected and reigning Christ ("In him the whole fulness of deity dwells bodily, and you have come to fulness of life in him" [Col. 2:10, RSV]). It is true that we fight against the "powers of this present darkness, against the spiritual forces of evil in the heavenly places" (Eph. 6:12), but it is also true that on the Cross, our Lord "disarmed the rulers and authorities, [for our sake] triumphing over them" (Col. 2:15). Therefore, we are to "take courage; [Christ has] conquered the world" (John 16:33). What Paul told the Christians in Corinth is true for us as well: "We do not wage war according to human standards, for the weapons of our warfare are not merely human [worldly, carnal], but they have divine power to destroy strongholds" (2 Cor. 10:3-4).

When I was a child, a woman named Hattie Moore could be seen walking the streets of my hometown, picking through garbage cans. Passing her one day, I said to my father, "Daddy, I feel very sorry for Hattie Moore." His response was surprising. "Son," he said, "don't feel sorry for her. Her husband was a wealthy doctor. He left all his wealth to Hattie when he died. She doesn't have to live that way!" That indelible moment eventually became a Christian parable for me.

Discipleship as this chapter has defined it will require appropriating all the resources Christ's victory has won for us. It will require unrelenting attention to the whole Christian Story.

Throughout Church history many fruitful paths to real-world living have been followed. The critical elements in all of them are that:

- They occur in and cultivate community.
- They engage the whole Christian Story.
- They equip disciples for practicing the Christian disciplines and prepare them for effective witness in the Church and in the world.

Christian discipleship involves learning to obey the law of liberty, the law of freedom. This paradox provides the key to a loving obedience that binds us to our Lord and to our neighbor (Gal. 5:1, 13-14). True Christian discipline springs from obedient faith and love and has nothing to do with bondage, legalism, or fear. Unmistakably, the New Testament tells us that the power of God working in us makes faithful discipleship a reality (Rom. 15:13; 16:25).

In the Wesleyan tradition we have access to rich treasures that are to be invested in real-world formation. They are grounded in our understanding of God and salvation.[463] We refer to these treasures as the means of grace or to participating in the means of grace. Wesley provided no exhaustive list of the means of grace because there is none. The means of grace are too varied and dependent upon the free God to permit codification. The Spirit may use any instrument He chooses to communicate God's strengthening grace to us. They include fasting, prayer, the Lord's Supper, and devotional readings. In early Methodism they included the class meetings, love feasts,[464] and special rules for holy living.[465]

Henry Knight has identified four formative markers of scriptural Christianity in the Wesleyan tradition:

- The Christian life is fundamentally lived in response to God's love.
- The Christian life flows from a transformation of the heart. Christians are more than forgiven sinners. They have been changed inwardly by God's grace. God's love cultivates in believers core affections and dispositions that govern Christian life.
- Christian affections are relational. That is, they are expressed as active love for God and for one's neighbor. Christian discipleship is inward but not isolated. It is maintained by "ongoing relationships of love to those outside the self. Christian affections are either social or nonexistent."
- Love for God and one's neighbor is Christian holiness. God is love. "To be a loving person is to be holy as God is holy." Holiness is the present experience of the rule of God in the heart. It is eternal life.[466]

Being formed by the real world—by the Story of God—defined the ministries of John and Charles Wesley. As young students at Oxford, they longed for lives wholly given to God. They were even members of the Holy Club.[467] They were mockingly called Methodists. They rigorously studied the Scriptures and earned the derisive names Bible bigots and Bible moths.[468] Judging by their efforts, they were no less zealous than Li Tianen and worlds apart from the German Christians. But like the apostle Paul, the two Wesley brothers came to see that being formed by the real world cannot be achieved through human efforts. In fact, like Paul, their strenuous efforts to achieve righteousness only increased their awareness of being sinners. But thanks be to God, the Holy Spirit showed them that "the abundance of grace and the free gift of righteousness" come first as God's free gift in Christ (Rom. 5:17). They first experienced the abundance of grace and the gift of righteousness in May 1738. Learning to live according to the real world followed from there. In line with the New Testament, their preaching and singing were marked by confidence that living victoriously as residents in God's alternative world is not a vain aspiration. It is realizable through "the Spirit of him who raised Jesus from the dead" (8:11). Good news! What they and many others have discovered is our heritage as well. Windy need not be our name.

For Reflection and Discussion

1. What are some of the false claims to reality that clamor for Christian allegiance today? Are there inherent limitations associated with reading the world through the Scriptures?
2. The question, "Do we read the world through the Scriptures, or the Scriptures through the world?" is a pivotal but difficult one. Identify some of the

major aspects of your culture against which the question has to be tested. What are some of the prime values communicated through the news and entertainment media that are directly at odds with the kingdom of God?

3. Survey the four Gospels to identify the moments in which Jesus tells His disciples they must make clear and firm choices regarding how they will be shaped.

4. What are some of the major resources for being shaped by the Story of God to which we have access? What specific contributions do they make to our formation as disciples?

5. What happens to the Christian faith when the rules of grammar are either ignored or taken lightly? What are some of the current examples of the outcome?

12

LIVING THE STORY IN A RELIGIOUSLY PLURALISTIC WORLD

Was there ever a storyteller like Jesus? His stories can become so deeply embedded in our memories that all we need to hear is the first line, and then the rest of the story plays out automatically. "A man was going down from Jerusalem to Jericho, and fell among robbers . . ." "A sower went out to sow his seed; and as he sowed . . ." "There was a man who had two sons . . ." (Luke 10:30; 8:5; 15:11). We call these stories parables.

But Jesus' stories must do more than capture our imagination. He wanted His disciples to enact them. The stories are supposed to get inside us, become incarnate, transform us, and take legs. Those who both hear *and* obey the stories are Jesus' disciples. Their lives become dramatic enactments of the gospel. They become Jesus' storied people. New Testament scholar N. T. Wright says that when Jesus told stories about the kingdom of God being at hand, He invited His hearers to audition for roles in the drama of divine fulfillment. They were to repent and become part of His kingdom story.[469] Through the "immeasurable greatness of his power" working in us, we are to be "conformed to the image of his Son" (Eph. 1:19; Rom. 8:29). Paul says that in this process, as we behold the glory of the Lord, we are being "changed into his likeness from one degree of glory to another" through "the Lord who is the Spirit" (2 Cor. 3:18, RSV).

Jesus told stories. But more importantly, He is the Story—the fulfilled Story of God. The New Testament declares that He isn't just one story among many others; He is the Master Story. He is God's definitive enactment of himself, the conclusion and interpretive key of the divine drama that has played through the ages. Jesus is the Father's grand parable, because when we see Him, we have seen the Father (John 14:9).

Have you ever seen a dramatic presentation in which the actors onstage invite members from the audience to come forward and join the story line? When this occurs the mood of the performance changes noticeably. That's what Jesus does. He isn't engaged in a monologue. He calls us to join Him onstage and assigns each of us an important role in the divine script. The Book of Acts tells us how the Church began to play its vital role in the continuing story of the risen Christ. The Epistles spell out our roles in the Story of God and tell us that our participation is reason for great joy and thanksgiving. One of the most amazing things about all this is that no one gets left out. The script is big enough for everyone to have a part. And no matter how clumsy an actor you or I might be, Jesus makes a place for us anyway. He inspires us, coaches us, corrects us, forgives us when we blow the lines or turn left when we should have turned right, and makes of us what neither we nor anyone else could have imagined.

I know of no better way to describe Christian discipleship than telling-by-living the Story of God. "Preach the gospel at all times and when necessary use words," Francis of Assisi instructed. Our participation in the Master Story should be evident in our lives—the gospel *received* becomes the gospel *reenacted*.

REENACTING THE MASTER STORY

Jesus told of some servants who owed debts to their master, and the master demanded they pay what they owed (Matt. 18:21-35). As the line moved along, the master called forward one servant who owed an enormous debt, *the equivalent of 150,000 years' wages!* Payment was impossible. In desperation the servant fell on his knees and begged, "Have patience with me, and I will pay you everything" (v. 26). How could a servant ever pay such a debt? How much patience would be necessary? His situation was hopeless.

Amazingly, instead of tossing the servant and his family into prison, the master, though it cost him, forthrightly forgave the servant "out of pity" (v. 27). Just like that! With one generous word of forgiveness, the incomprehensible debt was gone. The servant was free to go. Good news!

What impact should that moment have had on the servant? Jesus thought it should have reconstructed him from the ground up and sent him out to reflect such mercy in his own life. But did that happen?

Shortly after having been forgiven, the servant was walking down the road and spied a fellow servant. Immediately, his anger boiled. He seized the man by the throat. Servant number two must have been a miserable offender. What horrible offense had he committed? He was delinquent in a debt owed to servant number one. Given the first servant's level of anger, the debt must have been monumental. How much? *The equivalent of 100 days' wages!* We would probably assume that with a little mutual cooperation, in time the debt could have been retired.

Nothing doing! Instead, the first servant demanded full payment on the spot. Terrified, the second servant cried out, "Have patience with me, and I will pay you" (v. 29). (Sound familiar?) But servant number one had the debtor arrested and thrown into prison "until he would pay the debt" (v. 30).

Other servants standing nearby, who knew of the master's earlier forgiveness, observed the angry exchange. They beat a hasty path to the master and told him the whole sordid story. The master's anger was ignited. Calling the unforgiving servant into his presence, the master issued his judgment: "You wicked slave! I forgave you all that debt because you pleaded with me. Should you not have had mercy on your fellow slave, as I had mercy on you?" (vv. 32-33).

Then in disgust the master handed over the unforgiving servant "to be tortured until he would pay his entire debt" (v. 34). Given those conditions, he is probably still in jail.

The first servant had heard and received forgiveness. But he had accepted it for his own limited benefit. The master's astonishing forgiveness had not fundamentally *changed* him. He completely missed the importance of reenacting what had happened. He thought he could change his relationship with the master without changing his relationships with the people with whom he lived and worked. In Dietrich Bonhoeffer's words, he had "cheapened grace." He lost sight of the essential unity between *grace* and *obedience*.

The parable almost makes us cry out, "You foolish man. You ruptured the story; you didn't keep it going!" The parable shouts the inescapable relationship between faith and obedience. "Faith," said Bonhoeffer, "is only real when there is obedience, never without it, and faith only becomes faith in the act of obedience."[470] The master in the parable discovered the servant had tried to separate grace from its reenactment, its becoming enfleshed. And he abruptly put a stop to the servant's disjointed perception of the good news.

Unanticipated and unmerited forgiveness should have become the new story of the servant's life, even as it must become ours. As N. T. Wright explains, Jesus' forgiveness of sins was in itself a way of declaring that in and through Him, the kingdom of God was dawning. Isaiah (chaps. 40—50) declared that Israel would know that its long exile had ended when God finally forgave the sin that caused the exile. The hope of forgiveness anticipated the coming Kingdom. Jesus' command that His followers forgive as they had been forgiven would be their way of clearly affirming that this great, long-awaited event had arrived. To be a part of the new Kingdom community, Jesus' disciples would have to act the Kingdom even as they had received it.[471] What the master in the parable did for his servant could not be completed in some personal and private religious experience. It cried out to be publicly reenacted. Jesus said, "My mother and my brothers are those who hear the word of God and do it" (Luke 8:21). Loving Him and keeping His commandments are inseparable. "Those who abide in me and I in them bear much fruit, because apart from me you can do nothing" (John 15:5). That is what John Wesley meant when he said, "Christianity is essentially a social religion; . . . to turn it into a solitary one is to destroy it." Love for God must "shine forth in action." Attempts to reduce the gospel to one's own salvation and eternal security run "absolutely contrary to the design [of its] great Author."[472] To those who wanted to divorce the gospel from outward works, Wesley retorted, "Solitary religion is not to be found [in the Gospel of Christ]. 'Holy solitaries' is a phrase no more consistent with the Gospel than holy adulterers. The Gospel of Christ knows . . . no holiness, but social holiness."[473]

"True Christianity," Wesley insisted, "cannot exist without both inward experience and outward practice of justice, mercy and truth."[474] Long ago, God said through Jeremiah that to know Him is to "do justice and righteousness" by defending those who are "poor and needy" (Jer. 22:15, 16). After a performance by one of the greatest ballerinas of all time, someone asked her to explain the meaning of her dance. She responded, "If I could have said it, I wouldn't have needed to dance it."[475]

For the servant in the parable, as well as for us, living the Master Story should be a matter of happily bearing witness to the Master himself and to the new life His grace has created. The servant's neighbors, and ours, waited to see if he would become a storyteller.

That in a nutshell is what the Christian life and ethic are all about. It lies at the center of Jesus' ministry and all of the New Testament. The Christian ethic is a new way of doing that proceeds from a new way of being. The latter (forgiveness and the new birth) always comes first and is never to be replaced by doing. That error confuses Christian discipleship with legalism. But as Bonhoeffer and the Book of James (1:22—2:26) drive home, unless the new way of being (regeneration) expresses itself in a new way of doing, the new way of

being is in vain. This is the "indissoluble unity" between faith and obedience.[476]

The apostle Paul said this somewhat differently. To be in Christ by grace
through faith entails presenting "your bodies as a living sacrifice, holy and acceptable to God" (Rom. 12:1). This is the pattern throughout the New Testament. Christian discipleship itself proclaims the gospel, God's new order. It announces to all that the old things have passed away, and all things have become
new. Christians are "ambassadors" of the gospel (2 Cor. 5:20; see vv. 16-21).

A powerful and instructive account of the gospel reenacted in Jesus' disciples has recently emerged from the Burmese (Myanmar) jungles. Benedict
Rogers tells of visiting what was until recently a thriving community on the
Burmese side of the Moei River. The community had included a church,
school, houses, and a clinic. But when Rogers visited, he saw little more than
ashes. The Burmese Army had destroyed the community. Its inhabitants, part of
the Karen minority ethnic group, are among the nearly 4 million Burmese
Christians living under persecution. The army uses religion as a weapon of war.

This was not the first time the Christians had watched their village burn.
"We have to leave village after village, house after house," the pastor told
Rogers. "But it increases our faith." As before, the army had burned the houses, looted and destroyed the clinic, burned the crops, and set the church on
fire. The villagers had known the army was coming. Hurriedly, they had
crossed the river into Thailand and remained there until it was safe to return.
Had they not escaped, Rogers says, they would have been killed, raped, or
taken for forced labor. In time, they would move a few miles upriver and
build a new community, despite knowing that the army would eventually return to destroy the new village as well.

Kyow was among the soldiers who served the army's efforts to destroy
the Karen people. He had been forced into the Burmese Army at age 11. His
choice was to either join the army or go to jail. After three years, he decided
to escape. His officers had told him and his fellow soldiers that if they were
captured by the Karen Christians, they would suffer horrible retribution. In
spite of the warning, Kyow ran away and was indeed captured by the Karen.
But instead of abusing him as he had tortured them, the Karen Christians forgave him. Listen to 14-year-old Kyow's testimony: "With the Burma Army, life
was like hell. With the Karen, I feel safe, free and loved."[477]

The parable of the forgiving master and the unforgiving servant seems to
ask, "Do you like the way the first servant responded after the master's forgive-

ness?" Our answer is, "We don't like that part of the story at all. The servant should have continued the master's story." Jesus would respond, "Then rewrite that part of the story by telling it differently in your own lives."

In our pluralistic and postmodern world, our most important defense of the gospel will not be argumentation, even though we should be able to give an informed account of the faith we confess. The Church is deeply indebted to persons in every century who are gifted to formulate defenses of the Christian faith. While not forcing faith, they know how to challenge doubt, or perhaps answer those who simply ask about faith's meaning. The contributions of Athanasius, Augustine, Thomas Aquinas, C. S. Lewis, and Dorothy Sayers in the past, and Alister McGrath and John Polkinghorne in the present are just a few remarkable examples.[478] But each of these great defenders of the faith would quickly tell us that the most important defense happens when, through obedience to the Lord, we live the Story of God. Lacking reliance upon political privilege, coercion, and manipulation, the Story will advance on the strength of its attraction and excellence. And without fail, the Story will vindicate our trust.[479]

NINA'S AND ALLEN'S STORIES

Nina and Allen illustrate a rewrite of the servant parable's conclusion.[480] Nina Shea is touted to be the most doggedly influential advocate for religious freedom in the United States. She directs the Center for Religious Freedom (CRF) at Freedom House in Washington, D.C. Shea played a major role in brokering the 2005 end to the genocidal oppression of Christians and animists in southern Sudan.

Nina Shea is a Christian. But she has not always been. For a period of about 15 years during college, law school, and in her position with the International League for Human Rights, she didn't know any believing Christians. She describes herself during that time as a secular person who had little more than a nominal acquaintance with the Roman Catholic Church in which she was raised.

What happened to make the difference? What caused Shea to change from a secular person to a vibrant Christian who now invests her Christian faith in defending against religious persecution? The answer is simple and profound: She witnessed the faithfulness of persecuted Christians in Haiti, Nicaragua, the Dominican Republic, and elsewhere. In Haiti she met a Dutch priest and former classics professor who was starting schools and soup kitchens in "the worst slum of the Western world." In the Dominican Republic she observed a Pentecostal preacher living in a shack next to a garbage dump. "He was there, in the garbage dump, amidst the open sewers, trying to give dignity to people's lives." Shea observed Christians such as these, and many others, constantly living under the threat of violence. Yet they were steadfast in their places of witness and service, and acting out of love. "It had a powerful impact on me. I saw this repeated in country after country." Such lived-out witnesses to the power and truth of the gospel steadily led this once secular civil rights attorney to a confession of faith in Jesus Christ as Lord. Now in her 40s, her tireless advocacy for persecuted people everywhere is propelled by a love for Christ that expresses itself in love for others. "Out of a love for Christ," she says, "we are called to act."[481]

Allen owns a small manufacturing company that employs approximately 30 people. He does business in several European countries and in China. A Christian for nine years, Allen is a leader in his midwest congregation. He is 46, and he and his wife, Polly, have two teenaged children.

Like most small businesses, Allen's company was hit hard by the recession that stalled the American economy in the late 1990s. While business and profits sagged, costs for employee health insurance soared. The situation was bleak.

Out of loyalty to his employees, Allen had made a brave decision not to lay off anyone. But this required major "belt-tightening." For the company to remain competitive, cuts in salaries and benefits would have to be made. Allen planned to reduce everyone's pay and health care benefits by an across-the-board percentage.

As plans were developing, Allen participated in a Christian formation group led by one of the pastors of his congregation. Together, Allen, his minister, and seven other laypersons read and discussed *Just Generosity* by Ronald Sider.[482] They examined ways Christians could use their influence and education to practice justice and to love mercy in their spheres of influence. They studied the particular economic, domestic, and other obstacles many folk at the lower rungs of the economic ladder face each day.

Sensitive to the Holy Spirit, Allen saw dimensions of the Jesus Story that had never captured his attention before. Not only did he see, but he also acted. Unlike the selfish servant in Jesus' parable, Allen translated the Story into policy. Realizing that his lowest paid workers would be impacted by a flat percentage adjustment more than his executive team, Allen met with his leadership group. They restructured the plans to save the company.

The revised plan required the executive team—beginning with Allen—to take a higher percentage reduction in salary and benefits. As a result, the hourly employees were able to maintain suitable health coverage and to take a smaller cut in their pay. Executive compensation was capped at no more than four times the lowest amount paid to full-time employees.

The study also opened Allen's eyes to how restrictions on public transportation keep some individuals from seeking employment in his suburban company. He is now trying to make it possible for qualified people in low-income urban areas to have transportation to his plant.

In practical ways and without fanfare, Allen is extending the Jesus story to the shop floor of a midwestern American city.

EMPOWERED FOR STORYTELLING

What legitimate reason do we have for believing that our lives can tell, can reenact the Story? If we were to depend upon our own strength and wisdom, there would be none. We would be saddled with a commandment too grievous to be borne.

But the New Testament doesn't leave us to ourselves. It doesn't tell us that Jesus' expectation eventually proved to be unrealistic. And it doesn't leave us fumbling around for an answer. Rather, Jesus has now given to the Church the same Holy Spirit who empowered Him. Luke tells us that Jesus began His public ministry only after the Holy Spirit had empowered Him (Luke 3:21-22; 4:1, 18). This should not be surprising. Isaiah had prophesied this centuries before (Isa. 61:1-2; 58:6). Throughout His ministry Jesus relied upon the Holy Spirit. Through the power of the Spirit, He offered himself to the Father as atonement for our sins (Heb. 9:14). And the Father raised His Son from the grave by the power of the Holy Spirit (Rom. 8:11).

Is it any wonder why Jesus told His disciples they should not try to fulfill the Great Commission until they had been filled with the Holy Spirit? First, Jesus said, the disciples must be "clothed with power from on high" (Luke 24:49). That clothing occurred on the Day of Pentecost when the disciples were baptized with the Holy Spirit (Acts 2:1-4). In that event Jesus fulfilled the promise He had made. The risen Christ had come to the disciples through the Spirit's presence (John 14:18-24). The prophet Joel foretold this event (Joel 2:28-32; Acts 2:16-21).

Throughout the Book of Acts, as the gospel spreads from Jerusalem to Rome, the Holy Spirit inspires the Church's witness to its risen Lord (Rom.

15:19). There is a sense in which the Book of Acts remains an open book. It is still being written, and as members of Christ's Church, we today have a part in its continuation. Today, the Holy Spirit continues to fill the Church and to empower Jesus' disciples for effective witness. Nothing in the New Testament is more egalitarian than this: The Son freely sends the Holy Spirit upon all His disciples, sanctifying them as vessels of service and empowering them for holy living and effective witness. As Jesus' disciples, we have been sealed with the Spirit of promise, sealed until the day of our final redemption (Eph. 1:13; 4:30). As members of Christ's Body, the Holy Spirit is forming us as a habitation for God (2:22).

Lest there be any doubt about the power by which Christians are to live the Master Story, Paul says, "All who are led by the Spirit of God are children of God. For you did not receive the spirit of slavery to fall back into fear, but you have received the spirit of adoption" (Rom. 8:14-15). This describes the life of free, empowered, and obedient love through which the Master Story is told.

On June 16, 1976, a peaceful protest erupted into sheer violence in Soweto, a Black township 16 kilometers southwest of Johannesburg, South Africa. The uprising spread to other townships. Eventually more than 600 people were killed, making the riots the worst in South African history. The uprisings caused more destruction and deaths than any other disturbance in the country's history. They resulted from the injustices visited on "Blacks" and "Coloreds" by the apartheid laws and a long history of oppression. South Africa was teetering on the brink of all-out civil war.

In Newclare, a "Colored" township 15 kilometers away, high school student Patrick Thomas was being drawn into the rising tide of violence. Resentment against apartheid's racist universe and the oppression it had imposed on him and his people was turning Patrick into a radical. Hatred of what whites had done boiled in his soul. He was well on the way to being consumed by violence against whites and the oppression for which they stood.

But an obstacle stood in the way of Patrick's radicalization. In defiance of rigid social customs, three white missionary families had come into Newclare. Not only did they attend the churches, but they entered the people's homes to eat and fellowship with them. Knowingly violating apartheid norms, the three missionary families followed Jesus and identified with the people. Patrick could not fit these expressions of love into his accelerating hatred. The missionaries' bold acts of identifying with oppressed people turned the tide for Patrick. "On my way to violence," he says, "I could not get past their love.

They held me steady. The love they extended to an angry teenager and to my community packed salt against my soul and kept it from rotting in violence and hate."

Patrick Thomas went on to become the principal of a theological college in the Republic of South Africa. He is now completing a Ph.D. in theology, largely because, at risk to themselves, three missionary families told the Story by living it.[483]

For Reflection and Discussion

1. Christian ethics has been defined as a new way of doing that follows from a new way of being (namely, reconciled to God and made new creatures through Jesus Christ). In practical terms, what will doing the gospel involve? Why is it so important that these not be separated and that they be kept in order?

2. Identify and reflect upon persons in your experience who have reenacted the Story. How did they do this, and what was its impact on you and others?

3. Mahatma Gandhi is reported to have said that he would become Christian "if he could see one." He had been turned away from a Christian church because he was Indian. What are some of the more subtle and conspicuous ways we Christians have repeated the error that led to Gandhi's observation?

4. Can you identify persons in the public arena who are reenacting the Master Story through their lives? If so, how are they doing this, and what impact does their witness seem to have?

5. Dorothy Stang, a 73-year-old Catholic missionary, was slain in Brazil in 2005. Telling the Story cost Dorothy Stang her life. Study this modern-day martyr, or some other notable person in recent history whose life has told the Story. For an account of Dorothy Stang, go to <http://toledoblade.com/apps/pbcs.dll/article?AID=/20050215/NEWS08/502150333>.

13

ANTICIPATING THE STORY'S END

◆

"Let the heavens be glad, and let the earth rejoice" (Ps. 96:11).
"See, the home of God is among mortals" (Rev. 21:3).

At age five our granddaughter, Suzy, was beginning to experience the excitement of hearing tall tales and constructing her own. I come from a family of storytellers, and Suzy seems to have inherited the trait. Her eyes would widen as I told her about the one-armed Civil War soldier's ghost that wanders our island each full moon, looking for his lost arm.

Then, fired with imagination, Suzy would have her turn. She would sally forth to spin a yarn bigger than mine. But before long, she would run into trouble. Suzy had learned how to begin a story but not how to end it. Frustration would show. Desperately looking for a way out, she would make a sweeping but incoherent claim, hoping it would pass as a conclusion.

The Christian Story began with great promise. "Jesus came to Galilee, proclaiming the good news of God, and saying, 'The time is fulfilled, and the kingdom of God has come near; repent, and believe in the good news'" (Mark 1:14-15). But that was 2,000 years ago. Where is the Story headed now? Will its expectations be fulfilled, or have they derailed along the way?

And what about the way we have understood and spoken about the kingdom of God? Have we faithfully proclaimed its magnitude to the ends of the earth? Or have we reduced it to privatistic and parochial dimensions? Does the conclusion we anticipate fulfill the Story's confident beginning?

Throughout this book we have said that the gospel Story is for everyone, that it cannot be successfully lined up on the showroom floor as just one more religious option. The gospel is the doing of the One Eternal God and cannot be narrowly indexed to one culture or era. Instead, it applies to all cultures and eras, for it is God's good word about himself and about all people—more correctly, about *all creation*.

Let's be absolutely honest. Some ways in which Christians have told the gospel Story make it not worth telling. If it is told as a story about the superiority of one race, denomination, nation, or gender over another, then it is best left locked in the closet. If it is only told as a story about how God exists to meet *my* spiritual needs or support *my* religious causes, or about how God can coexist peacefully with the gods of greed, conflict, and oppression, then it ought to die in obscurity.

Many Christians today perpetuate another version of the gospel Story that, while popular, is not worth telling. This version of the gospel has good news for people but bad news for God's creation. It purports that God designed the gospel as an escape mechanism for people who want to "beat it out of here." Under this train of thought, the Old Testament hope for *shalom,* justice, and judgment upon the earth (Isa. 9:7) was simply wishful thinking. It isn't essential for the Story's completion. At the conclusion of all things, God will take us away from this earth to fulfill His kingdom. Let the world be damned. And that, supposedly, is how the Story ends.

Escape for us and hopelessness for God's creation—is that a Story we should be telling? Is it possible that for some of us the Story has taken a wrong turn or that some of us have confused a story of our own making with the Story of God? Even though some of us have fashioned a gospel that is world-denying, the Scriptures declare that the gospel of Jesus Christ is in fact world-affirming. Israel lived with the expectation that someday there would be renewed reason for the nations, for the heavens, for the coastlands to exult (Jer. 31:7-14). Jesus prayed, "Thy kingdom come. Thy will be done in earth, as it is in heaven" (Matt. 6:10, KJV).

This much is absolutely certain: a story of fear, escapism, and despair will hardly be heard by a pluralistic world as good reason to rejoice and embrace Christ. How could the wounded earth be set to singing by news like that? The question for us boils down to this: Is the Story of God grand enough to constitute good news for His world? The Church will have a Story worth telling only if the answer is a resounding *yes!* The next question is: Will we tell the Story as largely as its Author intends? Again, by the power of the Holy Spirit, the answer can be *yes!*—but only if God's Story is the one we tell. Before we set out to tell the Story in a religiously pluralistic and postmodern world, the Story needs to reexamine us, perhaps to correct us, even to transform us anew.

PROMISES, PROMISES

When the Bible talks about the reign of God, it has this world in mind as part of the package. It simply will not let anyone pit God against His creation or separate His kingdom from His world. The Bible includes the *world* in redemption. Much of popular Christianity has so minimized the importance of the kingdom of God and its relationship to the creation and has so reduced the gospel to individual dimensions that the importance of the world in God's plan has to be rediscovered all over again. Just what does the Bible say about how the world fits into God's Story?

The Old Testament

The Old Testament tells us that God created the world and called it good (Gen. 1—3). Ezra, speaking on the people's behalf, affirmed, "You are the LORD, you alone; you have made heaven . . . with all their host, the earth and all that is on it, the seas and all that is in them" (Neh. 9:6). Israel sang, "The earth is the LORD's and all that is in it, the world, and those who live in it; for he has founded it on the seas, and established it on the rivers" (Ps. 24:1-2; see 33:6; 136:1-9).

God the Creator is also God the Redeemer. Of all the titles Isaiah uses to speak of God, "Creator and Redeemer" are two of the most important. He is not one without being the other. Psalm 136 says that God's acts of creation and redemption manifest and vindicate His "steadfast love [that] endures forever." His faithfulness in creation *and* redemption declares that He alone is God. Psalm 33 affirms that the Lord who "loves righteousness and justice" has included "the earth" in His "steadfast love" (v. 5). Through this dual faithfulness, His name is manifest among the nations. Nothing can derail God's redemptive purposes regarding His creation.[484] Here He will reign as King.

The phrase *kingdom of God* doesn't appear in the Old Testament. But its root idea shows up often (e.g., 1 Chronicles, Psalms, Isaiah, Jeremiah, Daniel, Obadiah, and so forth). The Old Testament assumes God's reign over the creation and looks forward to a future manifestation of His reign that will achieve universal justice and righteousness. The anticipation of God's reign upon the earth carried clear implications for how Israel should structure its life in the present.[485]

But the conditions Isaiah, as well as Jeremiah, faced in Judah during its last years of existence certainly didn't show much promise for the kingdom of God on earth, and Judah certainly was not structuring its life according to Kingdom expectations. The people had flagrantly violated the covenant God made with His people, and their sin had bred more sin. They had joined themselves to their idols and had forsaken the God of steadfast love. Soon the Babylonians would destroy Judah, and many of the people would go into ex-

ile as captives. Brokenhearted, Isaiah interceded before God on behalf of rebellious Judah. He asked God to be merciful, to forgive the sins of the people,
and to restore them to faithfulness (Isa. 63:7—64:12). The answer God gave
was breathtaking. Not only would He restore His people to covenantal faithfulness, but He would also transform heaven and earth. He would "create
new heavens and a new earth" (65:17; cf. 66:22).

What became of all those grand promises? Uniformly, the New Testament declares that they are all fulfilled in Jesus Christ (2 Cor. 1:20), including,
as we shall see, the promise of new heavens and a new earth.

The New Testament

The Old Testament continuity between creation and redemption continues and even intensifies in the New Testament. The Gospel of John opens with
the words "in the beginning." This is the same phrase used in the Greek version of the Old Testament[486] to open the Book of Genesis. The verse in Genesis
ends, "God created the heavens and the earth" (1:1). John declares that the
Word of God who "became flesh and lived among us" (John 1:14) is the One
through whom God created the heavens and the earth. The astonishing claim
is that in Jesus of Nazareth, the Creator became one with His creation. He became the *created* without ceasing to be the *Creator* and revealed His glory
(doxa), His very person, in this way.

What happened on the first day of the week in Genesis? Creation began.
And what, according to John, happens on Easter morning, the first day of the
week? New creation begins. The Resurrected One whom death could not
contain, who was raised to new life by the Father, is the One through whom
the renewal of creation now proceeds. John is not alone in his confidence.
The anticipation that God will at last renew, or as Paul says, "unite all things
in him, things in heaven and things on earth" (Eph. 1:10, RSV), characterizes
the New Testament (Rom. 8; 1 Cor. 15; and Rev. 21—22).[487] This was part of
the early Christian gospel.

The nearness of Christ to His creation should settle all questions regarding its future and eliminate all thoughts regarding its abandonment. In eloquent terms, the Books of Colossians and Hebrews say that not only is Christ
the world's *origin* (Col. 1:15), but He is also its moment-by-moment *sustainer.*
"In him all things hold together," Paul said (Col. 1:17). He sustains "all things
by his powerful word" (Heb. 1:3).

That's how close Christ is to His creation. If any of us think and teach
otherwise—that the relationship between Christ and the creation is negligible

—we stray far from the Story of God. Contempt for the world finds no counterpart in the Bible.

The Incarnation forever establishes the bond between Christ and His creation. In the second century the Church struggled against a heresy known as Docetism.[488] The Docetists, as they were known, denied that God became incarnate in Jesus because they believed the creation to be unfit for such a reality. Against the Docetists, the Church insisted that any gospel that depreciates the creation, or leaves it behind, can be no gospel at all. Even now, the New Testament says, the Father in His Son is recapitulating (gathering back) all things to himself—"things in heaven and things on earth" (Eph. 1:10).

The most breathtaking statements of this hope occur in Romans and Revelation. Paul and John say that the promise God made to Isaiah regarding the transformation of the heavens and the earth will be fulfilled through Jesus Christ. In Rom. 8, Paul identifies the sons and daughters of God. He first talks about humankind's inheritance in Christ. Those who are led by the Spirit are children of God, for they are joint heirs with Christ (vv. 15-17). Then he expands the family circle; the creation also forms part of the children of God. It, too, has an inheritance in Christ. "The creation waits with eager longing for the revealing of the children of God" (v. 19). It has been "groaning in labor pains" (v. 22). But when Christ concludes His work, it will be clear that the creation's labor pains were not in vain, for it will be "set free from its bondage to decay and will obtain the glorious liberty of the children of God" (Rom. 8:21, RSV).[489]

In Rev. 21, the final vision given to John regards fulfillment of the promise made to Isaiah. The fulfillment will be part of the consummation of Christ's kingdom. "Then I saw a new heaven and a new earth; for the first heaven and the first earth had passed away, and the sea[490] was no more" (Rev. 21:1). So often Christians read this passage and interpret it as the destruction of the earth, but this is the language of renewal, fulfilling the promise to Isaiah. In the consummation, the creation will be freed from imperfections and transformed by the glory of God. Equally astonishing is the announcement made earlier in Revelation that the renewed creation will be the final dwelling place of our Lord. "Loud voices in heaven" announce that "the kingdom of the world has become the kingdom of our Lord and of his Messiah, and he shall reign forever and ever" (11:15). In response to this glorious fulfillment of God's ancient promises, the 24 elders, who symbolize the 12 patriarchs of the Old Testament and the 12 apostles, fall on their faces and worship God. Jesus' prayer, "Thy kingdom come," is fulfilled.

Isn't it amazing that even as the Roman juggernaut of persecution bore down upon the young Church, they continued to tell a Story that included promise for God's creation? Why did they do this? Because they believed that in Jesus Christ, the entire Story of God, all of His promises to us and to His creation, were being fulfilled, and they knew this to be good news for all. In the power of the Holy Spirit, such confidence was enough to compel the young Church to sing and tell of the Christ who is "making all things new" (21:5).

WAS THE STORY THIS BIG FOR JOHN WESLEY?

Did John Wesley faithfully follow in the wake of this world-affirming Story? Or did he, like so many of his theological descendents, shy away from the New Testament's promise? The answer is that Wesley rejoiced over the magnitude of redemption the Bible discloses, and he proclaimed its promise as central to the gospel. In a sermon titled "The General Deliverance," based on Rom. 8:19, Wesley declared, "He that sitteth upon the throne will soon change the face of all things, and give a demonstrative proof to all his creatures that 'his mercy is over all his works.' The horrid state of things which at present obtains will soon be at an end."[491] Wesley's sermon echoes Paul's words, affirming that the gospel applies to the creation even as it applies to us. "While God's creatures 'travail together in pain,'" He knows their suffering. He is "bringing them nearer and nearer to the birth, which shall be accomplished in its season."[492] Redemption of the creation and our redemption are inseparably joined, Wesley said. Theodore Runyon observes that for Wesley, Christians are commissioned by Christ to become partners with God in His determination to renew the fallen creation. Our own sanctification can be understood and lived out only in the larger context of a cosmic renewal of creation.[493]

A FLY IN THE OINTMENT

A universal restoration! A new creation! A story that doesn't fall apart at the end! Now that is a story worth telling far and near.

Not so fast. There is a fly in the ointment, and it seems to have stamped VETO on the New Testament's grand expectations. Based on the best evidence scientists now possess, hope and renewal seem to be absent from the creation's future. *The universe is dying.*

Physicist and theologian John Polkinghorne says, "The observable universe is condemned to eventual futility."[494] Because of what we know about the expanding universe and the life cycles of stars, we already know how the universe will end. Eventually, the universe will expand faster than gravity can hold it together,[495] halting the formation of any further stars or galaxies. Like a woman far beyond her ability to conceive, its life-bearing ability will cease, and the universe will peter out like a timer ticking down to the final second. The only remains will be the burned-out cinders of stars and the dead husks of planets. After more disintegration, only a featureless, infinitely large void will remain. And that will be the end of that.[496]

But long before all of this happens, life on earth will cease. Our middle-aged sun (about 5 billion years old) is burning its fuel at a rapid clip. We know what happens to stars like ours. When the sun's hydrogen core is depleted (in about 5 billion years), it will begin to burn the hydrogen in its shell and will brighten dramatically. Along the way, in about 1 billion years, the sun's increasing brightness will turn our earth into a hothouse. Plants will wither, carbon dioxide levels will plunge, and the oceans will begin to boil off. Life will expire. After a long series of expansions and contractions, the sun will become a red giant, 2,000 times brighter than it is now. Its atmosphere will expand to swallow Mercury and Venus, and eventually its atmosphere will envelop the Earth, reducing it to a red-hot charred ember.[497] Finally, after the sun's death has lingered for about another billion years, its core will collapse like a giant soufflé—poof! Like other dead stars, it will then become a dense and degenerate remnant.[498]

In other words, the creative and exuberant springtime our universe is currently experiencing will eventually be followed by a remarkable death. The world itself offers no reason to think that anything will happen to alter the sterility of a universe now running its mortal course.[499]

THE ANSWER FROM THE EMPTY TOMB

Unless we want to stick our heads in the sand like the proverbial ostrich, we have to admit that prospects for the New Testament's promises regarding the creation seem bleak. It appears that we now know something about the world that would have silenced the New Testament writers—had they only known. A greatly restricted Story now seems to be the wisest version.

As the death sentence for our universe becomes more generally known, we should not be surprised if thoughtful people conclude, "So much for the faithfulness of God!" and "So much for the world being His creation and the object of His care!" It will appear to many that God's faithfulness was just a fleeting blip on the screen, bracketed by eternal night. Thoughtful people might ask, "Is a dying universe compatible with, 'Bless the LORD, all his works, in all places of his dominion' (Ps. 103:22)?" Who should any longer believe that God established the sun, moon, and stars "forever and ever" (148:6)?

One tempting response to all this is to say, "Oh, well, given the length of time before our sun expires, and the even longer time before the universe runs down, the information has no practical bearing on Christian life and hope." True, it certainly doesn't immediately affect our lives or the lives of generations soon to come. But it certainly appears to place an eventual roadblock in the New Testament's path. But surely there are more urgent problems to confront, we might argue. Why not give our attention to ridding the world of disease or child abuse? Why not deal with problems worth tackling? Or someone might say, so what? My soul will be saved, and the fate of the Milky Way has nothing to do with that! Some might even say good riddance—this world was of no real value anyway.

So how should Christians respond to a dying universe? The same way we respond to the death of Jesus. *The answer is always resurrection.* Here the Christian Story either coheres magnificently or collapses pathetically. The Christian faith is either a resurrection movement or it is nothing at all (1 Cor. 15:12-19).

On Good Friday, no one had to explain to Jesus' traumatized disciples what His death meant. Death, not hope, had spoken the final word. See Him! There He hangs! Crucified like a common criminal, a victim of powers beyond His control! Dazed, broken, and confused, the disciples trudged home. The few who still had strength and interest made preparations for a respectable burial.

Had it ended there, the Story of God would have turned out to be history's grandest illusion. Death would have refuted the Son's witness regarding the Father. Anyone who thinks those exhausted disciples still had internal reservoirs of determination has not looked into their drained hearts. For all they knew, they had been hoodwinked big time.

But on the third day, the God who spoke the worlds into existence, and who upholds them by the word of His power, raised His Son from the grave (Heb. 1:2; 11:3). "He is not here, but has risen" (Luke 24:5). He is risen indeed! And *everything* changed. For the Christian Story, *everything* rises or falls with Jesus' crucifixion and resurrection. There all Christian hope resides.

When the Father raised His Son from the dead, He confirmed Christ's faithful testimony. All Jesus had said about the Father, about the Kingdom, about the gospel, and about God's reign are true. His resurrection definitively announces that the Creator—not death, sin, alienation, or decay—*has the final word in all creation* (Rom. 8:38-39). Death had celebrated prematurely, for the One who drained the bitter cup has now pillaged death and hell's stronghold. He has nailed sin and death to the Cross (Rom. 7:21—8:8; Col. 2:15). "The renewal of the earth," Dietrich Bonhoeffer said, "begins at Golgotha, where the meek One died, and from thence it will spread."[500] Easter is the time when the true light shines, and all darkness is put to flight (John 1:5; cf. 20:1; Heb. 2:13-15).[501]

> *Mighty Victim from on high, hell's fierce powers beneath Thee lie;*
> *Thou hast conquered in the fight, Thou hast brought us life and light;*
> *Now no more can death appall; now no more the grave enthrall;*
> *Thou hast opened Paradise, and in Thee Thy saints shall rise.*[502]

In the strength of Christ's resurrection *alone,* Christians confront death in *all* its forms—including the death of the universe. Jesus' resurrection was not something that happened just for Him. It has cosmic importance. Jesus' resurrection confirms that the Father has entrusted His Son with rescuing the world and bringing it to order. So, by the Spirit, Jesus spreads the fruit of His resurrection upon us and upon the whole creation. That is the Story, and the Church's mission is to faithfully tell this Story. Not salvation *from the world,* but salvation *of the world* is its joyous song.

On the authority of Christ's resurrection, Paul teaches that those who place their trust in Jesus will one day be raised from the grave, just as Jesus was. Paul calls Jesus' resurrection the firstfruits. This means there is more to come. The full harvest will look like the first and will include Jesus' followers. "In fact Christ has been raised from the dead, the first fruits of those who have died. For since death came through a human being, the resurrection of the dead has also come through a human being; for as all die in Adam, so all will be made alive in Christ. But each in his own order: Christ the first fruits, then at his coming those who belong to Christ" (1 Cor. 15:20-23).

Paul doesn't know exactly how this will happen and openly admits it. He knows that as far as human understanding can take us, the promise of our resurrection seems absurd, but no more absurd than Jesus' resurrection. Paul knows that the God who raised Christ from the grave "will give life to [our] mortal bodies also through his Spirit that dwells in you" (Rom. 8:11). He isn't much impressed by those who say, "I don't understand how this could happen, therefore it can't happen," or, "The data doesn't predict resurrection, therefore it won't occur" (1 Cor. 15:36).

Paul compares the Resurrection to planted seed. As any gardener knows, the seed that is sown is *not* what pops out of the ground after germination. "As for what you sow, you do not sow the body that is to be, but a bare seed, perhaps of wheat or of some other grain" (1 Cor. 15:37). But the gardener also knows that the plant that springs from the seed is *continuous* with what he or she planted. Both *discontinuity* and *continuity* are necessary for the seed's resurrection. If there were only *continuity,* the gardener would just get more seed. If there were only *discontinuity,* then he or she might harvest peanuts while expecting watermelons. The gardener counts on receiving the same and upon receiving much more.

So it is with the Christian hope of resurrection. "What is sown is perishable, what is raised is imperishable. It is sown in dishonor, it is raised in glory. It is sown in weakness, it is raised in power. It is sown a physical body, it is raised a spiritual body" (vv. 42-44). All of this is because of Jesus' resurrection. "The last Adam became a life-giving spirit" (v. 45).

What is true of Jesus' resurrection, the sprouting seed, and the hope of the resurrection *will also* be true of the creation's renewal. A real death and a real resurrection, a restoration and transformation, a new heaven and a new earth. The VETO a dying universe stamps on Christian hope certainly seems staggering, for none of the empirical data can underwrite Christian hope. But when has death ever inspired hope? We know nothing more about how God will fulfill His promise to His world than Paul knew about how grain sprouts from seed. But we know that the Christian pattern of *continuity* and *discontinuity,* of death and resurrection, will be followed again—all because of Easter. That is the way of the Creator-Redeemer God.

THE "END" OF THE STORY

Knowing that our hope lies in Christ's resurrection must shape the way we tell the Story. The Scriptures promise redemption for us and for the whole creation. The notion that somehow salvation is about me, and the world be damned, is a misrepresentation of the Story, and it is not a story that should be told to this broken, pluralistic world. If the story we tell is incoherent and incomplete, we should not be surprised if honest inquirers listen and then walk away. Of all people, Christians should demand credibility of themselves.

And unless we want to alienate much of the human race, we cannot show disregard for the world. Often, non-Christians show a greater regard for God's creation than do some of us who name God as the Creator. What God intends for His creation is something that has to be revealed and communicated through our lives, particularly in a postmodern world where people have rediscovered the creation. Think of the new age movement that emphasizes the unity between humans and nature. Many people perceive the Christian faith as standing over against nature, but this understanding is not faithful to the Christian Story. A prominent part of our world is waiting to hear the Good News. They already know about despair. Only a story of resurrection magnitude will attract their attention.

Not all religions seek redemption for creation, however. Hindus and Buddhists, for example, look forward to a release from this world. But the Story no more panders to their perceptions and expectations than it panders to ours. If that were the case, we could go around telling the Story to accommodate religious pluralism. But instead of accommodating our expectations, the Story transforms them. And if we are going to be storytellers, then we should tell the gospel Story as God defines it. This is really the only story the Holy Spirit is going to use. We have to be faithful to the biblical picture of restoration. If there is a portion of the creation that God just leaves behind, then we don't really have redemption; we have a salvaging expedition on our hands. But the kingdom of God Jesus inaugurates, the Kingdom sealed in His resurrection, leaves no part of creation behind.[503] But may explain it.

The pivotal importance of Jesus' resurrection brings us back to the chapter's beginning: What is the Story's end? Normally as we anticipate a story's conclusion we look forward to new information, to something the author has withheld until now. But the conclusion of the gospel Story cannot be found by flipping to page 300. Instead, we need to turn back to page 1. The *Alpha* is the *Omega*. Fundamentally, there will be no surprises because Jesus is the end of the Story.

The word *end* is one way of stating the Greek word for goal or purpose *(teleos)*. When something has achieved its purpose, it has achieved its end. So to say that Jesus is the end of the Story is to say that He fulfills the counsel of God's will (Eph. 1:11). God's design for His world has been revealed in Christ, and in Him, God's yes of redemption, of restoration, of new creation has been spoken. This is the way we should understand Paul's statement in Ephesians: "[God] has made known to us the mystery of his will, according to his good pleasure that he set forth in Christ, as a plan for the fullness of time, to gather up all things in him, things in heaven and things on earth" (1:9-10). Simply and grandly, the Christ revealed through the Spirit *is the future,* the end, of God. "You can bank on that," Paul says (the Holy Spirit is God's "earnest of our inheritance" [v. 14, KJV]). The future will be a faithful unfolding of the One who was dead, buried, raised, and who now sits at the right hand of the Father.

Knowing that Jesus is the end provides the basis for Christian hope, which has everything to do with joy and confidence and nothing to do with sensationalism, uncertainty, or shocking surprises. God's end for us in Christ, says theologian Michael Lodahl, is that love might flourish—"that we might become lovers of God and all of our neighbors."[504] In other words, our end is to look like God's end—Jesus. Every promise God has made to us and to His creation to bring about this end is founded upon the risen and ascended Lord.

Now there is a Story worth telling—to everyone!

For Reflection and Discussion

1. Examine the make-or-break importance of Jesus' resurrection in 1 Cor. 15.
2. Search Psalms and the Prophets for the promises God made to His creation. In Psalms, examine the voice of the creation as it praises God.
3. Interview five Christians and ask them about the role of the redemption of creation in the gospel Story. Also ask them to tell you what they believe the Book of Revelation teaches regarding the creation's future.
4. Examine the relationship between Jesus' resurrection and Christian hope in the Epistles of Paul and Peter.
5. Reflect on ways in which some Christians today portray the fulfillment of the kingdom of God in ways that don't actually parallel the New Testament.
6. Examine the ways in which the New Testament presents Jesus as the future of God, our future, and the future of the world.

CONCLUSION

When Martiyah, a Buddhist, moved to Bangkok from the northeastern province of Si Sake, she found a job as a housekeeper in a Chinese home located beside a church. Each morning she swept the sidewalk in front of the house as part of her chores. As she did, a man named Simon who worked at the church befriended her. In their conversations, Simon would tell Martiyah of his faith in Jesus Christ. One day he invited her to attend the Christmas program. With her employer's permission, Martiyah entered a church for the first time.

In time she began to attend Sunday services. She started asking how she, too, might know that her sins had been forgiven. As time permitted, Martiyah began to study the Bible with an older woman in the congregation. The more she studied, the more she understood why Jesus is called the Savior of the world. As Martiyah studied, the Holy Spirit was teaching her and drawing her to faith. Soon the day came when she confessed her faith in Christ and was born anew. She had been led with cords of love. Since then, Martiyah has continued to grow as a disciple. Now, says missionary Michael McCarty, she is telling others about Jesus and also teaching discipleship to new Christians.

Martiyah's story illustrates the reasons for telling the gospel Story that we explored in the preceding chapters. It shows why patient confidence in the grace of God will not disappoint. An amazing thing about those who faithfully tell the Story of God is that, as important as their witness is, they are not the primary storytellers—God is. This knowledge and confidence are why Christians should never accept the notion that the diversity of religions must be adopted as settled reality. Simon, who told the Story to Martiyah, was an instrument. The Holy Spirit reached through him, stretched beyond Martiyah's identity as a Buddhist, and provoked a hunger that only the Bread of Life could satisfy—as indeed He did. What is evident in Martiyah's story is that Simon respected her as a person even while being confident that the Story of Jesus was intended for her. His witness illustrates that the intersection between religious pluralism and the power of the gospel is our confidence in the Story's beauty and the Spirit's faithfulness. Simon and the others who led Martiyah to Christ knew how to embody Paul's statement in 2 Corinthians: "We refuse to practice cunning or to falsify God's word; but by the open statement of the truth we commend ourselves to the conscience of everyone in the sight of God" (4:2). Paul's confidence, and ours, was in the God who said, "Let light shine out of darkness," and who also shines in the hearts of believers "to give the light of the knowledge of the glory of God in the face of Jesus Christ" (v. 6).

No higher privilege is given the children of God than to become instruments through whom God tells the gospel Story, to be seized and fired by the gospel's promise and power of "new creation." This is a fundamental ministry to which Christ calls us all. It is the "priesthood of all believers."[505] If we are faithful to our charge, Charles Wesley sang, we will "glorify God" *and* "serve the present age."

Let us pray that the Holy Spirit will empower us for storytelling so that we may make known Christ's riches in all the earth. May the Good News be heard that the kingdom of righteousness and peace has begun and is now being fulfilled by Him who is Lord of all. And let us pray that the Father will endow us with a vision of transformation that matches the Story's magnitude and excellence. Amen.

NOTES

Introduction

1. I make a distinction between the ideology of religious pluralism and the fact of religious pluralism. Religious pluralism as such just describes the diversity of religions and our consciousness of that diversity as characteristic of our current situation. I understand *ideology* to mean "an integrated system of beliefs, assumptions, and values" that reflects "the needs and interests of a group or class at a particular time in history" (David Brion Davis, *The Problem of Slavery in the Age of Revolution 1770—1823* [Ithaca, N.Y.: Cornell University Press, 1975], 14). The term is not meant to be pejorative in any sense.

I recognize that *multicultural* is a term often used in conjunction with *religious pluralism*. Multicultural societies are also multireligious. But the two terms do not have the same meaning. Hence, I use *religious pluralism* throughout the book while recognizing that it includes multiculturalism.

2. Alan Race, *Christians and Religious Pluralism: Patterns in the Christian Theology of Religions* (Maryknoll, N.Y.: Orbis Books, 1982), 1.

3. Ibid., 3. Race cites Max Warren, then general secretary of the Church Missionary Society, as saying that the confrontation between Christian belief and agnostic science will turn out to be more like child's play when compared to the encounter between Christianity and the other world religions.

4. This "message" to Christians was foreshadowed by the 1932 report of the Layman's Inquiry, *Rethinking Missions*. Under the chairmanship of philosopher William Ernest Hocking, the report declared that the replacement of other religions by Christianity should yield to a process of mutual enrichment.

5. Gullah is an English-based Creole dialect that has been strongly influenced by West African languages such as Vai, Mende, Twi, Ewe, Hausa, Yoruba, Igbo, and Kikongo. It developed as a way for slaves in the Sea Islands of South Carolina, Georgia, and north Florida to communicate with Europeans and members of African tribes other than their own. The origin of the term is debatable. The Gullah-speaking people are called Geechees in Georgia. One can still hear Gullah spoken on some of the Sea Islands. Transliterated, the first part of the Lord's Prayer reads in Gullah: Ow-uh farruh, hu aht in heh-wn, hallow-ed be dy name, dy kingdom come, dy will be done on ut as it done in heh-wn.

6. *The LowCountry Weekly* (December 11-17, 2002).

7. David B. Barrett, ed., et al., *World Christian Encyclopedia: A Comparative Survey of Churches and Religions in the Modern World*, 2nd ed. (2 vols.) (New York: Oxford University Press, 2001). Barrett is affiliated with the Global Evangelization Movement in Richmond, Virginia, and with Pat Robertson's Regent University in Virginia Beach where he is a research professor of missiometrics—the science of missions.

8. The quote by Barrett is located in Toby Lister, "Oh, Gods," *Atlantic Monthly* (February 2002), *Atlantic Monthly Archives* located at <http://www.theatlantic.com/issues/2002/02/lester.htm>.

In 2004 an excellent guide to the many new religions that crowd our world was published (*New Religions: A Guide,* ed. Christopher Partridge [New York: Oxford University Press, 2004]). The book provides a brief introduction to a mind-boggling inventory of big and small religious groups.

9. Charles Krauthammer, "What the Uprising Generation Wants," *TIME* (November 21, 2005), 162. Krauthammer is quoting Bernard Lewis, the Cleveland E. Dodge Professor of Near Eastern Studies Emeritus at Princeton University and specialist in the history of Islam and the interaction between Islam and the West.

10. Ye'or is quoted by Niall Ferguson, "The Widening Atlantic," *Atlantic Monthly* (January/February 2005), 40-42; "A Muslim Europe?" *Atlantic Monthly* (January/February 2005), 58. Bat Ye'or, *Eurabia: The Euro-Arab Axis* (Cranbury, N.J.: Associated University Press, 2005).

11. Oriana Fallaci, *The Force of Reason* (New York: Rizzoli, 2005). Richard John Neuhaus points to a flourishing Roman Catholic Church in Poland as an important exception to this picture (Richard John Neuhaus, "The New Europes," *First Things* 156 [October 2005], 12-15).

12. Currently 5.2 million. This represents a decrease of 300,000 between 1993 and 2003. Based on the 2003 report of the National Jewish Population Survey. The Jewish population of the U.S. is older than in 1993, despite a large wave of immigrants from the former Soviet Union. Forty-seven percent of Jews marry non-Jews, and two-thirds of their children are not being raised as Jews (as reported in *First Things* 137 [November 2003], 83).

13. *Pluralism Project Newsletter* (October 20, 2005).

14. *American Passages: Diverse Origins and Common Destinies in the United States* (Time, Inc., 1995), 40-41.

15. Diana L. Eck, *A New Religious America: How a "Christian Country" Has Become the World's Most Religiously Diverse Nation* (San Francisco: HarperSanFrancisco, 2002), as quoted by the Pluralism Project of Harvard University <http://www.pluralism.org/publications/new_religious _america/index.php>). See also James A. Herrick, *The Making of the New Spirituality: The Eclipse of the Western Religious Tradition* (Downers Grove, Ill.: InterVarsity Press, 2003).

16. The Pluralism Project of Harvard University.

17. See William R. Hutchison, *Religious Pluralism in America: The Contentious History of a Founding Idea* (New Haven, Conn.: Yale University Press, 2003).

18. The Baha'i faith is an independent world religion with several million adherents worldwide, representing almost all nationalities, ethnic groups, classes, professions, and religious backgrounds.

19. See Margot Adler, *Drawing Down the Moon: Witches, Druids, Goddess-Worshippers, and Other Pagans in America Today* (New York: Penguin Group USA, 1997).

20. Wilfred Cantwell Smith, *The Faith of Other Men* (New York: Harper Torchbooks, 1972), 133. For a tour of contemporary American neo-pagan options go to <http://www.pluralism .org/weblinks/weblink_direct.php?tradition=Pagan>.

Smith rejected the notion of "ultimate revelations" binding upon all persons. He hoped for a worldwide religious community of "non-ultimate revelations." Islam would be seen as the personal ultimate for Muslims, Christ the personal ultimate for Christians, and so on through the religions.

21. Karl Barth, *Dogmatics in Outline* (New York: Harper and Row, Publishers, 1959), 80.

Part I (Introduction)

22. Ár nDraíocht Féin: A Druid Fellowship, Inc., 2003 <http://www.adf.org/core/>.

23. The German New Testament theologian Peter Stuhlmacher has given us an excellent summary of how Paul viewed the work of righteousness the Father accomplished in His Son by the Spirit. Stuhlmacher says that the gospel of righteousness Paul proclaimed is not exhausted in the message of the forgiveness of sins for individual Jews and Gentiles. More broadly, the gospel of God's righteousness involves the saving message that must be passed on to people everywhere, concerning the end-time rule of God that He will establish through Christ. Spreading the gospel of God's righteousness moves history toward its goal. God's justification (reconciliation) of sinners through His Son is the definitive manifestation of God's creative, gracious dealings with Gentiles and Jews. For Paul and for the New Testament generally, Christ is the "messianic Lord of the world appointed by God. As such, he has a threefold task. He is God's guarantor of the justification of all those who confess him as Lord and Savior from the day of his exaltation to the right hand of God until the final judgment (cf. 1 Cor. 1:30; Rom. 8:34). He is the judge of the world, appointed by God himself (cf. 2 Cor. 5:10; Rom. 2:16). And he has the mission of delivering 'all Israel' (cf. Rom. 11:26). The goal of his activity is the establishment of God's kingdom and reign (cf. 1 Cor. 15:23-28)" (Peter Stuhlmacher, *Revisiting Paul's Doctrine of Justification: A Challenge to the New Perspective* [Downers Grove, Ill.: InterVarsity Press, 2001], 30-31).

24. Paul Varo Martinson's *Families of Faith: An Introduction to World Religions for Christians* (Minneapolis: Fortress Press, 1999) provides a reliable basic introduction to the world religions. Michael Molloy's *Experiencing the World's Religions: Tradition, Challenge, and Change* (Mountain View, Calif.: Mayfield Publishing Company, 2002) is a more extensive introduction.

25. Paul F. Knitter, *No Other Name? A Critical Survey of Christian Attitudes Toward the World Religions* (Maryknoll, N.Y.: Orbis Books, 1985), 6.

26. Rev. Dr. George F. Regas, "Interpreting Christ in a Pluralistic World," a sermon delivered in the Washington National Cathedral, the Fifth Sunday of Easter, April 24, 2005. The full text of the sermon is available at <http://www.cathedral.org/cathedral/worship/gfr050424.html>.

27. Knitter, *No Other Name?* 4.

28. This picture of Europe stands in sharp contrast to the huge and growing Christian populations in the global south (the areas that we often think of primarily as the third world). See Philip Jenkins' discussion of the growth of Christianity in the global south in "The Next Christianity," *Atlantic Monthly* (October 2002), 53-68. The article is a condensation of Philip Jenkins, *The Next Christendom: The Coming of Global Christianity* (New York: Oxford University Press, 2002).

29. Jeff M. Sellers, "Letter from Spain: Stony Ground for the Gospel," *Christianity Today International/Books & Culture Magazine* (March 24, 2003) <http://www.christianitytoday.com /books/web/2003/mar24.html>. At least some of the opposition would stem from the fact that Spain is a predominantly Roman Catholic country. But much of it would spring from the fact that Spain is a country in the throes of advancing secularism. In 2004 Prime Minister Jose Luis Rodriguez Zapatero pushed for adoption of four draft laws designed respectively to introduce fast-track divorce, liberalize the existing abortion law, extend to same-sex couples the existing conjugal rights of heterosexual married couples, including the right to adopt children, and ending compulsory—Catholic—religious education in Spain's state schools. Archbishop Carlos Amigo of Seville charged, "The secular state was persecuting religion." Other church officials charged that the proposed laws constituted a road map for undermining religion and enforcing secularism in

Spain (Roland Flamini, "Spanish Church Battles New Laws," United Press International [October 8, 2004] <http://www.washtimes.com/upi-breaking/20041007-045313-6360r.htm>).

Chapter 1

30. Sydney E. Ahlstrom, *A Religious History of the American People* (New Haven, Conn.: Yale University Press, 1972), 154.

31. <http://www.bahai.org/features/intro>

32. "Woman Loves Diversity of Baha'i Faith," *Tennessean* (September 27, 2003), section 4A. Joyce Jackson is managing editor for School Age Notes, a publishing company specializing in materials for day-care centers.

33. Peter Berger, *The Sacred Canopy* (New York: Doubleday, 1967), 126.

34. D. A. Carson, "Christian Witness in an Age of Pluralism," *God and Culture: Essays in Honor of Carl F. H. Henry,* eds. D. A. Carson and John Woodbridge (Grand Rapids: Eerdmans, 1993).

35. Alister E. McGrath, "A Particularist View: A Post-Enlightenment Approach," *More than One Way? Four Views on Salvation in a Pluralistic World,* eds. John Hick, Dennis L. Okholm, and Timothy R. Phillips (Grand Rapids: Zondervan Publishing House, 1995), 152.

36. See James L. Fredericks, *Faith Among Faiths* (New York: Paulist Press, 1999), 104-8.

37. Race, *Christians and Religious Pluralism*, 1.

38. For example, Roman priests would examine the entrails of a goat to learn whether the shape of the liver indicated divine favor or disfavor for an anticipated action. This sort of religious involvement in public affairs extended to military campaigns. "Even local celebrations which included athletic contests, free food, jugglers, magicians, speeches and parades, would also include sacrifice to the local deities. For the people of Paul's world, any public activity that lacked a religious dimension would have been unthinkable" (Paul J. Achtemeier, Joel B. Green, and Marianne Thompson, *Introducing the New Testament: Its Literature and Theology* [Grand Rapids: Eerdmans, 2001]), 285-86.

39. Douglas Harink, *Paul Among the Postliberals: Pauline Theology Beyond Christendom and Modernity* (Grand Rapids: Brazos Press, 2003), 209. N. T. Wright says that in the Eastern Mediterranean where Paul ministered to the Gentiles, the imperial cult—the worship of Caesar, was "the fastest growing religion." He says that whereas in the West restraints were placed upon the imperial cult, this was not true in the East. "In the East—and the East here starts, effectively, in Greece, not just in Egypt—the provinces saw no need for restraint. With a long tradition of ruler-cults going back at least to Alexander the Great, local cities and provinces were in many cases only too happy to demonstrate their loyalty to the emperor by establishing a cult in his honour, and . . . by vying for the privilege of looking after his shrine" ("Paul and Caesar: A New Reading of Romans," originally published in *A Royal Priesthood: The Use of the Bible Ethically and Politically,* ed. C. Bartholemew [Carlisle: Paternoster, 2002], 173–93) <http://www.ntwrightpage.com/Wright_Paul_Caesar_Romans.htm>.

John D. Crossan and Jonathan L. Reed add that Roman imperial theology "consolidated the various parts of the empire into a single whole and was the glue that held the . . . civilized world together" (John Dominic Crossan and Jonathan L. Reed, *In Search of Paul: How Jesus's Apostle Opposed Rome's Empire with God's Kingdom* [New York: HarperSanFrancisco, 2004], 142).

40. The great triad composed of Jupiter, Juno, and Minerva held the supreme place. Others were added.

41. The one religion the Romans did suppress on occasion was Druidism, because of its practices of human sacrifice and cannibalism (Achtemeier, Green, and Thompson, *Introducing the New Testament,* 284).

For a statement of the rationale behind Rome's control over what it believed to be excessive forms of religion, see Crossan and Reed, 249-57.

42. How did the Romans justify their supposed superiority? They believed they were superior in reason. That is why they were able to triumph over all others. The Roman statesman, orator, and philosopher Cicero (103-46 B.C.) said the Romans won their empire because of "piety and religion," characteristics they included in how they understood reason (*Introducing the New Testament,* 288).

43. Harink, *Paul Among the Postliberals,* 209-10.

44. Thorsten Moritz, "Religious Pluralism and Universalism in Ephesians," *One God, One Lord: Christianity in a World of Religious Pluralism,* eds. Andrew D. Clarke and Bruce W. Winter (Grand Rapids: Baker Book House, 1992), 103.

45. Ibid., 91.

46. Niels C. Nielson Jr. et al., *Religions of the World* (New York: St. Martin's Press, 1983), 69-71.

47. Harink, *Paul Among the Postliberals,* 210.

48. Augustine, *The City of God,* Part Two, Book VI, Chapter 1 (Garden City, N.Y.: Image Books, 1958), 120.

49. The best description I have read of how Romans viewed the Christians they were persecuting is provided by Richard E. Rubenstein, *When Jesus Became God: The Struggle to Define Christianity During the Last Days of Rome* (New York: Harcourt, Inc., 1999), 27-34.

50. The Romans began the practice of deifying their dead rulers with Julius Caesar. In 44 B.C. he permitted erection of a statue of himself with the inscription, *Deo Invicto* ("to the unconquered god"). The adopted son of the deified Julius Caesar, Augustus Caesar (63 B.C.-A.D. 14), was titled *divi filius*—son of a god. Augustus did not personally claim divine status during his lifetime. Instead, he permitted the worship of his *genius* (his vital energy and generative power) and *numen* (divine will). After he died, his successor and adopted son, Tiberius, arranged to have him deified. In A.D. 185 Emperor Commodus issued a decree that "sacrifices should be made to the gods and to the statue of the emperor Commodus." Christians who refused to comply were persecuted without exception. They were tortured and many were massacred. But deification of the emperors was not uniform.

Acceptance of the national religion in antiquity was an obligation incumbent on all citizens; failure to worship the gods of the state was equivalent to treason. This universally accepted principle is responsible for the various persecutions suffered by Christians before the reign of Constantine. Christians denied the existence of the gods of the state pantheon and therefore refused to worship them. They were consequently regarded as atheists. It is true that the Jews also rejected the gods of Rome and yet escaped persecution. But from the Roman standpoint the Jews had a national religion and a national God, Jehovah, whom they had a legal right to worship.

51. During the persecution that included the martyrdom of St. Polycarp (A.D. 69-155) the persecutors cried out "Away with the Atheists; let Polycarp be sought for" (*The Martyrdom of Saint Polycarp, Bishop of Smyrna,* 3.2).

52. Achtemeier, Green, and Thompson, *Introducing the New Testament,* 286. The accusation appears in Tacitus, *Annals* 15:44, and Pliny, *Letters* 10:96.

53. *Paleopagan* is a term used to describe supposedly original polytheistic, nature-centered religious beliefs and practices of tribal Europe, Africa, Asia, the Americas, Oceania, and Australia. *Neo-pagan* is a term that describes contemporary efforts to revive and practice what many people believe paleopagan religions taught.

54. Ár nDraíocht Féin: A Druid Fellowship, Inc., 2003 <http://www.adf.org/core/>.

55. Douglas Harink discusses this distinction between the first-century Church and our day. He quotes Jonathan Wilson with whom he partly agrees. But Harink thinks the distinction between the two eras is not as sharp as Wilson thinks (*Paul Among the Postliberals,* 210-13).

56. Alfred N. Whitehead, *Process and Reality: An Essay in Cosmology* (New York: The Free Press, 1978), 342 [520]. J. N. Hillgarth says that one of the major reasons the gospel was attractive among the Greco-Roman masses was that the Church provided space for those the state had been unable to absorb. "The Greco-Roman world had seen the poor as negligible and slaves merely as 'talking-stock, who lived in barracks on large estates close to the animals ("semi vocal stock") and were hardly, if at all, better treated.'" By contrast, Christians insisted "on paying the same attention to their sick slaves' salvation as to that of their relations" (ed. J. N. Hillgarth, *Christianity and Paganism: The Conversion of Western Europe, 350-750* [Philadelphia: University of Pennsylvania Press, 1969], 4).

57. Musa Dube, *Postcolonial Feminist Interpretation of the Bible* (Duluth, Ga.: Chalice Press, 2000), 3.

58. Harink, *Paul Among the Postliberals,* 211.

59. Ibid., 212.

60. Marcia Z. Nelson, *The Gospel According to Oprah* (Louisville, Ky.: Westminster John Knox Press, 2005), 83. Nelson has written what has to be described as a surface treatment of Oprah Winfrey's religious beliefs. Surprisingly, she says, "I don't know what her personal religious beliefs are" (83). Speaking approvingly, Nelson says that "Oprah's gospel entertains; it's a gospel of good news" (86). Quoting Phyllis Tickle, Nelson says that Oprah's gospel has been good news for American culture for a long time. It is good news in part because it doesn't require sacrifice and discipline. "If entertainment required sacrifice and discipline, it wouldn't be entertainment" (86).

61. Ibid., 86.

62. "The Gospel According to Oprah," Watchman Fellowship of Alabama <http://www.wfial.org/index.cfm?fuseaction=artNewAge.article_1>.

63. "Woman Loves Diversity of Baha'i Faith," the *Tennessean* (September 27, 2003).

64. Bill Easum, *Leadership on the Other Side: No Rules, Just Clues* (Nashville: Abingdon Press, 2000), 73.

65. Told to the author by Floyd Cunningham, Ph.D., dean of the faculty, Asia-Pacific Nazarene Theological Seminary, May 1, 2003.

Chapter 2

66. Doug is regional communications coordinator for the Asia-Pacific Region, Church of the Nazarene. He oversees the production and/or facilitation of all broadcast, video, and literature projects in the region. He also teaches at Asia-Pacific Nazarene Theological Seminary, Manila, in the Christian Communications program. Doug and his wife, Angie, live in Singapore.

67. One of the most complete histories of religious pluralism in the West is *Religious Pluralism in the West: An Anthology,* ed. David George (Malden, Mass.: Blackwell Publishers, 1998). The history begins with the Bible and proceeds to post-World War II declarations.

68. Veli-Matti Kärkkäinen presents an excellent short history of how religious pluralism as we know it developed (Veli-Matti Kärkkäinen, *An Introduction to the Theology of Religions: Biblical, Historical, and Contemporary Perspectives* [Downers Grove, Ill.: InterVarsity Press, 2003], Part Two).

69. Knitter, *No Other Name?* 2.

70. In the course of several centuries after its founding, the Islamic world "became the center of Eurasian science as well as commerce. It was here, not in Europe, that the greatest achievements of classical Mediterranean philosophy and science were preserved for the future" (David Christian, *Maps of Time: An Introduction to Big History* [Los Angeles: University of California Press, 2004], 370-71). In Muslim-controlled Spain, for much of the 10th century Christians and Jews (called Dhimmi, non-Muslims) lived under measured toleration.

71. Christian, *Maps of Time,* 370. Manichaeism was one of the major ancient religions that began in Persia in the third century and quickly spread East and West, reaching Rome by A.D. 280. It was purported to be the true and fulfilling synthesis of all the known religions. Its founder was Mani (c. A.D. 210-276). He believed that he was the "Paraclete of the Truth" promised in the New Testament. Manichaeism professed to explain the origin, the composition, and the future of the world, and was a sworn enemy of Christianity. Basically Manichaeism taught that there are two everlasting, independent, and irreconcilable principles or realms of reality: the good principle of light and peace and the principle of darkness and conflict. The good principle dwells in the realm of light and accounts for all that is good and peaceful in the world. The evil principle dwells in the realm of darkness and accounts for all evil and conflict in the world. The two realms can never be reconciled. We can quickly see a major difference between Manichaeism and Christianity, which taught that there is only one God who created everything. For Christianity, evil in the world is the result of God's good creation being distorted by sin, not the result of an independent source and realm of being.

72. David Christian says that the huge volume of new information that flowed into Europe had its earliest and greatest impact on intellectual life and activity. "The digestion of this new mass of information transformed European intellectual life. Margaret Jacob writes that 'the cumulative effect' of the travel literature of the sixteenth and seventeenth centuries 'had been to call into question the absolute validity of the religious customs long regarded, specially by the clergy, as paramount'" (*Maps of Time,* 393). Christian is quoting Margaret Jacob, *The Cultural Meaning of the Scientific Revolution* (Philadelphia: Temple University Press, 1988), 109. Christian primarily credits the emergence of the modern scientific project to this explosion of information. "This infusion of new information and knowledge is the best available explanation for the radical skepticism about traditional accounts of reality that lies at the heart of the modern scientific project and that first becomes apparent in Europe in the sixteenth century" (*Maps of Time,* 393).

73. The science of religion (sometimes called comparative religion) was founded and given scientific respectability by Max Muller, *Comparative Mythology* (1856); *Introduction to the Science of Religion* (1873). Clinton Bennett observes that during the early phase of the scientific study of religions, scholars worked hard to maintain complete objectivity. They maintained a physical as well as a personal distance from the subject of their study. They worked to dispassionately describe what they saw. "The students of religions, ever anxious to stress the scientific status

of their discipline, left speculation about religious truth claims, or about any relationship between religions, and ultimate reality, to the theologians. Their task was descriptive, to reconstruct from texts and from classical sources the histories and belief systems of the world's religions." But under the light of postmodern scrutiny we see that the objectivity of the scientific study of religion wasn't as objective as the practitioners claimed. Their own Western biases affected what they saw and described. Much of what was offered as objective accounts of the "other" actually served, even if unintentionally, to enhance the idea of European superiority and consequently the interests of colonialism. Feminist scholars and others have exposed a tendency to judge or interpret other cultures and religions according to the criteria of one's own. This hidden agenda is called ethnocentrism. It has been extensively exposed by Edward Sa'id (Clinton Bennett, *In Search of the Sacred: Anthropology and the Study of Religions* [London: Cassell, 1996], 152-58).

74. Many Buddhists say that Buddhism is a philosophy and not a religion. Buddhism began as a philosophy of life, not as a religion. One major part of Buddhism, known as Mahayana Buddhism (also known as big raft or larger vehicle Buddhism), began to develop as a religion in the second century A.D., a little more than 600 years after the Buddha's death (c. 483 B.C.). The first step in the religious transformation of one part of Buddhism was to adore and worship Gautama (the Buddha's earthly family name) as a divine being who came to earth out of compassion for suffering humanity. Officially, Theravada Buddhists call this a corruption of the Buddha's original teaching. They say the Buddha taught his followers not to rely upon the gods. They, too, need enlightenment and final liberation in nirvana.

75. Charles Davis, *Christ and the World Religions* (New York: Herder and Herder, 1971), 25; as quoted in Knitter, *No Other Name?* 3.

76. Richard J. Plantinga, ed., *Christianity and Plurality: Classic and Contemporary Readings* (Malden, Mass.: Blackwell Publishers, 1999), 1.

77. Giambattista Vico, *The New Science*, 1725.

78. For an excellent tracing of how advanced secularism developed in Europe, see Benedict XVI, "Europe and Its Discontents," *First Things* 159 (January 2006), 16-22. He says that although advanced reductionistic European secularism passes itself off as scientifically dictated and humanistic, it actually "hides an intolerant dogmatism that views the spirit as produced by matter and morals as produced by circumstances. According to its dictates, morals should be defined and practiced on the basis of society's purposes, and everything is moral that helps to usher in the final state of happiness. This dogmatism completely subverts the values that built Europe. It also breaks with the entire moral tradition of humankind by rejecting the existence of values independent of the gods of material progress" (20).

79. David Christian says that "all forms of religious thought" trace back to humankind's ability to "imagine" (to abstract) and project its thought into a "nonhuman world" (*Maps of Time*, 189). Two recent illustrations of a clear-cut reductionist evaluation of religion can be found in *Breaking the Spell: Religion as a Natural Phenomenon* (Penguin, 2007) written by Tufts University philosopher Daniel Dennett, and *Moral Minds: How Nature Designed Our Universal Sense of Right and Wrong* (Ecco, 2006) written by Harvard biologist Marc Hauser. Hauser explores the "non-divine" origins of our sense of right and wrong.

80. One fascinating dimension of Constantius' support for the Arians was his sponsorship of the great Arian missionary Ulfila (c. 311-381) who translated most of the Bible into Gothic and who was hugely instrumental in winning the Visigoths to Arian Christianity. The Visigoths in turn converted the Ostrogoths, Burgundians, and Vandals to Arian Christianity.

The Nicene doctrine regarding the full deity of Christ made no sense to Constantius. In 353 he defeated Magnentius, successor to Constans, by a coup and became sole emperor of East and West. Richard E. Rubenstein says that, faced with theological division between the Greek East (largely Arian or semi-Arian) and the Latin West (mostly Nicene), Constantius hoped to establish moderate Arianism as the official Christianity of the empire. In 357 at the third Council of Sirmium it appeared the Arians had carried the day and that the Church would be officially Arian. The bishops gathered there formulated a distinctly Arian creed, though not as radical as Arius himself, for it did not declare Christ a creature. The council outlawed the use of *homoousios* (Nicene) and *homoiousios* (Arian). The third Council of Sirmium was the high-water mark for Arianism, but it did not end the controversy. The Latin bishops blasted the creed as the "Blasphemy of Sirmium" and rallied to the Nicene cause. At the same time, the Arians were theologically fragmenting in the East. In 359 at Rimini a majority of the gathered Latin bishops rejected as too Arian a compromise creed proposed by the East. Months later, and with winter coming on, under intense cajolery from the emperor and Arian churchmen, the Latin bishops surrendered and signed a creed saying the Son is simply "like the Father," but not in "all things," and not in "substance." In December the last Eastern signature was affixed and the Creed of Rimini-Seleucia was published. It was reconfirmed by East and West a few months later at Constantinople. Constantius had won, and a creed that Arians could sign had replaced the Creed of Nicea. Now bound to a creed engineered and enforced by the state, the Christian Church was officially moderately Arian—certainly not Nicene. An imperial desire for religious and political peace, not theology, had carried the day. Writing from Rome, St. Jerome said the Church awoke with a groan, as though rousing after a drunken party, to discover that it was now Arian (Rubenstein, *When Jesus Became God,* 191). Not until after the untimely death of Constantius, the subsequent interlude of Julian "the apostate," brief reigns by Jovian (a Nicene), Valentinian (West; a Nicene), Valens (East; an Arian), and finally the appearance of Theodosius I (c. 346-395), a formidable supporter of Nicene faith (tutored in Nicene Christianity by Ambrose of Milan), would the question—Arian or Nicene?—be settled. However, even before Theodosius, and even while violent conflict between radical Arians and pro-Nicene forces was on the upswing, three pro-Nicene Christian leaders in the East known to us as the Cappadocian Fathers were working creatively to chart a path forward that, while affirming Nicea, would make possible a reconciliation with the conservative Arians.

81. For a detailed, blow-by-blow account of the Arian controversy and the often lurid events associated with each segment of the conflict, read Rubenstein, *When Jesus Became God.*

82. Joseph Stephen O'Leary, *Religious Pluralism and Christian Truth* (Edinburgh: Edinburgh University Press, 1996), 13.

83. Ibid.

84. For a more complete history of religious pluralism, see Harold Netland, *Encountering Religious Pluralism: The Challenge to Christian Faith and Mission* (Downers Grove, Ill.: InterVarsity Press, 2001), 23-54.

85. For further study see Friedrich Schleiermacher, *On Religion: Speeches to Its Cultured Despisers* (Cambridge: Cambridge University Press, 1996 [first published 1799]); *The Christian Faith According to the Principles of the Evangelical Church,* trans. H. R. Mackintosh, ed. J. S. Stewart (Edinburgh: T & T Clark, Ltd., 2001, first published 1821-22).

86. Frederick Copleston, S.J., *A History of Philosophy,* Vol. 7, Part II (New York: Image Books, 1965), 142-46. Copleston quotes from the collection of Dilthey's *Works* 7:161.

87. John Frederick Denison Maurice, *The Religions of the World and Their Relations to Christianity* (London: J. W. Parker, 1847).

88. The History of Religion School made resources available for studying the great religions. Multivolume works, handbooks, compendia, and lexicons were produced.

89. Ernst Troeltsch, *The Social Teaching of the Christian Churches,* trans. Olive Wyon (Louisville, Ky.: Westminster John Knox Press, 1992; first published 1912).

90. For a more extended discussion of Troeltsch's thought and influence see Carl E. Braaten, *No Other Gospel: Christianity Among the World's Religions* (Minneapolis: Fortress Press, 1992), 27-29.

91. Ernst Troeltsch, "The Place of Christianity Among the World Religions," quoted from Plantinga, *Christianity and Plurality,* 216.

92. Paul Knitter discusses the importance of a lecture Troeltsch delivered at the University of Oxford in 1926, "The Place of Christianity Among the World Religions," in which he admitted he had been wrong regarding the superiority of Christianity. "To make such a judgment," Knitter says of Troeltsch, "One would have to crawl into the skin of that other religion and this is impossible." We are so caught in our own cultural skins that we cannot fully understand and appreciate another culture. We can never learn the "language" of another culture well enough to understand it or evaluate it. The truth or value of a religion depends on the knowledge one has who embraces it, and upon how well the religion fits the cultures in which it exists (*No Other Name?* 29-31). Carl E. Braaten says that John Hick has carried Troeltsch's "relativistic program to an extreme, with uncompromising consistency" (*No Other Gospel,* 38).

93. O'Leary, *Religious Pluralism and Christian Truth,* 15.

94. Richard Seager, Harvard University Doctoral Thesis on the Parliament, as quoted by Carl Teichrib, "Re-Creating Eden," September 14, 2004 <http://www.crossroad.to/articles2/04/teichrib-eden.htm>.

Seager refers to the parliament as "the dawn of religious pluralism." Richard Hughes Seager, ed., *The Dawn of Religious Pluralism: Voices from the World's Parliament of Religions, 1893* (Chicago: Open Court Publishing Company, 1992).

95. Swami Vivekanandam, Address at the World Parliament of Religions, Chicago, September 11, 1893 <http://www.searchforlight.org/Anubhuti/Anubhuti%20Vol%202/Viveka_chicago_%20Add.htm>.

96. Rev. De Jong's observations were communicated to the author via e-mail on Thursday, June 5, 2003.

97. "Declaration on the Relation of the Church to Non-Christian Religions, *Nostra Aetate,*" Proclaimed by His Holiness Pope Paul VI on October 28, 1965, paragraph 2, *Documents of the Second Vatican Council.*

98. Kärkkäinen, *Introduction to the Theology of Religions,* 114. If Benedict XVI is left to decide the Roman Catholic disposition toward other world religions, and toward other Christian bodies, an important document he released in August 2000 as Prefect of the Congregation for the Doctrine of the faith (CDF) probably reveals his position. In that year Joseph Ratzinger (Benedict XVI) released *Dominus Lesus,* a document that clearly stepped back from Vatican II. *Dominus Lesus* treats other Christian denominations (with the strange exception of the Orthodox) as essentially equal to non-Christian religions. "Faith" that is not Catholic is not Christian faith at all. Other churches and other religions are in a "gravely deficient situation." *Dominus Lesus* has met with

vocal criticism from some in the Roman Catholic Church, not the least of which is Cardinal Walter Kasper, leader of the Council for Promoting Christian Unity, and Roman Catholic theologian Gregory Baum.

99. R. S. Sugirtharajah, *Postcolonial Criticism and Biblical Interpretation* (New York: Oxford University Press, 2002), 1.

100. Wadi D. Haddad, Ph.D., "Tertiary Education Today: Global Trends, Global Agendas, Global Constraints." Haddad is the president of Knowledge Enterprise, Inc. (USA) <haddad @KnowledgeEnterprise.org>.

101. Plantinga, *Christianity and Plurality*, 2-3.

102. H. W. von der Dunk, *The Disappearing Heaven* (the Dutch title is *De Verdwijnende Hemel, Over de Cultuur van Europa in de Twintigste Eeuw* [Amsterdam: J. M. Meulenhoff, 2000]). Antonie Holleman discusses the book in an unpublished paper, "Sanctification and the Disappearing Heaven." The paper was delivered during the European Nazarene College Leadership Conference, 2003.

103. Karl Rahner, *Theological Investigations,* quoted in Plantinga, *Christianity and Plurality,* 290.

Chapter 3

104. *The Matrix* is a movie in which intelligent machines (artificial intelligence) have actually taken control of their creators—humanity. But few humans realize what has happened. The complex structure that has pacified, subdued, and now controls humanity is the Matrix. While persons go about what they believe to be normal, everyday life, the Matrix actually controls them and even draws their life from them as its source of power. But there are humans who remember what it was like before the Matrix existed, before it had taken over every dimension of human life. Those who know the truth are fighting at great personal risk to liberate all those who will see and listen, who are willing to join the struggle, and who are willing to live free of the Matrix. The movie is loaded with Christological, philosophical, Eastern, and science fiction imagery and themes.

105. Mark Tabb, "Postmodernism and the Matrix," *Kansas City Star* (November 22, 2003). Tabb's article is now available at <http://www.marktabb.com/what_is_the_matrix.htm>.

106. One Christian theologian who believes this to be the case is John Thornhill, recently retired head of the department of systematic theology at the Catholic Theological Union, Sydney, Australia. In *Modernity: Christianity's Estranged Child Reconstructed* (Grand Rapids: William B. Eerdmans Publishing Co., 2000), Thornhill argues that rather than abandoning modernity, the Church needs to rediscover it, for it still has much to offer civilization.

107. Richard Dawkins is a well-known confirmation of this. He is the Charles Simonyi Professor of the Public Understanding of Science at Oxford University. His confident atheism is on display in *The Blind Watchmaker: Why the Evidence of Evolution Reveals a Universe Without Design* (New York: W. W. Norton and Company, 1986). In *A Devil's Chaplain: Reflections on Hope, Lies, Science, and Love* (New York: Houghton Mifflin, 2003) Dawkins says, "To describe religions as mind viruses is sometimes interpreted as contemptuous or even hostile. It is both."

108. Others see the picture as quite mixed. James K. A. Smith says that although in important ways modernity is going through an "internal breakdown," it still thrives among persons in Europe and North America who treat the secular as though it were a religion, all the while accusing Christians of being "prejudiced" (*Introducing Radical Orthodoxy: Mapping a Post-Secular Theology*

[Grand Rapids: Baker Academic, 2004], 31, 43). While saying that the alleged death of modernity has been overstated, Smith also says that modernity is a "flawed, imploding project" (70).

109. Alister McGrath, *The Twilight of Atheism: The Rise and Fall of Disbelief in the Modern World* (New York: Doubleday, 2004), 218.

110. The Age of Reason is usually bounded by the publication of Isaac Newton's physics in the *Principia* (1685) and his theory of gravitation (1687) at one end, and the French Revolution (1789) at the other. The Age of Reason can be thought of as preceding the Enlightenment when we take into account the contributions of figures such as René Descartes (1596—1650), the "father of modern philosophy" and the "father of modern mathematics," and Benedictus (Baruch) de Spinoza (1632-77) who helped lay the foundations for the Enlightenment and modernity.

111. Space will not permit a discussion of just how varied the Enlightenment was. For many Enlightenment figures, commitment to enlightenment and to the Christian faith, even if reformulated, could and should be maintained. There were at least five "branches" of the Enlightenment: the British (including Scottish), French, Italian, German, and American. The British and American forms of the Enlightenment were probably most hospitable toward religion. But even then, one must consider the particular Enlightenment figure. Gertrude Himmelfarb has extensively discussed the complexity of the Enlightenment as it appeared in Britain, France, and America (Gertrude Himmelfarb, *The Roads to Modernity: The British, French, and American Enlightenments* [New York: Vintage Books, 2004]). She argues that chronologically the British Enlightenment preceded the French Enlightenment, and that the French themselves credited Bacon, Locke, and Newton with being the sources of the ideas that inspired their own Enlightenment. Reason played a major role in each form of the Enlightenment. But reason was not uniformly understood and applied. For many of the British Enlightenment figures (e.g., the Earl of Shaftesbury and Francis Hutcheson), reason played a secondary and supportive role to social virtues. Himmelfarb says the British, French, and American expressions of Enlightenment "shared some common traits: a respect for reason and liberty, science and industry, justice and welfare. However, these ideas took significantly different forms, and were pursued in different ways in each country" (20). What she says of Britain, France, and America could also be said of Germany, for there are important differences between Christian Wolff (1679—1754), Moses Mendelssohn (1729-86), and Gotthold Ephraim Lessing (1729-81).

112. Another factor that contributed to a loss of confidence in divine providence in history was the Great Lisbon Earthquake of 1755. It killed an estimated 100,000 people.

113. The Thirty Years War was the last phase of a series of wars involving religion. After the Reformation, as the religious differences among European people became established along national lines, political conflict intensified. In many instances, questions of religion served only as an excuse to wage war for political ends. The Thirty Years War was a savage struggle waged in Central Europe from 1618 to 1648. An important cause of the war was the failure of the Peace of Augsburg to settle the religious problems of Germany. The Peace (Treaty) of Westphalia (1648) ended the Thirty Years War.

114. This was particularly true of the French philosophes such as Voltaire, the Baron d'Holbach, Denis Diderot, and Jean le Rond d'Alembert in an accelerated measure. Gertrude Himmelfarb says that for them reason was not just pitted against religion, it was defined in opposition to religion. Reason was implicitly given the same absolute, dogmatic status as religion. Reason became for them the equivalent of the doctrine of grace. Himmelfarb notes that "there is

much truth in the familiar assertion that the *philosophes'* animus against religion was a by-product of their hostility to the Catholic Church, a church that was seen as authoritarian and repressive in itself, and even more so the accomplice of an authoritarian and repressive state." For the philosophes, "reason illegitimized not only the Catholic Church but any form of established or institutional religion, and beyond that any religious faith dependent on miracles or dogmas that violated the canons of reason" (*Roads to Modernity,* 152). Enlightenment may eventually liberate the masses from their blind servitude to religion. Although the English and American deists did not share the philosophes' animus toward religion, they certainly shared their belief that before a religious belief can be accepted it must successfully stand the test of reason.

115. John Locke, *Essay Concerning Human Understanding* (1690), IV, xix, 4, "Of Enthusiasm."

116. Immanuel Kant, "An Answer to the Question: 'What Is Enlightenment?'" Konigsberg, Prussia, September 30, 1784. Located in Immanuel Kant, *Foundations of the Metaphysics of Morals* and *What Is Enlightenment?* (New York: Macmillan Publishing, 1990). The full text is available at <http://www.fordham.edu/halsall/mod/kant-whatis.html>.

117. Some of the most notable architects of modernity were Francis Bacon (1561—1626), John Locke (1632—1704), Immanuel Kant (1724—1804), the Baron de Montesquieu (1689—1755), Voltaire (1694—1778), and Denis Diderot (1713-84). Thomas Hobbes (1588—1679) and René Descartes (1596—1650) were important precursors.

118. Voltaire was not an atheist. But he did vigorously oppose men's claims to possess special revelation from God that gives them privileges and powers over those who do not possess such insider information. Voltaire said, "My reason tells me that God exists: but it also tells me that I cannot know what He is," *On God, the Soul, and Innate Mortality, To Frederick, Prince Royal of Prussia* (October 1737).

119. "Those who can make you believe absurdities can make you commit atrocities," Voltaire <http://www2.lucidcafe.com/lucidcafe/library/95nov/voltaire.html>.

120. Kant, "What Is Enlightenment?"

121. Immanuel Kant, *Religion Within the Limits of Reason Alone,* 1793. In the preface, Kant said, "So far as morality is based upon the conception of man as a free agent who, just because he is free, binds himself through his reason to unconditioned laws, it stands in need neither of the idea of another Being over him, for him to apprehend his duty, nor of an incentive other than the law itself, for him to do his duty."

122. Bayle's greatest work is *Dictionnaire historique et critique (Historical and Critical Dictionary),* 1697, the single most popular work of the 18th century. Bayle is often referred to as the arsenal of the Enlightenment.

123. Diarmaid MacCulloch, *The Reformation* (New York: Viking Press, 2004), 674. Bishop Berkeley, Francis Hutcheson, Adam Smith, Bishop Butler, the Third Earl of Shaftesbury, and Edmund Burke are some of the British Enlightenment figures who advocated compatibility between Enlightenment and the Christian religion. Himmelfarb says that among the British Enlightenment figures "there was a conspicuous absence of the kind of animus to religion . . . that played so large a part in the French Enlightenment" (*Roads to Modernity,* 38). For Isaac Newton, God not only set the universe in motion but also is a living, active agent in it.

A host of Americans in the 18th century were adherents of the Enlightenment but saw no need to pit the Christian religion against reason and science, even if some of them (Jefferson,

Franklin, Paine) thought deism was the model for compatibility. But figures such as Jonathan Edwards, Benjamin Rush, John Witherspoon, and Ezra Stiles—evangelicals all—exploded the notion that Enlightenment and secular skepticism regarding religion necessarily travel together.

124. A summary of the major characteristics of modernity is as follows: (1) An abiding confidence in humankind's ability, through reason, to exercise power over nature's secrets, and to bring rational organization to all social relations. Humankind will achieve its salvation in this world through the inevitable march of progress. There is only one "reason." It transcends the individual, is universal, and is universally binding on all right-thinking persons; (2) confidence that reason is objective and dispassionate. In the search for knowledge, by permitting reason to rule in all things, the scientist or philosopher or ethicist can be set free from all self-interest, social, religious, and national biases. A right use of reason permits a person to transcend his or her location; (3) a determined development of the empirical, and later the social, sciences; (4) a universal basis for morality that relies on reason, not on divine revelation and laws; and (5) through the influence of René Descartes (1596—1650) an elevation of the individual self (the ego) as the arbiter of truth. The certainty of the self and the questionable quality of all other things establishes the ego as the primary certainty. All claims to knowledge must be assessed by the ego. Robert Webber notes correctly that establishing the self as that about which we are most certain contributed in large measure to the emergence of individualism and the assertion of the ultimate autonomy of each person (*Ancient-Future Faith: Rethinking Evangelicalism for a Postmodern World* [Grand Rapids: Baker Books, 1999], 18).

125. Richard Hofstadter, *Social Darwinism in American Thought* (Philadelphia: University of Pennsylvania Press, 1955; originally published 1944), 16.

126. England, 1688, 1830s; the United States, 1776; France, 1789, 1830, 1848, 1870; Canada, 1840s and 1850s; Germany, 1848, 1918; and Japan in the late 19th century and early 20th century.

127. J. Richard Middleton and Brian J. Walsh, *Truth Is Stranger than It Used to Be: Biblical Faith in a Postmodern Age* (Downers Grove, Ill.: InterVarsity Press, 1995), 18.

128. "Novalis" was the pseudonym of Baron Georg Philipp Friedrich Leopold von Hardenberg. Novalis' statement continues, ". . . discrediting by sarcasm the memory of all ennobling events and persons, and stripping the world of all colorful ornament" (quoted by Stephen Pickett, "A Faith That Feels," *Christian History* 86 [Spring 2005], 22).

129. Charles Darwin was indebted to Malthus and acknowledged his debt. He said that upon reading Malthus, "It at once struck me that under these circumstances favorable variations would tend to be preserved and unfavorable ones to be destroyed. The result of this would be the formation of new species" (*Life and Letters* 1:68, as quoted by Hofstadter, *Social Darwinism in American Thought*, 39). Later in the 19th century, Malthus' explanations were influential for many who applied the notion of "survival of the fittest" to social theory.

Historian Richard Weikart of California State University, Stanilaus, has recently argued that Darwin himself, and not just the "villain" Herbert Spencer, went a long ways toward promulgating a form of social Darwinism that anticipated the strongest living and the weakest dying, the "lower races" eventually being displaced "by the higher civilized races throughout the world" (Darwin in a letter to one William Graham, dated July 3, 1881). Richard Weikart, *From Darwin to Hitler: Evolutionary Ethics, Eugenics, and Racism in Germany* (Palgrave Macmillan, 2004).

130. Identifying Marx and Nietzsche as spokespersons for modernity has to be qualified. In

important ways they did represent modernity. But in other important ways they attacked what they believed to be its failures. Capitalism, for example, was a central feature of the modern world, and Marx was one of its most important critics. And some people say that Nietzsche is best seen a visionary herald of postmodernity. According to Frederick Copleston, S.J., Nietzsche spoke most directly as a representative of modernity during the second (1876-83) of three periods of his thought. In this period "Nietzsche prefers science to poetry, questions all accepted beliefs and pretty well plays the part of a rationalistic philosopher of the French Enlightenment" (Frederick Copleston, S.J., *A History of Philosophy,* Vol. 7, *Modern Philosophy, Part II: Schopenhauer to Nietzsche* [Garden City, N.Y.: Image Books, 1965], 166). Nietzsche's atheism is pronounced in the second and third periods. In *The Antichrist* (1888) Nietzsche says that the idea of God amounts to a declaration of war on human "life, Nature and the will to live! God is the formula for every calumny against this world and for every lie concerning a beyond" (as quoted by Copleston, 178).

131. Sigmund Freud, *The Future of an Illusion* (New York: W. W. Norton and Company; reissue ed., August 1989). Behind the notion that God must die if man is to live lies the modern erosion of belief that the world was created by God, that it manifests His glory, presence, and care, and that humankind is created in God's image *(imago Dei).* Rather than persons gaining their meaning from a unique relationship with God, they were increasingly viewed as self-constituting, autonomous subjects, disconnected from any defining relationship to God. Under these conditions, belief that being human can be properly understood only in relationship to God was unsustainable. Only a short step was needed to move from here to the belief that instead of humankind being created in God's image, it actually created God in its own image. God is just man writ large, a mere projection of humanity in cosmic dimensions. This reversal figured prominently in Ludwig Feuerbach (1804-72), Karl Marx, and Sigmund Freud (this explanation occurs in *Communion and Stewardship: Human Persons Created in the Image of God,* chap. 1, 2:18-19; 2004, The International Theological Commission of the Roman Catholic Church).

132. MacCulloch, *The Reformation,* 676.

133. Himmelfarb, *Roads to Modernity,* 126.

134. Henry D. Rack, *Reasonable Enthusiast: John Wesley and the Rise of Methodism,* 2nd ed. (Nashville: Abingdon Press, 1992), 32-33. Like MacCulloch, Rack singles out Jonathan Edwards and John Wesley as exhibit A of how effectively some 18th-century Evangelical leaders critically combined lessons from the Enlightenment with their orthodox faith. Both men drew heavily upon British philosopher John Locke (1632—1704), especially his empiricism (reflection operates on material introduced by sense experience, or sensation). Rack says that Wesley was a "paradox of a man who had absorbed some of the values and style of an 'age of reason,' but used them to defend a supernaturalist view of the world which went well beyond what was generally acceptable to his educated contemporaries" (33).

However, Rack also notes that Wesley's tolerance had important limits. For example, he had no patience with Dissenters from the Church of England who had chosen, had not been forced, to leave the Anglican Church. They had separated over opinions regarding church order and the like. He cautiously cooperated with some Dissenters more than others, apparently depending upon whether they concentrated on practical Christianity or opinions. Rack also leaves no doubt about Wesley's characteristic hostility toward what he believed to be popish distortions of apostolic Christianity. Wesley also shared the characteristic Protestant suspicion that Roman Catholic loyalty to the pope would make it impossible for British Catholics to be loyal to the crown. Supposedly, this jeopardized British liberty. Some of Wesley's actions toward Catholics, especially after 1778, actually damaged his reputation after 1780. Early in the 19th century Wesleyans were notorious for their anti-Catholic sentiments and opposition, a spirit that Rack says has to be laid in part at least at the feet of John Wesley himself. Nevertheless, Rack concludes that "for all his limitations, [Wesley] was genuinely and passionately opposed to physical persecution. This he owed more than he realized to the benevolent spirit of the eighteenth-century Enlightenment" (*Reasonable Enthusiast*, 309-11).

Following the lead of American historian Bernard Semmel (*The Methodist Revolution* [New York: Basic Books, 1973]), Gertrude Himmelfarb places John Wesley and 18th-century Methodism squarely in the ranks of the English Enlightenment of the British moral philosophers. "Whatever the differences between the moral philosophers and the Methodists—philosophical, theological, temperamental—in important practical matters, they tended to converge" (*Roads to Modernity*, 120). Himmelfarb also observes that Wesley's three-volume *Compendium of Natural Philosophy* was "naturalistic and empirical rather than theological" (125).

135. Cornelia Dean, "Scientists Speak Up on Mix of God and Science," *The New York Times on the Web* (August 23, 2005) <http://www.nytimes.com/>.

136. The list of critics who made this charge is long. It includes Karl Barth, Reinhold Niebuhr, Paul Tillich, and more recently David Tracy, Stanley Hauerwas, Michel Foucault, Catherine Pickstock, and John Milbank.

137. For example, the Swiss psychoanalyst Carl Jung (1875—1961) said that modernity's scientific and empirical preoccupation had grossly overstepped its bounds. It had all but suffocated humankind's deep-seated spiritual and religious dimension so necessary for human health and balance. Jung parted company with Sigmund Freud in 1913 because his view of religion was diverging from Freud's atheism. Jung believed there is a god-image in human "collective unconscious." It informs a religious dimension of human life, alongside other dimensions.

138. John Milbank, "Postmodern Critical Augustinianism: A Short Summa in Forty-two Responses to Unasked Questions," *The Postmodern God: A Theological Reader*, ed. Graham Ward (Malden, Mass.: Blackwell Publishers, 1997), 265. The statement is one of Milbank's indictments against modernity. He says that "the end of modernity, which is not accomplished, yet continues to arrive, means the end of a single system of truth based on universal reason . . ." (ibid.).

139. Theologian Catherine Pickstock assails modernity in its absolutist form for shutting down any reference to transcendence and undoing the liturgical or worshipful foundations of language (cited in Smith, *Introducing Radical Orthodoxy*, 72).

140. Dean, "Scientists Speak Up." Hauptman has no shortage of scientists ready to support his position. *The God Delusion* (Houghton-Mifflin, 2006) by Richard Dawkins, the Charles Simonyi professor for the public understanding of science at Oxford University, and *Six Impossible Things Before Breakfast* (W. W. Norton, 2007) by self-described "atheist-reductionist-materialist" Lewis Wolpert, represent what *TIME* describes as a recent "atheist literary wave" (*TIME*, "God vs. Science" [Nov. 13, 2006], 50).

141. See Theodore Roszak, *The Making of a Counter Culture: Reflections on the Technocratic Society and Its Youthful Opposition* (Berkeley, Calif.: University of California Press, 1995).

142. Jean-François Lyotard, a Canadian philosopher, made this point in *The Postmodern Condition: A Report on Knowledge* (*Theory and History of Literature*, Vol. 10), trans. Brian Massumi (Minneapolis: University of Minnesota Press, 1985).

143. Our discussion of postmodernity will concentrate on those features that affect a Wesleyan approach to telling and living the Story of the gospel. For those who desire access to more extensive discussions of postmodernity, the following sources will be helpful: Hans Bertens, *The Idea of the Postmodern: A History* (Routledge, 1995); David S. Dockery, ed., *The Challenge of Postmodernism: An Evangelical Engagement* (Victor, 1995); William Dunning, *The Roots of Postmodernism* (Prentice-Hall, 1996); Stanley Grenz, *A Primer on Postmodernism* (Eerdmans, 1996); Alister E. McGrath, *A Passion for Truth: The Intellectual Coherence of Evangelicalism* (InterVarsity, 1996); J. Richard Middleton and Brian J. Walsh, *Truth Is Stranger than It Used to Be* (InterVarsity Press, 1995); Joseph Natoli, *A Primer to Postmodernity* (Blackwell Publishers, 1997).

144. John Dewey, "Changing Human Nature," *Human Nature and Conduct: An Introduction to Social Psychology* (New York: Modern Library, 1922), 124.

145. In recent years, participants in a theological movement known as radical orthodoxy have unleashed a comprehensive attack on what they judge to be the idolatrous quality of much that defined modernity. Radical orthodoxy benefits from a postmodern critique of modernity, exposes the missteps of postmodernity, and then boldly goes far beyond mere critique. It is now mounting an effort to recover and restate the genius and power of the Christian faith for the Church and the public arena. On a broad front (economics, politics, theology, philosophy, and so forth), contributors challenge the modern notion that there is a secular domain from which God can and should be excluded. They charge that by claims made for the secular, modernity tried to create a story (liberal absolutism) so comprehensive and complete that God would just disappear. Those who led this effort failed miserably. Furthermore, they failed to admit their indebtedness to the Christian faith for much of what they tried to accomplish. In prophetic tones, radical orthodoxy charges that modernity was largely a project of pure arrogance and power. In thought, word, and deed it forcibly ejected the Church and the Christian faith from its necessary public arena. That proved to be a catastrophic sin, for only according to the truth and beauty of God as the Christian faith, through the Church, proclaims it, can the human soul and the human community be properly and truly formed. Nothing exists outside of our divinely ordained vocation of fellowship with God. All of existence must be viewed as participating in grace.

Radical orthodoxy is attempting to give a radically Christian account of social relationships, economic organization, political formation, aesthetic expression, and so on. It rejects dialogue with the secular if that means coming to terms with the autonomous space Enlightenment/modern secularity claims for itself.

For a comprehensive introduction to radical orthodoxy, see James K. A. Smith, *Introducing Radical Orthodoxy: Mapping a Post-Secular Theology* (Grand Rapids: Baker Academic/Paternoster, 2004). Radical orthodoxy has its own Web site, Radical Orthodoxy Online <http://www.calvin.edu/~jks4/ro/>.

An article by R. R. Reno provides a good introduction to radical orthodoxy: "The Radical Orthodoxy Project," *First Things* 100 (February 2000), 37-44. The article is available online at <http://www.firstthings.com/ftissues/ft0002/articles/reno.html>.

There are important criticisms of the orthodoxy of radical orthodoxy. One such critique has been lodged by Mark C. Mattes, "A Lutheran Assessment of 'Radical Orthodoxy,'" *The Lutheran Quarterly* (Autumn 2001), Vol. XV, No. 3. The article is available online at <http://www.lutheranquarterly.com/PreviousIssues/15-3-2001-Autumn.htm>.

146. McGrath, *Twilight of Atheism*, 271. McGrath counsels that when atheists correctly

expose intellectual, moral, and spiritual corruption in the Church, or point to the Church acting in harsh, vindictive, and unthinking ways, wise Christians will pay heed and move to "reform its ways," 277.

147. Harvey Cox, *Many Mansions: A Christian Encounter with Other Faiths* (London: Collins, 1988, 212), as cited in Bennett, *In Search of the Sacred*, 155.

148. *The Lancet* (international journal of medical science and practice), Vol. 366, No. 9481 (16 July 2005), 211-17. The study results were that distant prayer and the bedside use of music, imagery, and touch (MIT therapy) did not have a significant effect upon the primary clinical outcome observed in patients undergoing certain heart procedures. Therapeutic effects were noted, however, among secondary measures such as emotional distress of patients, rehospitalization, and death rates.

149. Paul Starobin, "The Accidental Autocrat," *Atlantic Monthly* (March 2005), 90-91.

150. For an illuminating overview of how postmodern critics have exposed the unrecognized, yet often harmful, biases of early scholars who engaged in the "scientific study of religions," see Bennett, *In Search of the Sacred*, 152-70. Critics have exposed how the myth of objectivity blinded many scholars to the ways in which their Eurocentric (ethnocentric) assessments of other cultures and religions painted pictures of subject races as not having the ability to know what was good for them. These scholars lent credibility to the notion of universal European superiority. Whatever appeared different, strange, or exotic in contrast to what was European was judged inferior (157).

151. For a recent illustration, consider the following: A "moral crime." That's how William V. Delaney Jr., M.D., labeled one recent illustration of how science and reason can be pressed into the service of the bottom line. More than 1.5 million Americans have an allergy to peanuts, and some can die in minutes if accidentally exposed. Each year many die as a result of the allergy. In 2005 the *Wall Street Journal* revealed how the U.S. biotech giant Genentech Inc. and Swiss drug maker Novartis killed the development of a drug that showed great promise of taming the allergy. Tanox Inc., a Houston biotechnology company, had produced an experimental drug, TNX-901. If further testing had proven successful, TNX-901 might now be nearing approval as the first effective treatment for people suffering from peanut allergy. Instead, the drug sits on the shelf, abandoned. Why? Because Genentech and Novartis, Tanox's corporate partners, told Tanox to kill TNX-901 in favor of a Genentech drug called Xolair. Xolair has yet to prove effective against peanut allergy. Tanox refused. Its two partners took Tanox to court. The court battle to kill TNX-901 lasted more than five years. It consumed well over $100 million in legal fees. The story of TNX-901 illustrates how the lust for profits can easily subvert the work of scientists and human well-being. Neither the sciences nor human reason are immune to their being used to advance commercial interests by stifling potential medical advances (David Hamilton, "Silent Treatment: How Genentech, Novartis Stifled a Promising Drug," *Wall Street Journal* [April 5, 2005], A1).

152. A 2005 poll conducted by Virginia Commonwealth University sheds interesting light on public reception regarding the sciences. The poll revealed that 85 percent believe that developments in science have helped make society better; as many as 56 percent agree that "scientific research doesn't pay enough attention to the moral values of society"; and 52 percent actually agree with the statement that "scientific research has created as many problems for society as solutions" (Nigel M. de S. Cameron, "The Great Stem Sell and Other Mistakes: What Americans Really Think About Science: Astonishing New Polling Data," *Christianity Today* (October 26, 2005) <http://www.christianitytoday.com/ct/2005/143/32.0.html>.

153. David B. Carmack, "Antibiotic-resistant pathogens increasing," American Academy of Orthopedic Surgeons <http://www.aaos.org/News/bulletin/feb05/fline3.asp>.

154. In the fall of 2005 the world was treated to an astonishing example of this. In May Dr. Hwang Woo-suk of Seoul National University, South Korea, had published a paper in the journal *Science* in which he announced that he and his associates had successfully developed 11 colonies of stem cells derived from embryos that were clones of 11 patients. His alleged success supposedly marked the first proof that it might be practical to create custom-designed stem cells to treat disease. The worldwide community of stem cell researchers and the press greeted Dr. Hwang's "achievement" with much fanfare and congratulations. But then the grand success began to fall apart. Questions about the dependability of his data surfaced. On Friday December 23 the star scientist resigned in disgrace from his professorship. An investigatory panel at Seoul National University had just announced that Dr. Hwang had falsified data for 9 of the 11 patient-derived embryonic stem cell colonies reported in *Science*. Later it was reveled that Hwang Woo-suk had falsified the data for all 11 of the alleged cell colonies. Unbridled thirst for personal and national acclaim, not scientific objectivity and reason, had driven him to professional self-destruction. (The South Korean government had promoted Dr. Hwang as a national hero and an international celebrity. It had invested about $65 million in his research before the collapse came.) It must also be noted that in spite of Hwang Woo-suk's deception, scientists were the ones who rigorously examined his claims and eventually exposed his fraud <http://www.nytimes.com/2005/12/25/science/25clone.html>.

155. For example, the Tuskegee Syphilis Experiment <http://www.dc.peachnet.edu/~shale/humanities/composition/assignments/experiment/tuskegee.html>.

156. Robert W. Jenson, "How the World Lost Its Story," *First Things* 36 (October 1993), 20.

157. Ibid., 21.

158. Adam Nicolson, "The Bible Tells Me So," *Wall Street Journal* (September 23, 2005), W13. The Bible Literacy Project, Inc., a nonpartisan, nonprofit endeavor to encourage and facilitate the academic study of the Bible in public schools, is working to reverse the situation Nicolson describes. Based in Fairfax, Virginia, and founded in 2001 by Chuck Stetson, the Bible Literacy Project, Inc., has published *The Bible and Its Influence* (2005) for use in public high schools. Amy A. Kass, Ph.D., senior lecturer at the University of Chicago, says the book is "a feast for the mind, the eye, and the heart. [It is] instructive, beautiful, and engaging!"

159. Lyotard, *Postmodern Condition*, xxiv.

Chapter 4

160. Karl Barth, *Church Dogmatics* I.1, trans. G. W. Bromiley (London: T & T Clark International, 2004), 295.

161. "Dalai Lama Touts Religion on Visit to Indiana Temple," *Chicago Tribune* (September 8, 2003), section 1, 16.

162. Arnold Toynbee, "What Should Be the Christian Approach to the Contemporary Non-Christian Faith?" *Attitudes Toward Other Religions: Some Christian Interpretations,* ed. Owen Thomas (Lanham, Md.: Roman and Littlefield, reprint 1986), 152.

163. Chester Gillis, *Pluralism: A New Paradigm for Theology* (Leuven: Peeters Press, 1993), 22.

164. Rev. Dr. George F. Regas, "Interpreting Christ in a Pluralistic World," a sermon delivered in the Washington National Cathedral, the Fifth Sunday of Easter, April 24, 2005. The full text of the sermon is available at <http://www.cathedral.org/cathedral/worship/gfr050424.html>.

165. The story was told by Rev. I. H. Belser in a sermon delivered on July 13, 2003. Rev. Belser is the rector of St. Michael's Church, Charleston, South Carolina. He said that many in the Charleston group "felt a spiritual oppression in the place, so they left the cathedral and had prayers on the bus."

166. Hick was a professor at Cornell University, Princeton Theological Seminary, Cambridge University, the University of Birmingham, and Claremont Graduate School.

167. John Hick, *The Metaphor of God Incarnate: Christology in a Pluralistic Age* (Louisville, Ky.: Westminster John Knox, 1993). See especially chapters 3 and 4 (pp. 27-46). In *The Metaphor of God Incarnate,* Hick traces what he believes to be the steps by which Jesus' followers transformed the crucified prophet from "Jesus" into "Christ."

168. Ibid., 1.

169. Ibid.

170. John Hick, *God and the Universe of Faiths* (New York: St. Martin's Press, 1973). Hick also states this position in *An Interpretation of Religion: Human Responses to the Transcendent* (New Haven, Conn.: Yale University Press, 1989).

171. John Hick, *God Has Many Names* (Louisville, Ky.: Westminster John Knox Press, 1986), 52. Hick's Copernican revolution overlooks the Christian affirmation that in Christ, and in Christ alone, do we encounter God incarnate. His effort to put distance between Christ and God ignores the very foundation of the Christian faith. Distance can be posited only by one who doesn't understand the Christian doctrine of the Incarnation and salvation.

172. A figure of speech that contains an implied comparison, in which a word or phrase ordinarily and primarily used of one thing is applied to another, as in Shakespeare's phrase, "All the world's a stage."

173. John Hick, *The Metaphor,* 105. Hick says that a myth is an "extended metaphor."

174. Ibid.

175. Ibid., 5. Here Hick relies upon E. P. Sanders, *Jesus and Judaism,* 1987.

176. Netland, *Encountering Religious Pluralism,* 221.

177. Ibid., 213.

178. O'Leary, *Religious Pluralism and Christian Truth,* 159-67.

179. John Sanders and Clark Pinnock, *No Other Name: An Investigation into the Destiny of the Unevangelized* (Grand Rapids: William B. Eerdmans Publishing Co., 1992).

180. Clark H. Pinnock, "An Inclusivist View," *More than One Way?* 97.

181. Ibid., 98.

182. Clark Pinnock identifies this form of inclusivism as modal inclusivism, meaning that while God's grace is operative beyond the confines of the Church, no prior judgment is made regarding *whether* or *how* God the Redeemer will utilize another religion.

183. Clark H. Pinnock, *A Wideness in God's Mercy* (Grand Rapids: Zondervan, 1992).

184. Pinnock, "An Inclusivist View," *More than One Way?* 97.

185. Ibid., 100.

186. Ibid., 98.

187. Ibid., 99. Pinnock cautions us against thinking that those who embrace inclusivism

agree on all points. They do not. "There is a spectrum of opinion within inclusivism about the activity of the Spirit in other religions and their precise *salvific* status."

188. Ibid., 99-100.

189. Wesleyan students of Karl Rahner are struck by the similarity between him and John Wesley in their doctrines of prevenient grace. Floyd Cunningham, for example, notes the similarity, even though he says that Rahner does not sufficiently distinguish between prevenient and saving grace. For Wesley, Cunningham says, "The Word is active even before becoming verbal or spoken, since it was from the beginning and always has been involved in the coming to be of all that exists. If God is at work among people there is a point of contact between God and persons prior to their conversion. Wesleyan thought, it seems to me, agrees with Karl Rahner that 'it would be wrong to regard the pagan as someone who has not yet been touched by God's grace and truth'" (Floyd T. Cunningham, "Christ, the Word, the Light, and the Message: A Wesleyan Reflection on World Mission," *Asia Journal of Theology* 5 [April 1991]: 106). Cunningham is quoting Rahner, "Christianity and the Non-Christian Religions," in *Christianity and Other Religions,* eds. John Hick and Brian Hebblewaite (Glasgow: Collins, 1980), 75. Cunningham also says that for Wesley, "Through the Word active in creation even those not privy to the stream of revelation flowing in the Hebrew's history of salvation are enabled by grace to perceive something of God. It is knowledge limited by sin. But grace is there sufficiently. At least men and women know that God exists, and that he is powerful. They are without excuse if they choose not to believe in him" ("Christ, the Word," 104).

190. Karl Rahner, *Theological Investigations,* a selection found in Plantinga, *Christianity and Plurality,* 291.

191. Ibid.

192. Ibid., 293.

193. Ibid., 295.

194. Ibid., 300.

195. Ibid., 301.

196. Ibid., 302.

197. Particularists are also referred to as restrictivists.

198. Hendrik Kraemer, *Why Christianity of All Religions?* trans. H. Hoskins, found in Plantinga, *Christianity and Plurality,* 253. Kraemer, following Karl Barth, insisted that the biblical faith, based on God's encounter with humankind, is radically different from all other forms of religious faith. Admitting that God's will shines through, albeit in a broken way, in the all-too-human attempts to know God in all religious life, Kraemer maintained that the only true way to know the revealed will of God is by responding to the divine intervention in history in Christ. World Council of Churches, Interfaith Dialogue <http://wcc-coe.org/wcc/what/interreligious/diction .html>. In the end, Christians must recognize that the other religions are inadequate gropings after the divine. Only in Christ has the divine-human chasm been bridged from the divine side.

199. R. Douglas Geivett and W. Gary Phillips rely specifically on Acts 4:12; John 3:16, 18; Rom. 10:9-15; John 14:6; 17:20. R. Douglas Geivett and W. Gary Phillips, "A Particularist View: An Evidentialist Approach," *More than One Way?* 229.

200. *The Westminster Confession* (1646) supports this position in conjunction with its doctrine of election: "Others, not elected, although they may be called by the ministry of the Word, and may have some common operations of the Spirit, yet they never truly come unto

Christ, and therefore cannot be saved: much less can men, not professing the Christian religion, be saved in any other way whatsoever, be they never [sic] so diligent to frame their lives according to the light of nature, and the laws of that religion they do profess. And to assert and maintain that they may, is very pernicious, and to be detested" ("Of Effectual Calling," chap. X:4).

201. Some of the biblical texts exclusivists believe support their position are: Exod. 20:3-6; 2 Chron. 13:9; Isa. 37:18-19; 40; Jer. 2:11; 5:7; 16:20; Acts 26:17-18; and Col. 1:13.

202. Ibid., 237-38.

203. Johannes Verkuyl is borrowing from Harold Netland, *Encountering Religious Pluralism,* 325, as quoted in Verkuyl, "The Biblical Notion of Kingdom: Test of Validity for Theology of Religion," *The Good News of the Kingdom: Mission Theology for the Third Millennium,* Van Engen, Dean S. Gilliland, Paul Pierson, Editors (New York: Orbis Books, 1993), 77.

204. Ibid., 321.

205. Ibid.

206. Ibid., 323.

207. John Stott and Timothy Dudley-Smith, eds. *Authentic Jesus* (Downers Grove, Ill.: InterVarsity Press, 1979), 83.

208. R. C. Zaehner, *Concordant Discord: The Interdependence of Faiths: Being the Gifford Lectures on Natural Religion Delivered at St. Andrews in 1967-1969* (Oxford: Oxford University Press, 1970); Wilfred Cantwell Smith, *Toward a World Theology* (reprint ed.; Maryknoll, N.Y.: Orbis Books, 1990); Ninian Smart and Steven Konstantine, *A Christian Systematic Theology in a World Context* (Minneapolis: Fortress Press, 1991).

209. In a century generously supplied with major Christian theologians, Karl Barth stood above them all in breadth and influence. In his 1917 *Commentary on Romans* he issued a thunderous challenge to 19th-century liberal theology and largely changed the direction of theology for the rest of the century. In his monumental *Church Dogmatics* and other works, Barth creatively and courageously led Christian theology back to the central and historic convictions of Christian faith.

210. Karl Barth, "The Revelation of God as the Abolition of Religion," *Church Dogmatics: The Doctrine of the Word of God,* trans. G. T. Thomson and H. Knight, ed. G. W. Bromiley and T. F. Torrance, a selection found in Plantinga, *Christianity and Plurality,* 236.

211. Ibid., 228-36.

Chapter 5

212. Rom. 16:17-18; 2 Cor. 11:12-21; Gal. 1:6-8; Eph. 4:14; Phil. 1:15-16; 1 Tim. 1:3-19; 2 Pet. 2:1-3; 3:16.

213. Harink, *Paul Among the Postliberals,* 43.

214. N. T. Wright, *The Challenge of Jesus* (Downers Grove, Ill.: InterVarsity Press, 1999), 24-25. The German New Testament scholar Peter Stuhlmacher says that "the Pauline doctrine of justification is the doctrine about the implementation of God's righteousness through Christ for the entire creation. Its goal is the establishment of the kingdom of God" (*Revisiting Paul's Doctrine of Justification,* 71).

215. According to the Gospel of Luke, when Jesus went through the cities and villages preaching, He preached the good news *(euangelion)* of the kingdom of God. When He gave the 12 disciples power and authority over all demons and to cure diseases, and then sent them out to preach, they were to proclaim the coming of the kingdom of God (Luke 9:1-6). When Jesus com-

missioned the 70 to go ahead of Him and preach in "every town and place where he himself intended to go," the evangelists were supposed to announce that "the kingdom of God has come near to you" (10:1, 9). And when He cast out demons, this was a sign that the kingdom of God had been inaugurated (11:14-23). The metamorphosis in the Christian faith that made it permissible to proclaim a gospel that is not the gospel of the kingdom of God, that promises individual salvation without any reference to the centrality of the kingdom of God found in the New Testament, is a reversal of monumental importance. But in much of popular Christian preaching and understanding, the metamorphosis isn't even recognized. We can see that the metamorphosis is far less demanding of Christians than is the New Testament order.

216. *Christianity Today*, ChristianityToday.com, Monday, February 2, 2004 <http://chris tianitytoday.com/ctmag>.

Chapter 6

217. Harink, *Paul Among the Postliberals,* 240.

218. During their Republican Period (510-44 B.C.) the Romans began to associate their devotion to Apollo, the Greek Sun God, with the Sibyl (from a Greek word that means prophetess) of Cumae. The books of prophecies kept in the Cumaean Sibyl's cave (called the Sibylline Oracles; the cave was located near the Greek city of Naples) were brought to Rome and deposited in the temple of Jupiter, Juno, and Minerva, where they were consulted in times of crisis. Counsel received from these prophecies prompted the importation of the statue of Cybele and the sacred stone.

219. The second of three wars between Rome and Carthage.

220. It was thought that participation in the rites of a religion other than one's own incurred disgrace and violated the god-given dignity of one's ancestral religion (Achtemeier, Green, and Thompson, *Introducing the New Testament,* 285).

221. Nielson, *Religions of the World,* 74. By the middle of the first century Caligula and then Claudius eased restrictions against Romans participating in foreign religions (Achtemeier, Green, and Thompson, *Introducing the New Testament,* 285).

222. This way of understanding the Church is in keeping with John Wesley's insistence that the Church is best defined *in action,* in its witness and mission, rather than by its form of government and institutional identity (Albert C. Outler, ed., *John Wesley* [New York: Oxford University Press, 1964], 307).

223. Harink, *Paul Among the Postliberals,* 240-42.

224. Robert E. Webber, *Journey to Jesus: The Worship, Evangelism, and Nurture Mission of the Church* (Nashville: Abingdon Press, 2001), 19.

225. Ibid., 20-21.

226. This story was contributed by Dr. Michael McCarty, formerly a missionary to Southeast Asia.

227. Greek philosophers such as the Cynics and Stoics would not have approved of such an extravagant exhibition. They would have called the priest's and people's response an expression of popular religion or superstition. At any rate, the response offers a glimpse into the religious pluralism that marked the city.

228. Bruce W. Winter, "In Public and in Private: Early Christians and Religious Pluralism," *One God, One Lord,* Clarke and Winter, eds., 130.

229. Paul spoke either before the council of the Areopagus or on the hill itself (Acts 17:16-34). If Paul was addressing the council of the Areopagus, his audience included the supreme governing council of Athens, which had responsibility for deciding religious questions.

230. A portico with a wall on one side and pillars on the other.

231. The history of Stoicism is divided into three periods. The Early Stoa: Zeno (b. 336/5-264/3), Cleanthes of Assos (331/30-233/2 or 231), Chrysippus of Soloi in Cilicia (281/278-208/205); the Middle Stoa (second and third centuries B.C.): Panaetius of Rhodes (c. 185-110/9 B.C.), Posidonius of Apameia (c. 135-51 B.C.); and the Later Stoa: Annaeus Seneca (d. A.D. 65), Epictetus of Hierapolis (c. A.D. 50-138), and Marcus Aurelius, Roman emperor from A.D. 161 to 180). The periods mark a steadily increasing attention to eclecticism, the practicality of philosophy, and moral principles that make for virtue. See Frederick Copleston, S.J., *A History of Philosophy: Greece and Rome,* Vol. 1, Part 2 (Garden City, N.Y.: Image Books, 1960).

232. Some of the important Roman Stoics who were alive in the first and second centuries were Seneca (4 B.C.-A.D. 65), Epictetus (A.D. 50-120), and Marcus Aurelius (A.D. 121-180). The Stoic concept of God was not like the Jews and Christians, for whom God and the world are not identical. By contrast, the Stoics identified God with the world. Although God rules the world by reason, the whole world forms God's substance. God (Absolute Reason) resides in matter; He spreads himself into matter and creates the beauty, purpose, and harmony we see in the world. Reason (the divine principle), which is God and which resides in matter, binds all things together by means of strict law. The Stoics believed the Logos to be the animating or active principle through which God rules and binds the universe together. So the Stoics would have attached their own meaning to Paul's statement that in God "we live and move and have our being" (Acts 17:28). They believed in both strict destiny and a measure of human freedom and were somehow able to balance both. The element of freedom made a place for providential acts by God on humankind's behalf.

233. Cleanthes, who succeeded Zeno as head of the Stoic school, wrote a hymn to Zeus that begins, "Of gods most glorious, known by many names" (Winter, *One God, One Lord,* 132).

234. Ibid. Winter is drawing upon the Stoic philosopher Balbus.

235. Ibid., 139-40.

236. Ibid., 137. The church in Ephesus was established under Paul's ministry during his third missionary journey. He pastored the church for over two years (Acts 19:1-40). His majestic testimony regarding his ministry there is recorded in Acts (20:18-35).

237. Ephesians was perhaps a circular letter to a number of churches in Western Asia Minor.

238. Moritz, "Religious Pluralism and Universalism in Ephesians," *One God, One Lord,* 102.

239. Ibid., 109.

240. Harink, *Paul Among the Postliberals,* 227.

241. Ibid.

242. Ibid.

243. Moritz, "Religious Pluralism and Universalism in Ephesians," *One God, One Lord,* 115-16.

Chapter 7

244. Kunta Kinte was kidnapped at age 16 in West Africa in the 18th century.

245. Don Aucoin, "Roots Made, Uncovered History," *Boston Globe,* Last Updated: Jan. 16, 2002 <http://www.jsonline.com/enter/tvradio/jan02/13055.asp>.

246. Theodore Runyon, *The New Creation: John Wesley's Theology Today* (Nashville: Abingdon Press, 1998), 207-14.

247. For a more complete discussion of Wesleyan theology than can be provided here, see William Greathouse and H. Ray Dunning, *Introduction to Wesleyan Theology* (Kansas City: Beacon Hill Press of Kansas City, 1988).

248. John and Charles were already Anglican priests and had served briefly as missionaries in Georgia before the occurrence of what they identified as their evangelical conversions.

249. John Wesley assured the clergy of the Church of England that they need fear no competition from him. "The rich, the honorable, the great, we are thoroughly willing . . . to leave to you. Only let us alone among the poor" (as quoted by Himmelfarb, *Roads to Modernity,* 120).

250. Known as the Holiness Revival.

251. Achtemeier, Green, and Thompson, *Introducing the New Testament,* 9.

252. *Manual, Church of the Nazarene,* Articles of Faith, IV. *The Holy Scriptures,* par. 4 (Kansas City: Nazarene Publishing House, 2001).

253. Achtemeier, Green, Thompson, *Introducing the New Testament,* 12. Someone might ask, "If this is true, how are we to account for all the marvelous stories the Gideons and missionaries tell about persons, far from a Christian congregation, who read the New Testament and subsequently confess faith in Jesus?" The answer is that it is the Church that has preserved and translated the Bible. It was the Church in the person of a Gideon or a missionary who placed the Bible where it could be read. Furthermore, we know that in order for the newly found faith to thrive as it ought to, the new believer will need to be joined to a Christian congregation for nurture, for hearing the Word, for baptism, for receiving the Lord's Supper, and so on.

254. Richard B. Hays, *The Moral Vision of the New Testament: A Contemporary Introduction to New Testament Ethics* (San Francisco: HarperSanFrancisco, 1996), 209.

255. Ibid., 210.

256. Nicea (325), Constantinople (381), Ephesus (431), Chalcedon (451), Constantinople II (553), Constantinople III (680), and Nicea II (787).

257. Hays, *Moral Vision of the New Testament,* 210.

258. Ibid.

259. We don't rest the work of God's saving work on subjective feelings, for God may very well carry out His work of redemption in us without there being any accompanying feelings and emotions.

260. *testimonium internum Spiritus Sancti*

261. Runyon, *New Creation,* 222.

262. Hays, *Moral Vision of the New Testament,* 211.

263. Alissa Monterroso, field operations assistant, Jesus Film Harvest Partners, relayed this story to the author on June 6, 2003.

264. Philip R. Meadows, "Candidates for Heaven: Wesleyan Resources for a Theology of Religions," *Wesleyan Theological Journal* 35, No. 1 (Spring 2000), 106.

265. Stuhlmacher, *Revisiting Paul's Doctrine of Justification,* 20.

266. Wesleyans are by no means alone on this score. Reformed (Calvinist) theologian G. C. Berkouwer condemns this understanding of justification as a gross misrepresentation of Re-

formed theology. The Reformation, he says, "restored sanctification in its true relation to faith. The immediate consequence of [salvation by grace through faith alone was to restore the] indissoluble bond between faith and sanctification." The forgiveness of sins, he says, must result in a true reorientation of life toward the grace of God and must lead to the restoration of a life that flourishes in God's abundant grace. This, he says, is the correct Reformed understanding of justification (G. C. Berkouwer, *Faith and Sanctification: Studies in Dogmatics* [Grand Rapids: William B. Eerdmans Publishing Company, 1952], 28).

267. Frank Gannon, "King of the Grill," *The AARP Magazine* (September/October 2003), 56 ff. "George Foreman's Christian Testimony" <http://poptohypermart.net/georgef.html>.

268. Dietrich Bonhoeffer, *The Cost of Discipleship* (New York: Simon and Schuster, 1959, reprinted 1995), 44.

269. Ibid., 45.

270. Atop Mount Defiance in May 2003, E. T. Morrel, an engineer for the area's public broadcasting station, told this story to Esther and me while we were visiting Fort Ticonderoga.

271. Hays, *Moral Vision of the New Testament,* 38.

272. Ibid.

273. Ibid., 44.

274. Ibid., see Rom. 8:1-4.

275. Theodore Runyon, ed., "Introduction: Wesley and the Theologies of Liberation," *Sanctification and Liberation: Liberation Theologies in Light of the Wesleyan Tradition* (Nashville: Abingdon Press, 1981), 17. Runyon draws from Wesley, "The End of Christ's Coming," *Works* 6:267-77.

276. Wesley's understanding of the Church can be observed in two sermons, "Of the Church" (sermon 74, *Works* 6:392-401) and "On Schism" (sermon 75, *Works* 6:401-24). All references to the *Works of John Wesley* will depend on *The Works of John Wesley,* 3rd ed., the 1831 Thomas Jackson ed. (Grand Rapids: Baker Book House Company, 2002 reprint).

277. Outler, *John Wesley,* 307.

278. Henry H. Knight III, *The Presence of God in the Christian Life: John Wesley and the Means of Grace* (Metuchen, N.J.: Scarecrow Press, 1992), 115.

279. Rob L. Staples, *Outward Sign and Inward Grace: The Place of Sacraments in Wesleyan Spirituality* (Kansas City: Beacon Hill Press of Kansas City, 1991).

280. Knight, *Presence of God.*

281. Wesley, *Works* 5:188.

282. Knight, *Presence of God,* 131.

283. Ibid. Knight says that Wesley's view of the sacraments "is a variation of the Reformed [Calvinist] doctrine of *virtualism,* mediated through Anglicanism. *Virtualism* holds that the elements remain unchanged, but Christ is nonetheless present through the Holy Spirit, using the elements as means of grace." *Virtualism* means that by *virtue (power)* of the Holy Spirit, faithful communicants are joined to Christ. They are lifted to heaven where Christ is seated at the Father's right hand. Theodore Runyon says that although John Wesley largely adopts Calvin's eucharistic doctrine as modified by the English Reformers, there is an important difference. He says that whereas for Calvin Christians are by the Spirit raised up to heaven, for John and Charles Wesley the direction is reversed. "Rather than our thoughts rising to Christ in heaven, the Spirit brings Christ to us, expressing the grace and love of God toward us through the means of bread and

wine" (Runyon, *New Creation,* 129-30). Given Calvin's insistence on "the real presence of Christ" in the Eucharist, we should be careful not to press this distinction too far.

284. Ibid., 131.

285. Ibid., 132.

286. Staples, *Outward Sign and Inward Grace,* 62-63.

287. Ibid., 64.

288. Knight, *Presence of God,* 131.

289. Wesley, *Works* 10:188.

290. Staples, *Outward Sign and Inward Grace,* 122.

291. Ibid., 224-28.

292. Wesley, *Works* 1:280. Staples presents an extended discussion of the Eucharist as a sacrament of sanctification in chapter 7, 201 ff.

293. Ibid., 203.

294. Knight, *Presence of God,* 131.

295. Staples, *Outward Sign and Inward Grace,* 226.

296. Ibid., 119.

297. K. Steve McCormick, "Along the Road," *Wesleyan Center for Twenty-First Century Studies* (Point Loma Nazarene University), Vol. 4, No. 3 (Spring 2003), 1.

Chapter 8

298. David McEwan, academic dean of Nazarene Theological College, in Queensland, Australia, sent this story to the author via e-mail, August 8, 2003. The story is used with the permission of Cheon-to, Kim (Ben).

299. Pronounced Stephon.

300. The film features Roland Joffé, Robert De Niro, Jeremy Irons, Ray McAnally.

301. Grande Ecole d'Ingénieur.

302. Stephane sent this story to the author via e-mail.

303. Randy Maddox, *Responsible Grace: John Wesley's Practical Theology* (Nashville: Abingdon Press, 1994). Maddox shows why, when speaking of Wesley's understanding of how God works to promote holiness, we are wiser to speak of way of salvation rather than order of salvation. The way of salvation indicates the "intertwined facets of an overarching purpose—our gradual recovery of the holiness that God has always intended for us" (158). It has been traditional for Wesleyan scholars to speak of order of salvation instead of way of salvation. For example, Lycurgus M. Starkey Jr. does this in *The Work of the Holy Spirit: A Study in Wesleyan Theology* (Nashville: Abingdon Press, 1962), 39-62. But Maddox, in agreement with much recent Wesleyan scholarship, shows why, for Wesley, the word *way* is more appropriate. It more correctly conveys "the gradual dynamics of Wesley's understanding of salvation." If we use order of salvation we should do so by defining it with a Wesleyan frame of reference (see Maddox, *Responsible Grace,* 157, footnote 2).

304. Staples, *Outward Sign and Inward Grace,* 152.

305. Quoted by Maddox, *Responsible Grace,* 157.

306. Staples, *Outward Sign and Inward Grace,* 152.

307. Barth, *Church Dogmatics* II.2, 94.

308. Ibid., 95.

309. Karl Rahner, *The Spirit in the Church* (London: Burns and Oates, 1979), 16.

310. Harink, *Paul Among the Postliberals,* 32.

311. Volodymyr relayed his testimony to the author in a June 2003 interview in Kansas City.

312. Rahner, *Spirit in the Church,* 16.

313. Wesley, *Works,* Sermon 128, "Free Grace": 7:373 (the capitalization belongs to Wesley).

314. Wesley believed that Adam was created in the natural, political, and moral image of God, all of which, because of the Fall, are now massively distorted in all persons. The natural image denotes the human spirit created in the image of God who is Spirit. It includes reason, will, and freedom. The political image denotes humankind's God-given capacity for social and political organization, for leadership and management, and for stewardship over God's creation. The moral image—the chief mark of humankind's relationship to God, denotes a relationship in which we continually receive His love, justice, and mercy, love God in return, and extend God's love, justice, and mercy to our neighbor and all creation. However, because of the Fall, all dimensions of our being have been thoroughly and totally infected by rebellion and spiritual darkness. Sin has enslaved every part of our existence, including our wills. There is no health in us. See Theodore Runyon's discussion of the three dimensions of the image of God (*New Creation,* 13-19).

315. Wesley, *Works* 6:509.

316. Meadows, "Candidates for Heaven," 102.

317. Wesley, *Works* 6:509.

318. Ibid., 7:188.

319. Importantly, John Wesley spoke of free grace and not free will, which would have been the Pelagian error. When Wesleyans erroneously speak of "man's free will" with reference to God they are justly accused of heresy. Persons who are dead in their sins have no free will to exercise toward God. Only if the Spirit of God makes the offer of faith and empowers the will to receive the gift of faith and redemption is there any hope at all. Persons who speak of free will are, perhaps unintentionally, still bogged down in works righteousness.

320. Wesley, *Works* 6:512. "There is no man that is in a state of mere nature; there is no man, unless he has quenched the Spirit, that is wholly void of the grace of God." ". . . every man has a greater or less measure of [preventing grace], which waiteth not for the call of man. Every one has, sooner or later, good desires; although the generality of men stifle them before they can strike deep root, or produce any considerable fruit. Every one has some measure of that light, some faint glimmering ray, which, sooner or later, more or less, enlightens every man that cometh into the world."

321. Starkey, *Work of the Holy Spirit,* 41.

322. Ibid., 39.

323. Wesley, *Works* 7:271.

324. Maddox, *Responsible Grace,* 29.

325. Flannery O'Connor, "Revelation," *The Complete Stories of Flannery O'Connor* (New York: Farrar, Straus, and Giroux, 1971), 488-509.

326. Wesley, *Works* 6:44. Justification and sanctification cannot be substantially separated. Veli-Matti Karkkainen says that one of the fruits of recent New Testament scholarship is the realization that "justification and sanctification cannot be distinguished from each other in the way Reformation theology—in contrast to both Roman Catholic and Orthodox theologies—has done.

Justification means primarily making just, setting a person in a right relationship with God and with others" (Veli-Matti Karkkainen, *One with God: Salvation as Deification and Justification* [Collegeville, Minn.: Liturgical Press, 2004], 16).

327. Ibid., 1:56.

328. Runyon, *New Creation,* 42.

329. Bonhoeffer, *Cost of Discipleship,* 64-65.

330. Wesley, *Works* 5:213-14.

331. Ibid., 7:253.

332. Runyon, *New Creation,* 42.

333. Ibid.

334. Harink, *Paul Among the Postliberals,* 257. Peter Stuhlmacher summarizes justification by grace through faith alone as "justification by virtue of the grace of God alone, which opens to people the saving way of faith and gives them the power to live this way by the Holy Spirit." Faith comes from hearing the gospel, and it is the gift of the Holy Spirit. It is active in the ministry of loving one's neighbor, in keeping God's commandment, and in the righteousness that is God's will (Gal. 5:6; 1 Cor. 7:19; Rom. 6:12-23) (Stuhlmacher, *Revisiting Paul's Doctrine of Justification,* 65-66).

335. Wesley, *Works* 7:5.

336. Maddox, *Responsible Grace,* 168.

337. Bonhoeffer, *Cost of Discipleship,* 63-69.

338. Starkey, *Work of the Holy Spirit,* 115-16.

339. Berkouwer, *Faith and Sanctification,* 23. Berkouwer invites us to consider the appeal in Leviticus: "Sanctify yourselves therefore, and be ye holy: for I am the LORD your God. And ye shall keep my statutes, and do them: I am the LORD which sanctify you" (Lev. 20:7-8, KJV).

340. It is also referred to as the principle of coinherence.

341. Runyon, *New Creation,* 55.

342. Starkey, *Work of the Holy Spirit,* 116.

343. Peter Stuhlmacher says the apostle Paul taught a "Spirit-inspired confession of Jesus Christ as Lord" (cf. 1 Cor. 12:3; Rom. 10:9-10). Stuhlmacher says that "as much as faith is directed toward the Spirit-filled word of God and is not a meritorious human achievement, one cannot deny that the apostle describes faith as a human act of obedience" (Stuhlmacher, *Revisiting Paul's Doctrine of Justification,* 66). This is precisely the spirit of Wesleyan theology on this point.

344. Barth, *Church Dogmatics* IV.4, 6.

345. Brian A. Wren, *The Episcopal Hymnal,* 603. Words copyright 1980 by Hope Publishing Company. All rights reserved. Used by permission of the publisher.

346. Peter Stuhlmacher warns us not to make a sharp distinction between justification and the new birth, or new creation. "Justification means the establishment of a new being before God (cf. 2 Cor. 5:17, 21). Therefore the controversial and . . . much discussed distinction between 'imputed' righteousness (which is only credited to the sinner) and 'effective' righteousness (which transforms the sinner in his or her being) cannot be maintained from the Pauline texts. Both belong together for the apostle" (Stuhlmacher, *Revisiting Paul's Doctrine of Justification,* 61-62). The justified, Stuhlmacher says, are "placed in the service of righteousness, which is God's will. Justification and sanctification are bound together and condition each other" (60). Stuhlmacher adds that Rom. 6:15-23 makes clear that "justification places people in sanctification and the service of righteousness. Through his atoning death on the cross, Christ 'sanctified' sinners for their en-

counter with God" (66). I believe the Wesleyan understanding of the relationship between justification and regeneration is in keeping with Stuhlmacher's reading of Paul.

347. Wesley, *Works* 6:44-45.

348. Berkouwer, *Faith and Sanctification,* 19.

349. Wesley, *Works* 6:45.

350. Berkouwer, *Faith and Sanctification,* 22.

351. Wesley, *Works* 6:44. See H. Ray Dunning, *Reflecting the Divine Image: Christian Ethics in Wesleyan Perspective* (Downers Grove, Ill.: InterVarsity Press, 1998), 43.

352. Hitoshi (Paul) Fukue is currently the president of Asia-Pacific Nazarene Theological Seminary, Philippines.

353. "As the Father grants pardon, as the Son offers himself as a pardoning sacrifice, so the Spirit completes and consummates the mission of the Son by raising up new life, not only adopting the believer into the family of God, but also imparting to the believer the clear awareness of this reconciled relationship" (Thomas C. Oden, *Life in the Spirit: Systematic Theology III* (San Francisco: HarperSanFrancisco, 1992), 200.

354. Wesley, *Works* 5:115.

355. Ibid., 8:106.

356. Ibid., 5:111.

357. Ibid.

358. Ibid., 114.

359. Runyon, *New Creation,* 67.

360. Ibid., 69.

361. Ibid, 160. See Runyon's treatment of *orthodoxy, orthopraxis,* and *orthopathy.* Runyon believes that distinctive of Wesley's theology, in addition to right belief and right practice, we must recognize the importance of right Christian experience. Runyon identifies six marks of orthopathy: (1) orthopathic experience must have its source in God. It must transcend subjectivism. Authentic religious experience "functions to register the reality of a spiritual world that transcends the self"; (2) it is inevitably life-transforming; (3) it is social, that is, it cannot be contained within the individual. God's love flows through us to all the world's creatures, especially to those in need and distress (orthopraxy); (4) orthopathic faith is rational, that is, experience of the living God as given to us by Christ through the Holy Spirit requires a rational element of reflection and interpretation holistically conceived (orthodoxy); (5) orthopathic faith is sacramental; and (6) it is directional. "It is on its way toward a goal. It incorporates us into the divine enterprise of renewing the world, and we know God as Creator as God becomes our Re-Creator" (*New Creation,* 160-67).

362. Harink, *Paul Among the Postliberals,* 35.

363. Ibid., 37.

364. Ibid., 35-36.

365. Ibid.

366. The Westminster Confession of Faith, 1646, Chapter XIII, "On Sanctification." It continues: "The dominion of the whole body of sin is destroyed, and the several lusts thereof are more and more weakened and mortified, and they more and more quickened and strengthened, in all saving graces, to the practice of true holiness, without which no man shall see the Lord."

367. Runyon, *New Creation,* 222.

368. For a comprehensive statement of the biblical foundations for Christian holiness, in-

cluding the hope of entire sanctification, see William M. Greathouse, *Wholeness in Christ: Toward a Biblical Theology of Holiness* (Kansas City: Beacon Hill Press of Kansas City, 1998).

369. Runyon, *New Creation,* 233. In *Relational Holiness: Responding to the Call of Love* (Beacon Hill Press of Kansas City, 2005) Thomas Jay Oord and Michael Lodahl show how all the dimensions of Christian holiness are anchored and fulfilled in the love of the Triune God we are called to receive, return, and extend to others.

370. Runyon, *New Creation,* 222.

371. Fanny Crosby, "Savior, More than Life to Me" (public domain).

372. John Wesley, *A Plain Account of Christian Perfection* in *Works* 11:395. "(3.) Every such mistake is a transgression of the perfect law. Therefore, (4.) Every such mistake, were it not for the blood of atonement, would expose to eternal damnation. (5.) It follows, that the most perfect have continual need of the merits of Christ, even for their actual transgressions, and may say for themselves, as well as for their brethren, 'Forgive us our trespasses.'"

373. Ibid. "None feel their need of Christ like" those whose love for God is "the sole principle of [their] action. None so entirely depend upon him."

374. Maddox, *Responsible Grace,* 165.

375. Ibid.

376. Staples, *Outward Sign and Inward Grace,* 202.

377. Wesley, *Works* 6:5.

378. Ibid., 5-6.

379. Bonhoeffer, *Cost of Discipleship,* 51.

380. Dunning, *Reflecting the Divine Image,* 43.

381. Rahner, *Spirit in the Church,* 16.

382. Between 1760 and 1830 the British Parliament enacted a series of laws called the Enclosure Acts. The Enclosure Acts had four major components: (1) They divided up the "common land" that had traditionally been shared by the community; (2) they redistributed plots of land in an effort to combine them into larger areas; (3) they revoked the poor peasant farmer's traditional right to scavenge food left behind on his or her landlord's fields (gleaning rights); and (4) they required all farmers to build an expensive gate around their lands. Seen from a pure perspective of economics, the Reform Acts led to a major increase in the rate of food production in Great Britain. The Reform Acts helped pave the way for the Industrial Revolution in England. But in the process many poor peasant farmers suffered because of the displacement. One by-product of the Enclosure Acts was to reduce the numbers of persons needed for food production and creating a pool of available labor for the new factories being built in the cities.

383. Theodore Runyon, ed., *Sanctification and Liberation,* 10.

384. Runyon, *New Creation,* 222.

385. Ibid., 8.

386. Wesley, *Works* 6:288.

Chapter 9

387. See Tae Hyoung Kwon, *John Wesley's Doctrine of Prevenient Grace: Its Impact on Contemporary Missiological Dialog,* an unpublished dissertation (Ann Arbor, Mich.: UMI Dissertation Services, 1996), 119-27.

388. John Wesley, "Caution Against Bigotry," *Works* 5:491. "If you will avoid all bigotry, . . .

whatever the instrument be, acknowledge the finger of God. And not only acknowledge, but rejoice in his work, and praise his name with thanksgiving. Encourage whomsoever God is pleased to employ, to give himself wholly up thereto. Speak well of him wheresoever you are; defend his character and his mission. Enlarge, as far as you can, his sphere of action; show him all kindness in word and deed; and cease not to cry to God in his behalf, that he may save both himself and them that hear him."

389. Meadows, "Candidates for Heaven," 100.

390. Ibid., 98-101.

391. Barth, *Dogmatics in Outline,* 80.

392. Wesley, *Works* 12:453. Letter to John Mason, Nov. 21, 1776: "No man living is without some preventing grace; and every degree of grace is a degree of life."

393. Ibid.

394. Mark Powell Royster, *John Wesley's Doctrine of Prevenient Grace in Missiological Perspective,* unpublished dissertation (Ann Arbor, Mich.: UMI Dissertation Services, 1998), 239.

395. Meadows, "Candidates for Heaven," 120.

396. A good example of this is John Cobb, *Christ in a Pluralistic Age* (Louisville, Ky.: Westminster John Knox Press, 1983).

397. Runyon, *New Creation,* 35. Runyon draws on Randy Maddox, "Wesley and the Question of Truth, or Salvation Through Other Religions," *Wesleyan Theological Journal* 27/1-2 (Spring-Fall 1992).

398. Meadows, "Candidates for Heaven," 102.

399. Runyon, *New Creation,* 32. Runyon says that the claims and content of conscience must be tested against the spirit of Christ. This applies to Christians and non-Christians alike.

400. Wesley, *Works* 5:17-18.

401. Harink, *Paul Among the Postliberals,* 251. See Douglas Harink's discussion of Paul's position. Wesley is in harmony with the way Harink explains Paul.

402. Meadows, "Candidates for Heaven," 126. See Floyd T. Cunningham's discussion of the role of prevenient grace in social laws and structures. Floyd T. Cunningham, "Christ, the Word, the Light, and the Message: A Wesleyan Reflection on World Mission," *Asia Journal of Theology* 5 (April 1991): 106.

403. Wesley, *Works* 6:41.

404. This account of C. S. Lewis's movement to Christian faith is given by J. I. Packer and Jerry Root, "Mind in Motion," *Christian History,* Issue 88 (Fall 2005), 17.

405. Maddox, *Responsible Grace,* 159.

406. Wesley, *Explanatory Notes on the New Testament,* Acts 10:34-43.

407. Pinnock, *Wideness in God's Mercy,* 92.

408. Wesley, *Explanatory Notes.*

409. Meadows, "Candidates for Heaven," 105.

410. Maddox, *Responsible Grace,* 32.

411. John Wesley makes this distinction in his sermon "On Faith," Sermon 106, 1:10. I believe Philip Meadows goes too far in his interpretation of what the workings of prevenient grace might accomplish in someone who has not heard and received the gospel. Meadows comes all too close to eliminating the distinction between the faith of a servant and the faith of a son. He thinks Wesley's emphasis on the prevenient work of Christ supports "an openness to the

saving presence of the Spirit dispensed among non-Christian peoples. It is in this sense that other ways of being religious can be seen as having *providential roles* in God's plan of salvation for the world" ("Candidates for Heaven," 125, italics added). Meadows thinks Wesley would have even supported the possibility of sanctification among those who have never heard the gospel: "We might extend Wesley's hints about the possibility of true religion among non-Christians, such that the idea of sanctification (as the pursuit of holiness and the definition of salvation proper) can become the primary category for both including and evaluating the quality of all religious life. In other words, the distinction between 'external' religion and true religion does not distinguish non-Christian religion *per se,* but applies to both, albeit in different ways and to different degrees" (ibid., 124). In my opinion, Meadows has carried Wesley further than Wesley intended. He has come perilously close to collapsing any qualitative distinction between prevenient grace and a full revelatory encounter with Jesus Christ. Meadows's extrapolation all but collapses the new birth and regeneration into the possibilities of prevenient grace. See especially pages 125-26.

412. Ibid., 112-14.

413. Wesley, *Works* 7:198-99. In substance Karl Barth agrees with Wesley. When referring to Rom. 2:13, Barth says, "These men are justified as doers of the Law, and they will stand in the judgment. They are Gentiles, and as such they are people who in an astonishing way do what is demanded by the Law; without having the Law, they are law to themselves. They give evidence that the work of the Law is written in their hearts" (*Church Dogmatics* IV.4, 7).

414. Wesley, *Works* 5:21, "As many of this place can testify; using diligence to eschew all evil, and to have a conscience void of offence; redeeming the time; buying up every opportunity of doing all good to all men; constantly and carefully using all the public and all the private means of grace; endeavouring after a steady seriousness of behaviour, at all times, and in all places; and, God is my record, before whom I stand, doing all this in sincerity; having a real design to serve God; a hearty desire to do his will in all things; to please him who had called me to 'fight the good fight,' and to 'lay hold of eternal life.' Yet my own conscience beareth me witness in the Holy Ghost, that all this time I was but *almost a Christian.*"

415. Ibid.

416. Staples, *Outward Sign and Inward Grace,* 253.

417. Wesley, *Works* 5:9.

418. Ibid., 5:353.

419. Ibid., 7:45-46.

420. Ibid., 5:80.

421. Harink, *Paul Among the Postliberals,* 228.

422. Catherine of Siena (1347-80) was recognized for whipping herself three times a day, once for her own sins, once for the sins of the living, and once for the sins of the dead.

423. Pinnock, *Wideness in God's Mercy,* 90.

Chapter 10

424. Leonard Sweet, *SoulTsunami* (Grand Rapids: Zondervan, 2001, originally 1999), 44.

425. Stephen L. Carter, *The Culture of Disbelief* (New York: Anchor, 1994). Carter says that "post-Christian" can also surface as "anti-Christian." Benedict XVI says that "in European society today [he could have just as easily added North America], thank goodness, anyone who dishonors the faith of Israel, its image of God, or its great figures must pay a fine. The same holds true for

anyone who dishonors the Koran and the convictions of Islam. But when it comes to Jesus Christ and that which is sacred to Christians, freedom of speech becomes the supreme good" (Benedict XVI, "Europe and Its Discontents," *First Things* 159 [January 2006]), 21.

426. Brian D. McLaren, *The Church on the Other Side: Doing Ministry in the Postmodern Matrix* (Grand Rapids: Zondervan Publishing House, 2000), 74.

427. Easum, *Leadership on the Other Side*, 70-71.

428. Daniel Hill, "Reaching the Post-Christian," *Leadership Journal* (Fall 2004), also located at LeadershipJournal.net <http://www.christianitytoday.com/le/2004/004/17.71.html>.

429. McLaren, *Church on the Other Side*, 74-75.

430. John Fischer, *Fearless Faith: Living Beyond the Walls of "Safe" Christianity* (Eugene, Oreg.: Harvest House Publishers, 2002), 221-23.

431. Cunningham, "Christ, the Word, the Light, and the Message," 107.

432. Williston Walker, *A History of the Christian Church,* revision eds. C. C. Richardson, W. Pauck, and R. T. Handy (New York: Charles Scribner's Sons, 1959), 459.

433. McLaren, *Church on the Other Side*, 74.

434. Daniel Hill, "Reaching the Post-Christian."

435. Not his real name.

436. Harink, *Paul Among the Postliberals,* 253.

437. Barth, *Dogmatics in Outline,* 80.

438. Ibid., 247.

439. Meadows, "Candidates for Heaven," 128.

440. Ibid.

441. Jeff Sellers, "The Church as Culture," *First Things* 142 (April 2004), 31.

Chapter 11

442. Harink, *Paul Among the Postliberals,* 218.

443. A group of Communist party leaders in the People's Republic of China who were arrested and removed from their positions in 1976 after the death of Mao Zedong. They were blamed for the social mayhem associated with the Cultural Revolution.

444. David Aikman, *Jesus in Beijing: How Christianity Is Transforming China and Changing the Global Balance of Power* (Washington, D.C.: Regnery Publishing, Inc., 2003), 67-70.

445. *Reich* means "realm or empire." The Protestant Reich Church was founded in 1933 by Adolf Hitler. It brought together into one church 29 regional churches. The Protestant Reich Church was largely based on Nazi ideas. It sought to rid Christianity of all Jewish ideas. Some wanted to eliminate the Old Testament. The merger was the result of work by the German Christians, an organization founded in 1932. The German Christians were led by Nazi clergy who wanted to bring the Lutheran church into line with the political and ideological goals of National Socialism. After 1937 the Protestant Reich Church became less and less an important tool of the Nazis.

The record of the German Roman Catholics and Pope Pius XII constitutes its own story. Three Roman Catholic bishops led Catholic opposition to Nazi anti-Semitism, the Gestapo, and killing the infirm. They were Bishop von Galen of Munster, Bishop von Preysing of Berlin, and Bishop Josef Frings of Cologne. Bishop von Galen preached a famous sermon called "The Anvil Sermon" in which he said, "At this moment we are the anvil rather than the hammer. Other men, strangers, renegades, are hammering us. . . . The anvil cannot and need not strike back: it must only be firm, only hard!" One succinct treatment of Roman Catholic opposition is, "Hitler's Hammer, the Church's Anvil," Justus George Lawler, *First Things* 157 (November 2005), 31-36.

446. Located in Donald W. Musser and Joseph L. Price, eds., *A New Handbook of Christian Theology* (Nashville: Abingdon Press, 1996), 88.

447. Augustine, *The City of God.* Christian theologian and ethicist Stanley Hauerwas deals extensively with two different cities or societies (he uses the Latin word *polis*). The Church is the visible expression of the *polis* of God and is animated by the Holy Spirit. Its goal is friendship with God and neighbor. True relationships of love and service are possible in this community because the Holy Spirit spreads abroad the love of God in its members. This society has its own purpose and goal and cannot be made to serve the purposes of the civil state, a secular economy, or any idol of human making. The *polis* of God doesn't have a social ethic, it is a social ethic, crafted by its Lord and none other. The *polis* of God is a Kingdom that the old order of violence and greed opposes and in which it cannot participate (Stanley Hauerwas, *The Peaceable Kingdom: A Primer in Christian Ethics* [Notre Dame, Ind.: University of Notre Dame Press, 1984]). James K. A. Smith says the society *(polis)* or community *(koinonia)* the Spirit creates is marked by a distinct story that is told in distinct practices, a distinct goal that transcends the old order, and the common presence of the Holy Spirit among its members through the Word and the Sacraments (*Introducing Radical Orthodoxy,* 239).

448. Hans W. Frei, *The Eclipse of Biblical Narrative: A Study in Eighteenth and Nineteenth Century Hermeneutics* (New Haven, Conn.: Yale University Press, 1974).

449. Ibid., 1.

450. Ibid.

451. John Milbank, *The Word Made Strange: Theology, Language, Culture* (Malden, Mass.: Blackwell Publishers, 1997), 250.

452. Harink, *Paul Among the Postliberals,* 220.

453. Achtemeier, Green, and Thompson, *Introduction to the New Testament,* 20.

454. Ronald J. Sider, *Scandal of the Evangelical Conscience: Why Are Christians Living Just Like the Rest of the World?* (Grand Rapids: Baker Book House, 2005), 14.

455. Ibid., 64-68, 94-110.

456. Ibid., 74, 77.

457. Ibid.

458. Webber, *Journey to Jesus,* 73. Webber identifies five markers that should characterize a congregation if it is effectively to tell the gospel story in a pluralistic world (67-80). **First,** the congregation must have a missional self-understanding. **Second,** evangelism requires a renewed congregation. To effectively tell the gospel story the congregation must pay careful attention to renewing its inner life. Renewal by the Holy Spirit will mean becoming the kind of Christian community in which new Christians can, in a relational and communal atmosphere, be "Christianized." The congregation should ask, "What will happen to new Christians in our midst? Will they find here a demonstration that Christ has defeated the powers of evil, of hatred and alienation? Will they be received into the community? Will they encounter Christian hospitality? Will they be comprehensively nurtured in the Christian Story?" **Third,** a church should call disciples to commit to their social networks. In what Webber calls "gossip-evangelism," as opposed to "confrontational-evangelism," a missional church must "exhibit an enthusiastic willingness to tell other people

in their immediate social networks about the church and its people." **Fourth,** a congregation should establish a reputation for servanthood. **Fifth,** a congregation must establish a process for the formation of new Christians.

459. Henry H. Knight III, *A Future for Truth: Evangelical Theology in a Postmodern World* (Nashville: Abingdon Press, 1997), 202.

460. Robert Sutton's story is found in a Prison Fellowship letter to supporters, dated July 24, 2003.

461. Webber, *Ancient-Future Faith,* 132-33.

462. Augustine, *Confessions,* Book Ten, Chapter XXIX.40. Augustine also said, "If thou, O God, dost show thyself to him who loves thee as thou hast commanded—and art sufficient for him—then, such a one will neither turn himself away from thee nor turn away toward himself" (Book Twelve, Chapter XV.19).

463. For a model of spiritual formation that draws extensively on the Wesleyan understanding of Christian formation, see Wesley D. Tracy, E. Dee Freeborn, Janine Tartaglia, and Morris Weigelt, *The Upward Call: Spiritual Formation and the Holy Life* (Kansas City: Beacon Hill Press of Kansas City, 1994). Beginning in Chapter 11, the authors discuss the importance of the Wesley Bands, small groups, accountability, and mentoring.

464. Maddox, *Responsible Grace,* 210. The love feasts were a standard expression of communal support in early Methodism. Wesley thought the love feasts to be a continuation of the early Christian agape meal. Wesley borrowed the service from the Moravians who used nonconsecrated bread and water in the meal. The love feast service was a time for praise and fellowship. At first it was an occasional service in the Methodist bands (i.e., convinced Christians). Eventually the love feast became a monthly service open to the whole society. A few serious outsiders were also invited.

465. Ibid., 192.

466. Knight, *Presence of God,* 18-20. At the risk of making the means of grace appear more codified than Wesley intended, we can identify their two branches: doctrine and discipline. The *Manual of the Church of the Nazarene* calls them "faith and practice" (par. 27.1).

The distinction between doctrine/faith and discipline/practice roughly parallels the New Testament distinction between the foundations of Christian faith and the life built upon those foundations.

1. **Doctrine (Faith).** Doctrine has principally to do with the character and actions of God that we confess as Christian faith. It involves God's self-disclosure, the history of His deeds on behalf of the creation, and His mighty saving acts in Jesus Christ. Doctrine is the living faith of the Church, made known to the apostles, preserved in the Scriptures, safeguarded by the Church, and communicated to us through the Holy Spirit. (In the Church of the Nazarene, *doctrine* includes the 16 Articles of Faith [*Manual,* pars. 1-22].)

Doctrine is not mere intellectual assent. It is the living faith of the Church. It includes the whole range of faithful responses Christians give to the gospel. As active, faithful response to God, doctrine expresses itself in inward holiness and outward holiness—all by grace alone. This distinction is seen in the phrase "holiness of heart and life." Inward holiness means loving God with all one's heart, soul, mind, and strength, and loving one's neighbor as oneself. The *Manual of the Church of the Nazarene* states inward holiness in the following way: "They shall evidence their commitment to God by . . . Loving God with all their heart, soul, mind, and strength, and one's neighbor as oneself" (V, The General Rules, par. 27.1 [1]).

Outward holiness refers to actions that flow from the heart (James 1:18-25) that God has transformed. Outwardly they evidence gracious transformation. A central feature of Wesleyan spirituality is that "love must be active; it is something which is done. There can be no 'inward' love without a corresponding change in one's active relationship with God and neighbor" (Knight, *Presence of God,* 4).

Outward holiness takes two complementary forms. The first is works of piety (works done for God such as corporate worship and praise, listening to sermons of edification, the Lord's Supper, singing hymns, formal prayers, studying the Scriptures, fasting, accountability, and a daily devotional life). The second form is works of mercy (works done for one's neighbor that express love for God). One of the most notable early Methodist works of mercy was the Foundry in London. In 1738 John Wesley either rented or purchased the building and then organized the Methodist Society there. In addition to religious services, the Methodists conducted a school for poor children. From the Foundry they dispensed money from a loan fund for poor people to keep them from paying exorbitant interest to others.

    2. **Discipline (Practice).** Discipline involves (by grace) cultivating our relationship with God through a disciplined life. It means denying oneself, taking up the cross, and following Jesus daily. It includes losing one's life for Christ's sake (Luke 9:23-27; Matt. 16:24; Mark 8:34). It involves being conformed to the image of Christ and having our minds renewed by Christ (Rom. 12:1-2). In Romans Paul describes discipline as "present[ing] your members to God as instruments of righteousness" (6:12-14). Peter admonishes "be holy yourselves in all your conduct" (1 Pet. 1:16). Wesley summarized Discipline for the Methodists in the General Rules. They are three in number:

- Avoid all known sin.
- Do as much good as one can (conduct works of mercy).
- Attend all the ordinances of God (works of piety).

467. To read John Wesley's account of how the Holy Club was formed, go to *The Journal of John Wesley* online at <http://www.ccel.org/w/wesley/journal/htm/vi.htm>.

468. Wesley, *Works* 7:203.

Chapter 12

469. Wright, *Challenge of Jesus,* 43.

470. Bonhoeffer, *Cost of Discipleship,* 64.

471. Wright, *Challenge of Jesus,* 69-70.

472. Wesley, *Works* 5:296, 302.

473. Ibid., 296.

474. Ibid., 4:174.

475. Wright, *Challenge of Jesus,* 169.

476. Bonhoeffer, *Cost of Discipleship,* 64.

477. Benedict Rogers, "Burma's Almost Forgotten," *Christianity Today* (March 2004), Vol. 48, No. 3, 52. Copyright © 2004 *Christianity Today* <http://www.christianitytoday.com/ct/2004/003/7.52.html>.

478. Persons who serve the gospel in this way are called apologists. The Greek word from

which this comes is *apologia*. It means "to give an answer or reason for, to make a defense of" something. It could be a statement, a theory, a position one has taken, or anything like that. An apology is made in response to those who make enquiries and present challenges. In the second century a group of Christian thinkers appeared who offered a defense of the Christian faith against its accusers. They are known as the apologists and include Quadratus, Aristides, Justin, Tatian, Melito, and Athenagoras. Like all apologists, they served the gospel by using their learning to frame a coherent defense of the faith. One risk an apologist runs is that in an effort to present the faith in a coherent manner, its scandal may be forfeited in the interest of making the meaning of the Christian faith accessible to those who do not believe. But this need not happen.

479. Alan Jacobs says that over time he came to be uneasy with his reputation as an undefeatable debater and indeed with the idea of proving Christian truths by scoring points (Alan Jacobs, *The Narnian: The Life and Imagination of C. S. Lewis* [San Francisco: HarperSanFrancisco, 2005], as reviewed by Richard John Neuhaus, *First Things* 159 [January 2006], 75).

480. Allen's name has been changed to protect privacy. The story was reported to the author in a paper written for a doctor of ministry seminar at Nazarene Theological Seminary. The story is used by permission.

481. Sheryl Henderson Blunt, "The Daniel of Religious Rights," *Christianity Today* (August 26, 2005) <http://www.christianitytoday.com/ct/2005/009/18.52.html>.

482. Ronald J. Sider, *Just Generosity* (Grand Rapids: Baker Book House, 1999).

483. Patrick Thomas told this story to the author on September 27, 2003, in Nashville.

Chapter 13

484. Bernard Anderson, *Understanding the Old Testament*, 3rd ed. (Englewood Cliffs, N.J.: Prentice-Hall, Inc., 1975), 451.

485. Achtemeier, Green, and Thompson identify five factors that were common to Old Testament expectations regarding the kingdom of God: First, the Old Testament assumes God's reign over the creation and looks forward to a future, unmistakable manifestation of His reign. Second, not only will God's rule be established upon the earth, but it will achieve universal justice and righteousness. Third, God's rule will have specific, concrete, and visible consequences for Israel. Fourth, visions and hopes for the future carry with them implications for the present ordering of Israel's life. And fifth, God's reign will come as salvation for the righteous and judgment for the wicked (*Introducing the New Testament*, 216-17).

486. The Septuagint, the version John most likely would have used.

487. Wright, *Challenge of Jesus*, 116. For the early Christian theologians, the cycles of the week seemed to symbolize the meaninglessness of earthly existence taken into itself. Like the legendary Greek image of the snake swallowing its own tail, the seven-day week returns to itself, repeating its cycle. So the patristic tradition proposed the eighth day, which broke open the cyclical chain of seven days. The seven-day week represented the history of the created world; the eighth day symbolized eternity. Sunday, the day of the resurrection of Christ, was the first and the eighth day at the same time. Sunday is the day of the sun, the source of life, the first day of the week, and symbolically the first day of creation. It is also the eighth day, the day of the new creation, the day of resurrection, which initiated all creation to eternal life. The eighth day breaks the monotonous cycle of time and liberates time from bondage to boredom and death. There is no longer evening or morning to mark the bounds of the day, no sun or moon to determine the course of day or night.

488. The word *Docetist* derives from the Greek word *dokeo,* one meaning of which is "appearance or semblance." The Docetists taught that Christ only appeared or seemed to be a man. His sufferings and death were mere appearance. "If he suffered he was not God; if he was God he did not suffer."

489. Peter Stuhlmacher explains that the expression "groaning in labor pains" used in 8:22 continues the Jewish and early Christian expectation that the Messiah's coming would be preceded by a period of "messianic birth pangs." They would afflict human and all living creatures. By "creation," Paul means "the whole creation that was subjected to futility and death with Adam's fall. It will be set free from 'futility' and 'bondage to decay' and will 'obtain the freedom of the glory of the children of God'" (8:21) (Stuhlmacher, *Revisiting Paul's Doctrine of Justification,* 72).

490. The sea is a symbol of turbulence and unrest.

491. Wesley, *Works* 6:248. All of John Wesley's sermons are available online at <http://gbgm-umc.org/umhistory/wesley/sermons/serm-060.stm>.

492. Ibid., 250.

493. Runyon, *New Creation,* 214. Wesley would have welcomed the research results of Marc Bekoff, an ethologist at the University of Colorado who has shown that many animals demonstrate patterns of altruism, empathy, and a sense of fair play. Bekoff and other researchers such as Frans de Waal at Emory University in Atlanta are demonstrating that some animals (e.g., dogs, chimps, hyenas, monkeys, and dolphins) possess not just raw emotions but also subtler and more sophisticated mental states, including envy, empathy, altruism, and a sense of fair play (Michael D. Lemonick, "Honor Among Beasts," *TIME* [July 11, 2005], 55-56).

494. John Polkinghorne, "Eschatology: Some Questions and Some Insights from Science," *The End of the World and the End of God: Science and Theology on Eschatology (Theology for the Twenty-First Century)* John Polkinghorne and Michael Welker, eds. (Harrisburg, Pa.: Trinity Press International, 2000), 31.

495. This is because the force of antigravity is increasing in volume while gravity remains constant. Antigravity was a concept originally proposed, and later abandoned, by Albert Einstein. He thought the idea to be the greatest blunder of his life. This force, now called dark energy, is making the universe fly apart faster and faster. Not only does dark energy swamp ordinary gravity, but an invisible substance known to scientists as dark matter seems to outweigh the ordinary matter of stars, planets, and people by a factor of 10 to 1. These discoveries raise more questions than they answer. Even though scientists know dark matter is there, they are far from understanding what it really is. The same goes for dark energy.

496. Called an open universe. It will take trillions of years for the universe to fade away. For more detail than the text includes, the following will be helpful: Long before all of this happens, life on earth will have ceased. Our middle-aged sun (about 5 billion years old) is burning its fuel at a rapid clip. Based on what astronomers know happens to stars like ours, they say that for another 5 billion years our sun will continue to consume the hydrogen at its core. When the hydrogen core is depleted (burnt to helium), the sun will begin to burn the hydrogen in its shell, brightening dramatically in the process. About 1 billion years from now the increased luminosity will turn our earth into a hothouse. Plants will wither. Carbon dioxide levels will plunge, and the oceans will begin to boil off. The sun's core will contract and rise in temperature. The burning will continue to eat outward and will increase the sun's brightness. Increased brightness, added to the rising inner temperature, will cause the sun's outermost atmosphere to expand and cool.

The sun will become a red giant. Its atmosphere will expand to swallow Mercury and Venus. Eventually the red giant's atmosphere will either envelop or nearly envelop the Earth, turning it into a red-hot charred ember. Life having expired, the sun will have become 2,000 times brighter than it is now.

As the hydrogen shell burns out, the red giant will shrink. As it compresses, the core will heat to 100 million degrees. At that temperature helium will begin to burn. What was once the life-giving sun will have become a pulsating yellow giant, well advanced in its death throes. Once most of the helium is exhausted, the sun will again enter a red giant phase, becoming even brighter and larger than it was in its first red giant phase. It will extend beyond the earth's current orbit. The cool outer layers of the star will be pushed away from the sun to form a planetary nebula (a cloud of interstellar gas or dust).

In our absence, the red giant phase of the dying sun will go on for about 1 billion years. Eventually, in one final gasp, the sun's core will collapse like a giant soufflé. It will become a dense and degenerate remnant.

497. Polkinghorne and Welker, *The End of the World and the End of God.*

498. Frederic Golden, "How Long Will We Be Around?" *TIME* Magazine Archive (June 25, 2001).

499. Christian, *Maps of Time,* 489.

500. Bonhoeffer, *Cost of Discipleship,* 110.

501. N. T. Wright, *The Resurrection of the Son of God* (Minneapolis: Augsburg Fortress Press, 2003), 334-35.

502. "At the Lamb's High Feast We Sing," Latin text, 1632, trans. Robert Campbell (1814-1868).

503. A word of caution is in order. The language here should not be confused with universalism. I am speaking of the created world. It is indeed God's will and provision that all persons come to repentance and everlasting life. But, to paraphrase Karl Barth, many persons commit the "possible impossibility" by rejecting the Lord of life. This, John said, is because they love darkness rather than light (John 3:19).

504. Michael Lodahl, *God of Nature and of Grace: Reading the World in a Wesleyan Way* (Nashville: Kingswood Press, 2004). I am referencing chapter 7: "To (Pre)serve the Present Age: Eschatology in a Wesleyan Way." I received the chapter electronically from the author. The quoted material is used with the author's permission.

Conclusion

505. The priesthood of all believers is an essential doctrine of Protestant theology. Martin Luther said that the alleged superiority of the spiritual estate (papacy, clergy, monks, etc.) over the temporal (the normal trades and occupations of life) was a hoax. The secular estate is just as good and important as the spiritual estate as a field for service to God. In one's occupation, a Christian can and should render service to God and to the gospel. Through such sanctified service, he or she renders priestly service to God (Martin Luther, *To the Christian Nobility of the German Nation,* 1520).

BIBLIOGRAPHY

Books

Achtemeier, Paul J., Joel B. Green, and Marianne Thompson. *Introduction to the New Testament: Its Literature and Theology.* Grand Rapids: Eerdmans, 2001.

Adler, Margot. *Drawing Down the Moon: Witches, Druids, Goddess-Worshippers, and Other Pagans in America Today.* New York: Penguin USA, 1997.

Ahlstrom, Sydney E. *A Religious History of the American People.* New Haven, Conn.: Yale University Press, 1972.

Aikman, David. *Jesus in Beijing: How Christianity Is Transforming China and Changing the Global Balance of Power.* Washington, D.C.: Regnery Publishing, Inc., 2003.

Anderson, Bernard. *Understanding the Old Testament,* 3rd ed. Englewood Cliffs, N.J.: Prentice Hall, Inc., 1975.

Augustine. *The City of God,* Part Two, Book VI, Chapter 1. Garden City, N.Y.: Image Books, 1958.

_____. *Confessions.* Trans. and ed. Albert C. Outler, 1955 (public domain) <http://www.fordham.edu/halsall/basis/confessions-bod.html>.

Barrett, David B., George T. Kurian, Todd M. Johnson, eds. *World Christian Encyclopedia: A Comparative Survey of Churches and Religions in the Modern World* (2 vols.). New York: Oxford University Press, 2001.

Barth, Karl. *Church Dogmatics,* I.1. Trans. G. W. Bromiley. London: T & T Clark International, 2004.

_____. *Church Dogmatics,* II.2, 94.

_____. *Church Dogmatics,* IV.4, 6.

_____. *Dogmatics in Outline.* New York: Harper and Row, Publishers, 1959.

Bennett, Clinton. *In Search of the Sacred: Anthropology and the Study of Religions.* London: Cassell, 1996.

Berger, Peter. *The Sacred Canopy.* New York: Doubleday, 1967.

Berkouwer, G. C. *Faith and Sanctification: Studies in Dogmatics.* Grand Rapids: William B. Eerdmans Publishing Company, 1952.

Bonhoeffer, Dietrich. *The Cost of Discipleship.* New York: Simon and Schuster, 1959, reprinted 1995.

Braaten, Carl E. *No Other Gospel: Christianity Among the World's Religions.* Minneapolis: Fortress Press, 1992.

Carson, D. A., and John Woodbridge, eds. *God and Culture: Essays in Honor of Carl F. H. Henry.* Grand Rapids: Eerdmans, 1993.

Carter, Stephen L. *The Culture of Disbelief.* New York: Anchor, 1994.

Christian, David. *Maps of Time: An Introduction to Big History.* Los Angeles: University of California Press, 2004.

Clarke, Andrew D., and Bruce W. Winter, eds. *One God, One Lord: Christianity in a World of Religious Pluralism.* Grand Rapids: Baker Book House, 1992.

Cobb, John. *Christ in a Pluralistic Age.* Louisville, Ky.: Westminster John Knox Press, 1983.

Copleston, Frederick, S.J. *A History of Philosophy: Greece and Rome,* Vol. 1, Part 2. Garden City, N.Y.: Image Books, 1960.

_____. *A History of Philosophy: Modern Philosophy,* Vol. 7, Part II: *Schopenhauer to Nietzsche.* New York: Image Books, 1965.

Cox, Harvey. *Many Mansions: A Christian Encounter with Other Faiths.* London: Collins, 1988.

Crossan, John Dominic, and Reed, Jonathan L. *In Search of Paul: How Jesus' Apostle Opposed Rome's Empire with God's Kingdom.* New York: HarperSanFrancisco, 2004.

David, Charles. *Christ and the World Religions.* New York: Herder and Herder, 1971.

Davis, David Brion. *The Problem of Slavery in the Age of Revolution 1770–1823.* Ithaca, N.Y.: Cornell University Press, 1975.

Dawkins, Richard. *The Blind Watchmaker: Why the Evidence of Evolution Reveals a Universe Without Design.* New York: W. W. Norton and Company, 1986.

_____. *A Devil's Chaplain: Reflections on Hope, Lies, Science, and Love.* Houghton Mifflin, 2003.

"Declaration on the Relation of the Church to Non-Christian Religions, *Nostra Aetate,*" Proclaimed by His Holiness Pope Paul VI on October 28, 1965, paragraph 2, *Documents of the Second Vatican Council.*

Dewey, John. "Changing Human Nature," *Human Nature and Conduct: An Introduction to Social Psychology.* New York: Modern Library, 1922.

Dube, Musa. *Postcolonial Feminist Interpretation of the Bible.* St. Louis: Chalice Press, 2000.

Dunning, H. Ray. *Reflecting the Divine Image: Christian Ethics in Wesleyan Perspective.* Downers Grove, Ill.: InterVarsity Press, 1998.

Easum, Bill. *Leadership on the Other Side: No Rules, Just Clues.* Nashville: Abingdon Press, 2000.

Eck, Diana L. *A New Religious America: How a "Christian Country" Has Become the World's Most Religiously Diverse Nation.* San Francisco: HarperSanFrancisco, 2002.

Editors of *TIME Magazine. American Passages: Diverse Origins and Common Destinies in the United States. TIME Magazine,* 1995.

Fallaci, Oriana. *The Force of Reason.* New York: Rizzoli, 2005.

Fischer, John. *Fearless Faith: Living Beyond the Walls of "Safe" Christianity.* Eugene, Oreg.: Harvest House Publishers, 2002.

Flemming, Dean. *Contextualization in the New Testament: Patterns for Theology and Mission.* Downers Grove, Ill.: InterVarsity Press, 2005.

Fredericks, James L. *Faith Among Faiths.* New York: Paulist Press, 1999.

Frei, Hans W. *The Eclipse of Biblical Narrative: A Study in Eighteenth and Nineteenth Century Hermeneutics.* New Haven, Conn.: Yale University Press, 1974.

Freud, Sigmund. *The Future of an Illusion.* New York: W. W. Norton and Company; reissue ed., 1989.

Fukuyama, Francis. *The End of History.* New York: Free Press, 2006.

Geivett, R. Douglas, Alister E. McGrath, Clark H. Pinnock, and W. Gary Phillips. *More than One Way? Four Views on Salvation in a Pluralistic World,* eds. John Hick, Dennis L. Okholm, and Timothy R. Phillips. Grand Rapids: Zondervan Publishing House, 1995.

George, David, ed. *Religious Pluralism in the West: An Anthology.* Malden, Mass.: Blackwell Publishers, 1998.

Gillis, Chester. *Pluralism: A New Paradigm for Theology.* Leuven: Peeters Press, 1993.

Greathouse, William M. *Wholeness in Christ: Toward a Biblical Theology of Holiness.* Kansas City: Beacon Hill Press of Kansas City, 1998.

Greathouse, William, and H. Ray Dunning. *Introduction to Wesleyan Theology.* Kansas City: Beacon Hill Press of Kansas City, 1988.

Harink, Douglas. *Paul Among the Postliberals: Pauline Theology Beyond Christendom and Modernity.* Grand Rapids: Brazos Press, 2003.

Hauerwas, Stanley. *The Peaceable Kingdom: A Primer in Christian Ethics.* Notre Dame, Ind.: University of Notre Dame Press, 1984.

Hays, Richard B. *The Moral Vision of the New Testament.* San Francisco: HarperSanFrancisco, 1996.

Herrick, James A. *The Making of the New Spirituality: The Eclipse of the Western Religious Tradition.* Downers Grove, Ill.: InterVarsity Press, 2003.

Hick, John. *God and the Universe of Faiths.* New York: St. Martin's Press, 1973.

————. *God Has Many Names.* Louisville, Ky.: Westminster John Knox Press, 1986.

————. *An Interpretation of Religion: Human Responses to the Transcendent.* New Haven, Conn.: Yale University Press, 1989.

————. *The Metaphor of God Incarnate: Christology in a Pluralistic Age.* Louisville, Ky.: Westminster John Knox Press, 1993.

Hillgarth, J. N., ed. *Christianity and Paganism, 350-750.* Philadelphia: University of Pennsylvania Press, 1969.

Himmelfarb, Gertrude. *The Roads to Modernity: The British, French, and American Enlightenments.* New York: Vintage Books, 2004.

Hofstadter, Richard. *Social Darwinism in American Thought.* Philadelphia: University of Pennsylvania Press, 1955, originally published 1944.

Hutchison, William R. *Religious Pluralism in America: The Contentious History of a Founding Idea.* New Haven, Conn.: Yale University Press, 2003 (noted).

Kant, Immanuel. "An Answer to the Question: 'What Is Enlightenment?'" Konigsberg in Prussia, 30th September, 1784. Located in Immanuel Kant, *Foundations of the Metaphysics of Morals and What Is Enlightenment?* New York: Macmillan Publishing, 1990.

————. *Religion Within the Limits of Reason Alone,* 1793.

Kärkkäinen, Veli-Matti. *An Introduction to the Theology of Religions: Biblical, Historical, and Contemporary Perspectives.* Downers Grove, Ill.: InterVarsity Press, 2003.

————. *One with God: Salvation as Deification and Justification.* Collegeville, Minn.: Liturgical Press, 2004.

Knight, Henry H. *A Future for Truth: Evangelical Theology in a Postmodern World.* Nashville: Abingdon Press, 1997.

————. *The Presence of God in the Christian Life: John Wesley and the Means of Grace.* Metuchen, N.J.: Scarecrow Press, 1992.

Knitter, Paul F. *No Other Name? A Critical Survey of Christian Attitudes Toward the World Religions.* Maryknoll, N.Y.: Orbis Books, 1985.

Kwon, Tae Hyoung. *John Wesley's Doctrine of Prevenient Grace: Its Impact on Contemporary Missiological Dialog* (an unpublished dissertation). Ann Arbor, Mich.: UMI Dissertation Services, 1996.

Locke, John. *Essay Concerning Human Understanding* (1690), IV, xix, 4, "Of Enthusiasm."

Lodahl, Michael. *God of Nature and of Grace.* Nashville: Kingswood Press, 2004.

Lyotard, Jean-François. *The Postmodern Condition: A Report on Knowledge (Theory and History of Literature,* Vol. 10.). Trans. Brian Massumi. Minneapolis: University of Minnesota Press, 1985.

MacCulloch, Diarmaid. *The Reformation.* New York: Viking Press, 2004.

Maddox, Randy. *Responsible Grace: John Wesley's Practical Theology.* Nashville: Kingswood Books, 1994.

Manual of the Church of the Nazarene. Kansas City: Nazarene Publishing House, 2001.

Martinson, Paul Varo. *Families of Faith: An Introduction to World Religions for Christians.* Minneapolis: Fortress Press, 1999.

Maurice, John Frederick Denison. *The Religions of the World and Their Relations to Christianity.* London: J. W. Parker, 1847.

McGrath, Alister. *The Twilight of Atheism: The Rise and Fall of Disbelief in the Modern World.* New York: Doubleday, 2004.

McLaren, Brian D. *The Church on the Other Side: Doing Ministry in the Postmodern Matrix.* Grand Rapids: Zondervan Publishing House, 2000.

Middleton, J. Richard, and Brian J. Walsh. *Truth Is Stranger than It Used to Be: Biblical Faith in a Postmodern Age.* Downers Grove, Ill.: InterVarsity Press, 1995.

Milbank, John. "Postmodern Critical Augustinianism: A Short Summa in Forty-two Responses to Unasked Questions," *The Postmodern God: A Theological Reader.* Ed. Graham Ward. Malden, Mass.: Blackwell Publishers, 1997.

_____. *The Word Made Strange: Theology, Language, Culture.* Malden, Mass.: Blackwell Publishers, 1997.

Molloy, Michael. *Experiencing the World's Religions: Tradition, Challenge, and Change.* Mountain View, Calif.: Mayfield Publishing Company, 2002.

Musser, Donald W., and Joseph L. Price, eds. *A New Handbook of Christian Theology.* Nashville: Abingdon Press, 1996.

Nelson, Marcia Z. *The Gospel According to Oprah.* Louisville, Ky.: Westminster John Knox Press, 2005.

Netland, Harold. *Encountering Religious Pluralism: The Challenge to Christian Faith and Mission.* Downers Grove, Ill.: InterVarsity Press, 2001.

Nielson, Niels C., et al. *Religions of the World.* New York: St. Martin's Press, 1983.

O'Connor, Flannery. *The Complete Stories of Flannery O'Connor.* New York: Farrar, Straus, and Giroux, 1971.

Oden, Thomas C. *Life in the Spirit: Systematic Theology III.* San Francisco: HarperSanFrancisco, 1992.

Okholm, Dennis L., John Hick, and Timothy R. Phillips. *More than One Way? Four*

Views on Salvation in a Pluralistic World. Grand Rapids: Zondervan Publishing House, 1995.

O'Leary, Joseph Stephen. *Religious Pluralism and Christian Truth.* Edinburgh: Edinburgh University Press, 1996.

Oord, Thomas Jay, and Michael Lodahl. *Relational Holiness: Responding to the Call of Love.* Kansas City: Beacon Hill Press of Kansas City, 2005.

Outler, Albert C., ed. *John Wesley.* New York: Oxford University Press, 1964.

Partridge, Christopher, ed. *New Religions: A Guide.* New York: Oxford University Press, 2004.

Pinnock, Clark H. *A Wideness in God's Mercy.* Grand Rapids: Zondervan, 1992.

Plantinga, Richard J., ed. *Christianity and Plurality: Classic and Contemporary Readings.* Malden, Mass.: Blackwell Publishers, 1999.

Polkinghorne, John, and Michael Welker, eds. *The End of the World and the Ends of God: Science and Theology on Eschatology.* Harrisburg, Pa.: Trinity International Press, 2000.

Race, Alan. *Christians and Religious Pluralism: Patterns in the Christian Theology of Religions.* Maryknoll, N.Y.: Orbis Books, 1982.

Rack, Henry D. *Reasonable Enthusiast: John Wesley and the Rise of Methodism,* 2nd ed. Nashville: Abingdon Press, 1992.

Rahner, Karl. *The Spirit in the Church.* London: Burns and Oates, 1979.

Royster, Mark Powell. *John Wesley's Doctrine of Prevenient Grace in Missiological Perspective* (unpublished dissertation), Asbury Theological Seminary. Ann Arbor, Mich.: UMI Dissertation Services, 1989.

Roszak, Theodore. *The Making of a Counter Culture: Reflections on the Technocratic Society and Its Youthful Opposition.* Berkeley: University of California Press, 1995.

Rubenstein, Richard E. *When Jesus Became God: The Struggle to Define Christianity During the Last Days of Rome.* New York: Harcourt, Inc., 1999.

Runyon, Theodore. *The New Creation: John Wesley's Theology Today.* Nashville: Abingdon Press, 1998.

_____, ed. *Sanctification and Liberation: Liberation Theologies in the Light of the Wesleyan Tradition.* Nashville: Abingdon Press, 1981.

Sanders, John, and Clark Pinnock. *No Other Name: An Investigation into the Destiny of the Unevangelized.* Grand Rapids: William B. Eerdmans Publishing Co., 1992.

Schleiermacher, Fredrich. *On Religion: Speeches to Its Cultured Despisers.* Cambridge: Cambridge University Press, 1996, first published 1799.

_____. *The Christian Faith According to the Principles of the Evangelical Church.* Trans. H. R. Mackintosh, ed. J. S. Stewart. Edinburgh: T & T Clark, Ltd., 2001, first published 1821-22.

Seager, Richard Hughes, ed. *The Dawn of Religious Pluralism: Voices from the World's Parliament of Religions: 1893.* Chicago: Open Court Publishing Company, 1992.

Sider, Ronald J. *Just Generosity.* Grand Rapids: Baker Book House, 1999.

_____. *Scandal of the Evangelical Conscience: Why Are Christians Living Just like the Rest of the World?* Grand Rapids: Baker Book House, 2005.

Smart, Ninian, and Steven Konstantine. *A Christian Systematic Theology in World Context.* Minneapolis: Fortress Press, 1991.

Smith, James K. A. *Introducing Radical Orthodoxy: Mapping a Post-Secular Theology.* Grand Rapids: Baker Academic/Paternoster, 2004.

Smith, Wilfred Cantwell. *The Faith of Other Men.* New York: Harper Torchbooks, 1972.

_____. *Toward a World Theology.* Maryknoll, N.Y.: Orbis Books, 1990.

Staples, Rob L. *Outward Sign and Inward Grace: The Place of Sacraments in Wesleyan Spirituality.* Kansas City: Beacon Hill Press of Kansas City, 1991.

Starkey, Lycurgus M. *The Work of the Holy Spirit: A Study in Wesleyan Theology.* Nashville: Abingdon Press, 1962.

Stott, John, and Timothy Dudley-Smith, eds. *Authentic Jesus.* Downers Grove, Ill.: InterVarsity Press, 1979.

Stuhlmacher, Peter. *Revisiting Paul's Doctrine of Justification: A Challenge to the New Perspective.* Downers Grove, Ill.: InterVarsity Press, 2001.

Sugirtharajah, R. S. *Postcolonial Criticism and Biblical Interpretation.* New York: Oxford University Press, 2002.

Sweet, Leonard. *SoulTsunami.* Grand Rapids: Zondervan, 2001.

Thomas, Owen, ed. *Attitudes Toward Other Religions.* Lanham, Md.: Roman and Littlefield, reprint 1986.

Thornhill, John. *Modernity: Christianity's Estranged Child Reconstructed.* Grand Rapids: William B. Eerdmans Publishing Co., 2000.

Toynbee, Arnold. "What Should Be the Christian Approach to the Contemporary Non-Christian Faith?" *Attitudes Toward Other Religions.* Ed. Owen Thomas. Lanham, Md.: Roman and Littlefield, reprint 1986.

Tracy, Wesley D., E. Dee Freeborn, Janine Tartaglia, and Morris Weigelt. *The Upward Call: Spiritual Formation and the Holy Life.* Kansas City: Beacon Hill Press of Kansas City, 1994.

Troeltsch, Ernst. *The Social Teaching of the Christian Churches* (2 vols.). Trans. Olive Wyon. Louisville, Ky.: Westminster John Knox Press, 1992 (originally published 1912).

Verkuyl, Johannes. "The Biblical Notion of Kingdom: Test of Validity for Theology of Religion," *The Good News of the Kingdom: Mission Theology for the Third Millennium,* Charles Van Engen, Dean S. Gilliland, Paul Pierson, eds. New York: Orbis Books, 1993.

Vico, Giambattista. *The New Science.* 1725.

von der Dunk, H. W. *The Disappearing Heaven.* Dutch title: *De Verdwijnende Hemel, Over de Cultuur van Europa in de Twintigste Eeuw.* Amsterdam: J. M. Meulenhoff, 2000.

Walker, Williston. *A History of the Christian Church.* New York: Charles Scribner's Sons, 1959.

Webber, Robert E. *Ancient-Future Faith: Rethinking Evangelicalism for a Postmodern World.* Grand Rapids: Baker Books, 1999.

_____. *Journey to Jesus: The Worship, Evangelism, and Nurture Mission of the Church.* Nashville: Abingdon Press, 2001.

Weikart, Richard. *From Darwin to Hitler: Evolutionary Ethics, Eugenics, and Racism in Germany.* New York: Palgrave Macmillan, 2004.

Wesley, John. *Explanatory Notes on the New Testament*. Grand Rapids: Baker Publishing Group, 1983 reprint.

_____. *Works of John Wesley*. Grand Rapids: Baker Book House Company, 2002 reprint.

Whitehead, Alfred N. *Process and Reality: An Essay in Cosmology*. New York: Free Press, 1978.

Wright, N. T. *The Challenge of Jesus*. Downers Grove, Ill.: InterVarsity Press, 1999.

_____. *The Resurrection of the Son of God*. Minneapolis: Fortress Press, 2003.

Zaehner, R. C. *Concordant Discord: The Interdependence of Faiths: Being the Gifford Lectures on Natural Religion Delivered at St. Andrews in 1967-1969*. Oxford: Oxford University Press, 1970.

Ye'or, Bat. *Eurabia: The Euro-Arab Axis*. Cranbury, N.J.: Associated University Press, 2005.

Journals/Magazines

Cunningham, Floyd T. "Christ, the Word, the Light, and the Message: A Wesleyan Reflection on World Mission," *Asia Journal of Theology* 5 (April 1991).

Ferguson, Niall. "The Widening Atlantic," *Atlantic Monthly* (January/February 2005), 40-42.

Gannon, Frank. "King of the Grill," *The AARP Magazine* (September/October 2003). George Foreman's Christian testimony at <http://poptohypermart.net/georgef.html>.

Golden, Frederic. "How Long Will We Be Around?" *TIME* Magazine Archive (June 25, 2001).

Hillgarth, J. N. *Christianity and Paganism: The Conversion of Western Europe*. Philadelphia: University of Pennsylvania Press, 1969.

Jenkins, Philip. "The Next Christianity," *Atlantic Monthly* (October 2002), 53-68.

Jenson, Robert W. "How the World Lost Its Story," *First Things* 36 (October 1993), 19-24.

Krauthammer, Charles. "What the Uprising Generation Wants," *TIME* (November 21, 2005).

Lawler, Justus George. "Hitler's Hammer, the Church's Anvil," *First Things* 157 (November 2005).

Lister, Toby. "Oh, Gods," *Atlantic Monthly* (February 2002), *Atlantic Monthly* Archives, located at <http://www.theatlantic.com/issues/2002/02/lester.htm>.

McCormick, Steve. "Along the Road," *Wesleyan Center for Twenty-First Century Studies*. Point Loma Nazarene University, Vol. 4; No. 3 (Spring 2003).

Meadows, Philip R. "Candidates for Heaven: Wesleyan Resources for a Theology of Religions," *Wesleyan Theological Journal* 35, No. 1 (Spring 2000).

Packer, J. I., and Jerry Root. "Mind in Motion," *Christian History* 88 (Fall 2005), 17.

Pickett, Stephen. "A Faith that Feels," *Christian History* 86 (Spring 2005).

Pluralism Project Newsletter (October 20, 2005).

Sellers, Jeff M. "The Church as Culture," *First Things* 142 (April 2004), 31-36.

_____. "Letter from Spain: Stony Ground for the Gospel," *Christianity Today* (Week of March 24, posted 03/24/2003). Copyright © 2003 by the author or *Christianity*

Today International/Books & Culture Magazine (March 24, 2003) <http://www
.christianitytoday.com/books/web/2003/mar24.html>.

Starobin, Paul. "The Accidental Autocrat," *Atlantic Monthly* (March 2005), 82-92.

The Lancet 366 (international journal of medical science and practice), No. 9481 (16
July 2005), 211-17.

Newspapers

Aucoin, Don. *Boston Globe.* Last Updated: Jan. 16, 2002 <http://www.jsonline.com
/enter/tvradio/jan02/13055.asp>.

"Dalai Lama Touts Religion on Visit to Indiana Temple," *Chicago Tribune* (September 8,
2003), section 1, 16.

LowCountry Weekly (December 11-17, 2002).

Nicolson, Adam. "The Bible Tells Me So," *Wall Street Journal* (September 23, 2005),
W13.

Prison Fellowship, "A Letter to Supporters," July 24, 2003.

Tabb, Mark. "Postmodernism and the Matrix," *Kansas City Star* (November 22, 2003).

Tennessean (September 27, 2003), section 4A.

Internet Sources

Ár nDraíocht Féin: A Druid Fellowship, Inc. <http://www.adf.org/core/>.

Carmack, David B. "Antibiotic-resistant pathogens increasing." American Academy of
Orthopedic Surgeons. <http://www.aaos.org/News/bulletin/feb05/fline3.asp>.

Contemporary American neo-pagans. <http://www.pluralism.org/weblinks/weblink
_direct.php?tradition=Pagan>.

Blunt, Sheryl Henderson. "The Daniel of Religious Rights." *Christianity Today* (August
26, 2005) <http://www.christianitytoday.com/ct/2005/009/18.52.html>.

Dean, Cornelia. "Scientists Speak Up on Mix of God and Science," *The New York
Times on the Web* (August 23, 2005) <http://www.nytimes.com/>.

Documents of the Second Vatican Council <http://www.ewtn.com/library/COUN
CILS/V2ALL.HTM>.

Haddad, Wadi D. "Tertiary Education Today: Global Trends, Global Agendas, Global
Constraints" <haddad@KnowledgeEnterprise.org>.

Hill, Daniel. "Reaching the Post-Christian," *Leadership Journal* (Fall 2004), also located
at LeadershipJournal.net <http://www.christianitytoday.com/le/2004/004/17.71
.html>.

Regas, George F. "Interpreting Christ in a Pluralistic World," a sermon delivered in the
Washington National Cathedral, the Fifth Sunday of Easter, April 24, 2005 <http://
www.cathedral.org/cathedral/worship/gfr050424.html>.

Rogers, Benedict. "Burma's Almost Forgotten," *Christianity Today* 48 (March 2004),
No. 3, 52. Copyright © 2004 Christianity Today <http://www.christianity
today.com/ct/2004/003/7.52.html>.

The Pluralism Project of Harvard University <http://www.pluralism.org/publications/
new_religious_america/index.php>.

Swami Vivekanandam Address at the World Parliament of Religions, Chicago (September 11, 1893), <http://www.searchforlight.org/Anubhuti/Anubhuti%20Vol%202/ Viveka_chicago_%20Add.htm>.

Tabb, Mark. "Postmodernism and the Matrix," *Kansas City Star* (November 22, 2003). Tabb's article is now available at <http://www.marktabb.com/what_is_the_ma trix.htm>.

Teichrib. "Re-Creating Eden" (September 14, 2004). <http://www.crossroad.to/arti cles2/04/teichrib-eden.htm>.

The Festival at Eleusis <www.mystae.com/restricted/streams/scripts/eleusis.html>.

"The Gospel According to Oprah," Watchman Fellowship of Alabama <http://www .wfial.org/index.cfm?fuseaction=artNewAge.article_1>.

Wright, N. T. "Paul and Caesar: A New Reading of Romans." <http://www.ntwright page.com/wright_Paul_Caesar_Romans.htm>.